Rein

Internationalization, Cu

MW01595464

Gesellschaftliche Transformationen
Societal Transformations

herausgegeben von/edited by

Eckhard Dittrich, Nikolai Genov, Raj Kollmorgen,
Ingrid Oswald, Heiko Schrader, Melanie Tatur

Band/Volume 8

LIT

Reinhard Golz (Ed.)

Internationalization, Cultural Difference and Migration

Challenges and Perspectives
of Intercultural Education

LIT

Bibliographic information published by Die Deutsche Bibliothek
Die Deutsche Bibliothek lists this publication in the Deutsche
Nationalbibliografie; detailed bibliographic data are available in the
Internet at http://dnb.ddb.de.

ISBN 3-8258-8755-3

A catalogue record for this book is available from the British library

© LIT VERLAG Münster   2005

Grevener Str./Fresnostr. 2   48159 Münster
Tel. 0251-62 03 20   Fax 0251-23 19 72
e-Mail: lit@lit-verlag.de   http://www.lit-verlag.de

Distributed in North America by:

Transaction Publishers
New Brunswick (U.S.A.) and London (U.K.)

Transaction Publishers   Tel.: (732) 445 - 228(
Rutgers University   Fax: (732) 445 - 3138
35 Berrue Circle   for orders (U. S. only
Piscataway, NJ 08854   toll free (888) 999 - 6

Table of Contents

Introduction: Educational Transformations Without the Consideration of International Experiences Seldom Last

Reinhard Golz

The processes of globalization and migration are altering the relationships among cultures and ethnic groups. Thus, the international and intercultural aspects of education are becoming increasingly important. The international cooperation relations are changing and extending accordingly. These processes express themselves in the personal composition of this book, in which the articles contribute in specific ways to an international and interdisciplinary research project ("Transformation Societies in Europeanization and Globalization Processes") conducted at the University of Magdeburg (Germany). The focus points of this project are the current transformations in post-socialist Central and Eastern Europe. Most East European countries, due to social systems that came to an end in the years 1989-90, were insufficiently prepared for the democratic and pluralistic approaches to cultural heterogeneity. Together with the new opportunities for social and individual advancement, the unknown risks of a liberal social order also became a realization. Unemployment and a sense of lost perspectives went hand in hand with underdeveloped administrative and individual strategies for overcoming conflicts, all of which were further complicated by migration and rising levels of multiculturalism.

In almost all of these countries a part of the population and of the political establishment greets this development as something normal and desirable, and as a source of cultural, social and finally economic enrichment. Another part of the population regards this development as a threat to the social and economic status quo. The arguments of the opponents of a multicultural society are becoming increasingly questionable, although the proponents, as well, sometimes find themselves in difficulty, particularly when they assume radical relativist positions. The situation becomes even more complicated when both parties discuss the term 'integration', and when, for example, opponents of the multicultural society say integration when they mean assimilation.

In any event, integration and intercultural education are becoming the key concepts in discussions on the consequences of migration. It is thus becoming increasingly important to define intercultural education not only in the sense of integration for the migrants to the receiving society, but also to help the members of the majority culture to become more tolerant and less prejudiced. It is important to overcome hostility towards foreigners, and people with a different cultural background.

It seems that there is little in common regarding the pedagogical concepts to solve the integration problems of cultural minorities and of migrants, and that there are no universal recipes for an intercultural pedagogy. However, history has shown that educational transformations without critically constructive consideration of international pedagogical developments seldom last. The pedagogical system of a nation does not consist of an amalgamation of external (international) influences and it cannot be restricted to a merely national level. However, any tendency towards isolating such a system from international transformations, perspectives and experiences leads to an academic stand still.

This is not only relevant for the former socialist countries, but also for those countries not subjected to a comparable pressure of change through societal transformation. It would hardly be realistic to believe in continual receptive processing of western academic publications about education. And yet it is a matter of learning from experience and developments in other education systems, in order to improve one's own system. This should be done carefully, to avoid lending quite different functions to borrowed elements in their new context. This international comparison can be a critically constructive corrective for national thoughts and actions, it can fulfil a consultative function towards national policies of migration and education.

There is no alternative to mutual appreciation as a precondition for mutual understanding. This is especially true concerning the problems arising from the growing interculturality of all societies. Intercultural education should look more closely into the experiences of classic immigration countries such as Canada. This should be done without copying those experiences and uncritically importing theoretical approaches. Using these experiences critically will help to understand people in their cultural identity crisis, to accept and empower people not only in their cultural and national identity, but also in their interculturality and potential world citizenship.

The contributions to this book were developed between 2004 and 2005, mostly following an international conference of the already mentioned interdisciplinary research project "Transformation Societies ...". The conference, which took place in May of 2004, had four focus points; the first two being: „Societal Transformations in Conceptual and Comparative Perspectives" and „Economy, Culture, Ethics – Preconditions and Consequences of the economic Transformation". The contributions to these two focus points are published by Raj Kollmorgen, the speaker for the project (cf. Kollmorgen 2005; for further information about the goals, contents, problems and perspectives of the project refer to: Dittrich 2003, 2001; Kollmorgen/Schrader 2003; http://www.uni-magdeburg.de/research/forsch.shtml).

Two other focus points of the conference were "Politico-cultural and Human Rights Conflict Fields and Solution Strategies" and "Migration, Interculturality and Education in Historical and Current Contexts". The contributions made to these two focus points were further discussed and compiled in the book at hand where they serve its title in a variety of ways.

The articles of the first part of this book discuss intercultural and educational challenges in migration and transformation processes of selected transformation countries, such as (East)Germany, Czech Republic, Poland, Russia, Moldova and Kosovo, but also countries such as Portugal, and Spain, which are effected by these transformation processes, because of having an increasing amount of migrants from the former socialist countries. In the second part of the book authors from Canada, Germany, Ethiopia, and Kenya discuss problems of Human Rights, the increasing Cultural Diversity and the thereby developing identity crisis and developments as well as the thereby resulting pedagogical and socio-psychological issues. This book refers also to the new relastionships in research contexts on globalization and migration processes and their challenges and per-spectives for the intercultural education. The contributions are also a reflection of the particularly intense scientific co-operation in the teaching and research areas between the represented universities and the editor.

I would like to thank my colleagues for their help to organize the conference and the publication process, first of all Junior-Professor Dr. Raj Kollmorgen, the speaker for the research project "Transformation Societies ..." (University of Magdeburg). I am also most grateful to Dr. Wolfgang Mayrhofer, Melanie Lahne and Aline Hannemann (all from the University of Magdeburg) for their assis-tance in the technical editing and preparation of the papers for publication. Thanks also to Christina Koblbauer and Andrea Michel (Simon Fraser Univer-sity, Burnaby) for corrections of the English texts.

Literature

Kollmorgen, Raj (Hg./2005): Transformation als Typ sozialen Wandels. Postso-zialistische Lektionen, historische und interkulturelle Vergleiche. Münster: LIT Verlag.

Dittrich, Eckhard (2003): Transformationsforschung in Magdeburg. In: Kollmor-gen, Raj/Schrader, Heiko (Hg.): Postsozialistische Transformationen: Gesell-schaft, Wirtschaft, Kultur. Würzburg: Ergon: 285-292.

Dittrich, Eckhard (Hg./2001): Wandel, Wende, Wiederkehr. Transformation as Epochal Change in Central and Eastern Europe: Theoretical Concepts and Their Empirical Applicability (Transformationen. Gesellschaften im Wandel, Bd. 2) Würzburg: Ergon.

Kollmorgen, Raj/Schrader, Heiko (Hg./2003): Postsozialistische Transformationen: Gesellschaft, Wirtschaft, Kultur. Theoretische Perspektiven und empirische Befunde (Reihe: Transformationen. Gesellschaften im Wandel, Bd. 6). Würzburg: Ergon.

Reinhard Golz (University of Magdeburg, Germany)

Integration of Migrants: Social and Educational Challenges in Processes of Societal Transformations

Abstract:
Following the political change, the former socialist countries were prepared differently for democratic and pluralistic approaches to cultural heterogeneity. Together with the new opportunities for social and individual advancement, the unknown risks of a liberal society also came into being. Unemployment and a sense of lost perspectives went hand in hand with underdeveloped administrative and individual strategies for overcoming conflicts, all of which was further complicated by migration and rising levels of multiculturalism. Integration of people with different cultural backgrounds and intercultural education are becoming key concepts regarding the consequences of migration and globalization processes. It is not only a matter of compensating for social and educational deficits of cultural minorities, but also of familiarizing the dominant group with cultures of minorities, and of helping the members of the majority culture to overcome hostility, discrimination and racism. There are no universal (international) recipes for intercultural learning, however history has shown that transformations without critically constructive consideration of international developments seldom last.

1. Reasons and Factors of the Migration

When people shift their life emphasis and social activity space over a longer time period and over a larger area, then the causes for this serious decision lie in different push- and pull-factors.[1] However, it mostly concerns a complex entwinement of this and further factors. Migration is a global, cyclic, and dynamic feature. Under the different migration types and/or motivations for migration, the following are particularly important: the religious migration, the workers' migration and emigration for economic-social reasons, the political emigration, the refugee migration (e.g. the migration of the Jewish contingent refugees from the former Soviet Union to Germany) etc. Different economic, political, social, demographic and other factors thus obviously play the dominating role in migration movements from different governing systems. The reasons and factors mentioned, however, cannot explain why, for example, only one part of a population disadvantaged in a society emigrates or why already once emigrated individuals (or single families) tend to emigrate once again (e.g. Russian-Germans to America - see Janssen 1997). Psychoanalytic bases can contribute to the understanding

---

[1] Push factors: political persuit, displacement, flight etc.; Pull factors: emigrants, unemployed searching better working opportunities in different countries, regions, etc.

of these phenomena. Afterwards, the distinction is made between "external" explanation models (migration causes are looked for outside of the person) and "internal" (psychoanalytic) explanation models. There are two basic tendencies in the human psyche: While some people love to clasp themselves onto something solid if they believe his security is in danger, others love the wide range and distance, the free spaces and challenges; they are interested in giving up and regaining security (cf. Balint 1972). Accordingly, migration would not exclusively be hardships. Migration can refer both to the crossing over of state borders as well as movement within states. It must therefore not only affect "foreigners". An example is the strengthened inner migration in the area of the former Soviet Union, mostly in the direction of the Russian federation and its larger cities. Another, although thereby not comparable phenomenon, is the east-west migration in Germany since 1989/90.

2. Controversies on Integration of Migrants

Life in East European transformation countries like East Germany, Czech Republic, Poland etc. are not only characterised by the transformation to a market economy, democratic civil societies and processes of europeanization and globalization. There are the additional challenges of the migration processes and therefore the permanently increasing interculturality of the societies. In this tension-fraught context, the projects of the integration of migrants (etnically/culturally different people) have to answer quite complex and controversial questions, of which the following are especially crucial:

Is migration and the growing interculturality of society a ...

... cultural, social, economical enrichment, desirable phenomenon of social life in the context of globalization?	... socio-economical and cultural burden, national threat, and danger against which to be warned?

Should immigration ...

... be controlled, with an equilibrium between economically/demographically wished for immigrants and those who *must* be helped due to human rights?	... not only be drastically reduced, but in the end even stopped – in the interest of the allegedly „hard-pressed, native majority"?

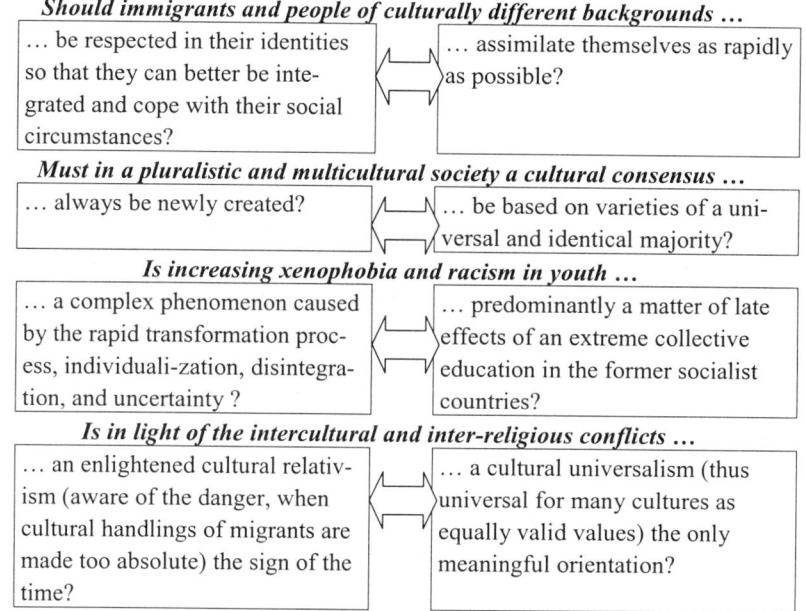

Should immigrants and people of culturally different backgrounds ...

... be respected in their identities so that they can better be integrated and cope with their social circumstances?	... assimilate themselves as rapidly as possible?

Must in a pluralistic and multicultural society a cultural consensus ...

... always be newly created?	... be based on varieties of a universal and identical majority?

Is increasing xenophobia and racism in youth ...

... a complex phenomenon caused by the rapid transformation process, individuali-zation, disintegration, and uncertainty ?	... predominantly a matter of late effects of an extreme collective education in the former socialist countries?

Is in light of the intercultural and inter-religious conflicts ...

... an enlightened cultural relativism (aware of the danger, when cultural handlings of migrants are made too absolute) the sign of the time?	... a cultural universalism (thus universal for many cultures as equally valid values) the only meaningful orientation?

These questions and controversies around migration and its consequences for integration and thus for an intercultural education worthy of this name may not be referred to in the same way (universally) in all post-socialist countries. However, they influence the discussions particularly strong around current integration and intercultural education. Migration and growing multicuturalism is much influenced by the ongoing globalisation process. However globalisation and migration may be judged, we are still faced with the question of whether a corresponding multicultural society will be a desirable cultural enrichment and factually existent or a necessary evil, an economic, social and cultural burden (cf. Globalisierung [...] 1999, Obrazovanije 2004, Suárez-Orozco / Quin-Hilliard 2004).

3. Problems of the Integration and Intercultural Education in Germany with Special Reference to East Germany

In the context of globalisation factors and demographic trends in Germany, the arguments of the opponents of a multicultural society are becoming increasingly questionable. However, the proponents, too, sometimes find themselves in difficulty, particularly when they assume radical relativist positions. The situation becomes even more complicated when both parties discuss the term integration. While assimilationist positions are more and more rarely taken up openly, pleas are made for integration by supporters and opponents of the multicultural society, albeit with a different interpretation. The opponents, taking an intellectually circuitous route, say integration when they mean assimilation. In any event, in discussions on the consequences of migration and intercultural education, integration of migrants, and taking into account both equality and diversity (cf. Wenning 2004) is becoming *the* challenge to pedagogy.

Integration can be the only way for cultures to live together in a pluralistic and democratic society. Integration of migrants into the society of the receiving (host) country is apparently successful when the specific values and equal rights of the individual cultures are acknowledged, and when integration „does not mean uprooting or faceless assimilation. Integration is also an alternative to incompatible cultures living side by side without any interaction" (cf. Rau 2000). Integration has much to do with the problem and the development of cultural identity. Belonging to a culture (or even to more than one culture) gives one not only a psychologic orientation, it is also important for the capability to act in a complex and diverse society. But it is not to be ignored that the development of an identity is connected to an ongoing change, and that cultural identities are eventually changeable entities (attitudes). To recognize and strengthen the cultural identity of migrants and members of minority cultures does not mean to hinder their complex and complicated integration process into their new cultural setting (cf. Auernheimer 1989).

For the more radical universalists, what finally ties us together in society is an identity, a basic consensus. Only within this identity and this basic consensus can people live together lastingly. From a relativistic standpoint the thorny question arises as to whether a community that is founded on identity is really a community, whether a society made up of variations of a universal and identical majority can exist in the long run (cf. Masschelein 1995: 117 ff.). People have to continually find a consensus. Cultural identity perpetually changes (cf. ibid.: 122, Demorgon 1999: 25). One's own and others' identities have to be accepted as they have developed, but also as changeable entities.

Accepting and respecting another world interpretation and value system and culture is not possible without questioning one's own culture. People must always be able to critically scrutinize their own world views. At the *cognitive* level, it concerns the recognition of one's own ethnocentrism, and the abolishment of a cultural „we-"border in global responsibility and the awareness of characteristics of intercultural communication. At the *affective-emotional* level it concerns the foundation of tolerance and respect of people from other cultures as well as acceptance of interculturality as a characteristic of a pluralistic society. At the *action-related* level it has something to do with the emphasis and the realization of the common interests, with organization of knowledge and experience of mutual cultural enrichment, with the practice of intercultural solidarity and of a rational dealing with the displeasure and the overcoming of intercultural conflicts (cf. Nieke 1995: 198 ff.).

Intercultural education should thus be *the* pedagogical and social task of our time in an increasingly multicultural German society, and of the coming generations in the new democratic countries. Intercultural education should have long ago stopped being defined only in the sense of integration of *migrants* into the receiving society. It concerns the participants of the German *majority* culture of the receiving country more strongly to have intercultural tolerance (respect), and to overcome xenophobia, discrimination and racism.

Migration after the reunification is in Germany sometimes regarded as a warning sign of a new crisis. Some consider such a society to be desirable, to be worth striving for, and in keeping with the times, while others feel that it is a threat to the West and its humanistic foundations (cf. Nieke, 1995: 81). Many foreign workers, immigrants, and asylum-seekers experience everyday life in Germany partly as a threatening reality on account of language and cultural distance. Migration is „a starting point for public disputes, in which very controversial phenomena are discussed and can no longer be settled easily, because they have already become a reality: the multiculturality of German society or the indisputable fact that the Federal Republic, willingly or unwillingly, has long since been a land of immigration" (Bade, 1992: 5). Thus Germany has been a starting point as well as a final stop for large waves of immigrants for a long time.[1]

Germany currently has (if Russia is not counted completely as a European country) the highest population in Europe, with 82.1 million inhabitants; but the trend of demographic development is negative, Germany now having the lowest birth rates in the entire world. This situation was aggravated by the dramatic demographic breakdown of East Germany (the former GDR), especially in the first

---

[1] From 1945 to 1990, over 30.5 million people moved to the former West Germany. But we must put this figure into perspective. We are talking about a period of 45 years and about very heterogeneous migration. There were displaced persons, refugees and people who wanted to re-settle, leaving the former GDR with and without permits. Then there were returning settlers, with German statehood, and ethnic Germans, who lost their homes in Eastern and South-Eastern Europe. Some of the latter came as late as after 1993 ("belated returning settlers", in German *Spätaussiedler*) claiming German nationality or ethnicity. In the above-mentioned figure (30.5 million from 1945-1990) we must also include the migrant workers, *Gastarbeiter*, from Italy (after 1953), from Yugoslavia (after 1954) and from Greece, Portugal, Spain and Turkey (after 1960). Since 1990 two groups have grown noticeably - asylum seekers and returning settlers. Today the population of Germany (varying regionally) consists of about 90% Germans. In 2002 altogether 7.3 million immigrants lived in Germany, making up about 9 % of the entire population. 28.1 % of them were Turkish, 11.1 % from the former Yugoslavia, 8.2 % Italian, and 5.0 % Greek. The largest concentration of foreigners is in cities like Frankfurt/Main or Offenbach, where they constitute a quarter of the population.

years after reunification, and is still influencing German society. The question has been (and still is) debated whether the influx of many young immigrants compensates for the decline and ageing of the German population.

However, the biggest problem is the increasing unemployment rate in Germany as a whole, especially in East Germany:

Unemployment Rate (West Germany)   *Unemployment Rate (East Germany)*
(Angaben in Prozent)

	(2000)	(2004)	(2005*)		(2000)	(2004)	(2005*)
Baden-Wuerttemberg:	5,2	6,2	7,2	Brandenburg:	16,7	18,7	20,5
Bavaria:	5,0	6,9	9,1	Mecklenburg-Pom.:	17,1	20,5	23,6
Schleswig-Holstein:	8,0	9,8	12,7	Saxony:	16,4	17,8	20,1
Berlin:	15,8	17,6	19,6	Saxony-Anhalt:	19,8	20,3	22,8
Bremen:	12,7	13,3	18,5	Thuringia:	14,7	16,7	19,4
Hamburg:	8,7	9,7	10,6				
Hessen:	7,1	8,2	9,3				
Lower Saxony:	8,8	9,6	12,3				
North Rhine-Westph.:	8,9	10,2	12,3				
Rheinland-Palatine:	6,9	7,7	9,8				
Saarland:	9,6	9,2	11,3				

Gesamt (2005): 5,2 Mio. = 12,6%; West: 3,4 Mio. = 10,4 %; East = 1,8 Mio = 20,7 %
(2005*): Previous receivers of social welfare are now counted as unemployed people.

(Source: Bundesanstalt für Arbeit, May 2000 and February 2005;
http://www.statistik-portal.de/Statistik-Portal/de_jb02_jahrtab13.asp)

In a time of high unemployment the temptation was and is great to exclude asylum applicants and refugees from the world of work. However, this would only make the former more dependent on welfare. It would lead to a reduction in the social budget and therefore in the finances for asylum applicants, thereby partially leading the latter into crime. In the history of the FRG there has always been a connection between economic downturn and the growth of animosity towards foreigners (cf. Marshall 2000).

Actually there is no real basis for the heated discussions concerning migration and immigration. The annual number of immigrants with longer-range perspectives stands at around 250,000 persons per year.[2] For a long time now, „immigra-

---

[2] This number breaks down into 98,000 „belated returnees" (*Spätaussiedler)* and their dependents and 157,000 new foreign immigrants (among them 82,000 foreign family-members, ca. 35,000 Unionsbürger,

tion" has been taking place, as it were, in the delivery room. If Germany had had a liberal policy regarding the right to national citizenship in the last 25 years, it would now have around 4 million foreigners and a foreign-born population quota just touching the 5% mark (cf. http://www.integrationsbeauftragte.de).

The actual quota is now about 9 % (7,3 Mio.). However, statements like „The boat is full" can only be seen as extremely demagogic. Other, related aspersions led (and lead) equally astray, such as the claim that foreigners take away work and housing from the indigenous population, misuse the social system, to which they have contributed little if anything, and are responsible for a rise in crime. Or – seen from another perspective – what contribution have foreigners made to the German economy?

In this regard there is an interesting result from a survey from the year 2001 made by the "European Monitoring Centre on Racism and Xenophobia (EUMC). 1000 citizen in East and West Germany were asked about their acceptance of migrants and minorities. Two of the main results are: First, in general there are hardly any big differences between East and West, but intolerance is a phenomenon of **young** East Germans and - **older** West Germans. Second, the acceptance of migrants is in general quiete low all over Germany, not only in the East! Refer to the first mentioned result this scheme:

23,000 recognized refugees und 17,000 Jewish immigrants). The number of foreigners after the application freeze of 1973 was estimated at around 4 million, in 2001 at 7.3 million. The percentage of foreigners in the total population rose from 6.4% to 8.9%. This is high in comparison with other European countires. But the number of foreigners is not simply dependent on the net-figure of immigrants, but also on naturalization practices. A glance at the figures on duration of residency shows the following: one third of foreign-born residents have lived longer than twenty years in Germany, more than half longer than ten years. 1.6 million or 22 % of them were born within Germany. One could say: most foreigners long ago became natives.

"Minorities are to blame for grievances"			
	yes	*not*	*don´t know*
Instructions qualities in schools with "to			
many" children of migrants is decreasing			
(West)	*60*	*26*	*14*
(East)	*48*	*35*	*17*
Minority groups trade the social system			
(West)	*54*	*28*	*18*
(East)	*60*	*22*	*18*
The presence of minority			
groups is a factor of insecurity			
(West)	*42*	*37*	*21*
(East)	*51*	*32*	*18*
Minority groups are precedenced			
by Authorities			
(West)	*26*	*55*	*19*
(East)	*26*	*51*	*23*
Minority groups increase the			
unemployment			
(West)	*57*	*27*	*16*
(East)	*65*	*22*	*13*
Migrants are above the average			
involved in crims			
(West)	*57*	*29*	*14*
(East)	*67*	*19*	*14*

(cf. EUMC 2001)

In Germany each tenth child lives in relative poverty according to data of the UN child welfare organization UNICEF. In the USA the portion, being each fifth child, is the largest. The lowest child poverty is in Denmark and Finland with under three percent. UNICEF classifies poor households as those which must get along with less than half of the national average income. In Germany, according to the study, particularly children from immigrant families and children raised by one parent suffer under poverty: 40 percent of them are poor. Beside material things, they often lack the allowance of upbringing and education. In addition, these children more frequently have health problems, cannot concentrate in instruction, and even drop out from school. With children of foreign parents, language problems are another added factor. Unsatisfactory training and thus bad career opportunities continue the path of poverty.

For many varied reasons, the children of immigrants urgently need special attention to prevent them from falling behind in school. It has been shown that the success in school of foreign children on the basis of immigration and its connected challenges, is well below their potential. In the meantime, thirty percent of school children in Germany have an immigrant background and, as a case in point, „forty percent of non-German youths with a diploma from a Hauptschule (at approx. age 16) do not find an apprenticeship" (Rau 2000). Learning to live together should be well prepared for in the context of immigration. In this situation, pedagogy must fulfil its responsibilities and make a contribution to intercultural understanding in a virtually multicultural society. Intercultural understanding is one of the most important conditions for future international cooperation, not only in the educational sector, but also in a larger social-political view. These problems are also strongly connected with the process of inner-German unification, where there are many problems which can be identified. Among these, nothing was more controversially discussed than the causes of increased xenophobia and youth criminality towards foreigners, returning settlers, asylum-seekers and other migrants among young East Germans. Although attempts to explain this phenomenon have been complex and contradictory, much like the actions against foreigners themselves, we can nevertheless isolate — without going into respective detail — the following partly contradictory points of reference in the debate:

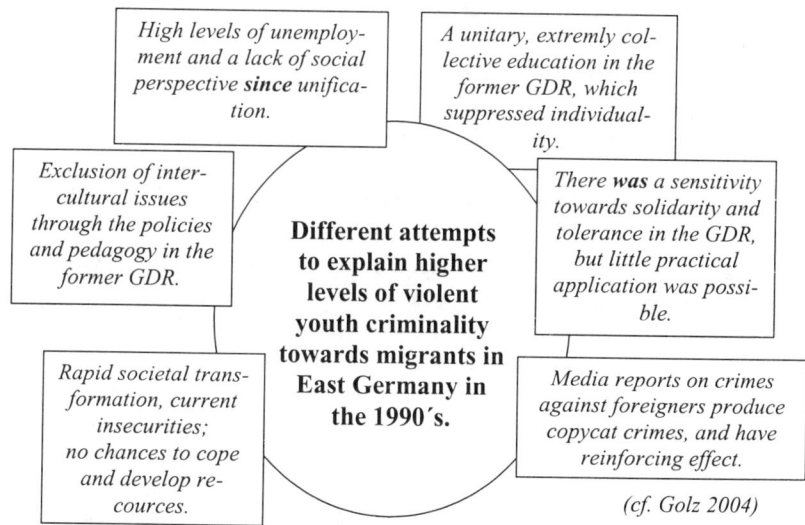

*High levels of unemployment and a lack of social perspective **since** unification.*

A unitary, extremly collective education in the former GDR, which suppressed individuality.

Exclusion of intercultural issues through the policies and pedagogy in the former GDR.

Different attempts to explain higher levels of violent youth criminality towards migrants in East Germany in the 1990´s.

*There **was** a sensitivity towards solidarity and tolerance in the GDR, but little practical application was possible.*

Rapid societal transformation, current insecurities; no chances to cope and develop recources.

Media reports on crimes against foreigners produce copycat crimes, and have reinforcing effect.

(cf. Golz 2004)

As for the causes of increased xenophobia, the truth lies perhaps somewhere between the positions sketched above.

A core problem in handling immigrants from other cultures is the approach to integrating these people into the society of the Federal Republic. First we will deal with what integration is *not* and/or *should not be*: assimilation. Even if the term, assimilation, is rather avoided in the meantime by opponents of a multicultural society, it by no means has only historical meaning. Dominating concepts up to the 1980's and to a certain degree today not completely overcome "Ausländerpaedagogik" ("special pedagogy for foreigners") could and can be understood as national state oriented assimilations pedagogy - a universal tendency pedagogy of the adjustment of the cultural minorities to the majority culture of the immigration country. We know that in the best scenario assimilation happens over very long historical periods (for instance with the Huguenots in Germany) but that it otherwise – with the short term expectation of assimilation of a host country - only rarely, if at all was ever successful in history. That applies even to the classical immigration countries. One must certainly add that there can also definitely be an expectation of assimilation coming from immigrants themselves, as one can observe, for example, with the Russian-Germans, at least up to a certain time in their emigration process. This self assimilation expectation, however, often turns into assimilation disappointment. The language barriers cannot be overcome, the difficulties with the vocational acknowledgment - particularly in a time of high unemployment - is added, and so one often goes neither the way of assimilation, nor the way of integration, but lands directly in segregation.

Above all it has to do with the exchange and appropriation of intercultural competence in meeting with cultural unfamiliarity. Finally, for example, culture-conditioned conflicts, must be resolved. One cannot *not* act; casualness, turning one's back, when people from other cultures are discriminated against or threatened physically, are also forms of action. Openness, adaptability, exchange, contact and interaction can every now and then be connected with the necessary agreement of a universalistic legitimised, moderate and enlightened minimal consensus (cf. Nieke 1995).

As previously already stressed, the concern here is not of violations of the law through immigrants, but around culture-conditioned conflicts of the everyday life. To overcome such conflicts, but also simply for the better integration of cultures in daily life, background knowledge of the cultures and environments of the immigrants in addition to that of one's own culture, is necessary. "Only he who is able to tolerate can to some extent be safe. Only he who has reliable orientations, tolerantly bears the knowledge of the other one." (P. Atteslander, quoted in Nieke

1995, S. 216) On the other hand there is an argument, that an acceptance of other world interpretations and world systems in other environments and cultures without disconcertion of one's own positions, is not possible. One must thus to a certain extent always be able to critically analyse one's own life perspective.

Intercultural education and communication become in an increasingly multicultural society an important task of future generations. They do not only have to shape the *internal* (mental) German agreement, they also have to master the complicated processes of the europeanization and globalisation as well as the constant new challenges in the context of the migration processes.

Intercultural education should no longer be defined only in the sense of the integration of immigrants into the receiving society. The concern becomes ever increasingly stronger, to help the members of the majority culture of the host country have more intercultural tolerance (respect) and fewer prejudices, and to overcome hostility towards strangers, discrimination and racism. Intercultural education should more strongly consider the theoretical conceptions and practical experiences of classical immigration countries - without copying and uncritically accepting. It could help to better understand people in their cultural and national identity, in their interculturality, or also in their cultural identity crisis.

Germany needs „education concepts which acknowledge that pupils from German families with a Western Christian background are no longer the normal case everywhere." This must be given greater attention in basic and continuing training for teachers. „Education is, after all, the key element of any encounter between cultures worthy of this name. Only education can help to overcome prejudice. It is the best protection against fundamentalism and racism." (Rau 2000) „Integration does not mean uprooting or faceless assimilation. Integration is also an alternative to incompatible cultures living side by side without any interaction." It is the commitment, which must be renewed over and over again, to live by common values. (idem.) The laws of the receiving country do have a universalistic character. They have to have the basic consensus, even if the case is that nothing is so good that it can not be changed for the better. However, we also have to consider that cultural traditions and ways of life are to be seen as relativistic. What should the basic (universalistic) consensus of the different cultural traditions be? Would it not ultimately be the dominant culture of the (German) country of immigration? These questions are obviously discussed not only in Germany and especially in East Germany, but in other newly democratic countries as well.

4. Education of Migrants and People from Different Cultures in Germany and Other Transformation Countries, with Reverence to the PISA-Survey

Often enough the relatively shameful showing of Germany in the recent PISA-study (PISA: „Programme for International Student Assessment", cf. PISA 2000) is attributed to the high percentage of badly educated and socially problematic immigrant children in the schools. In the Mathematics and Natural Sciences Rankings Germany placed 21st out of the 31 participating countries and in Reading competencies it placed 20th (cf. Deutsches PISA-Konsortium 2001).

In Germany there is an unusually strong connection between social heritage, educational participation, and gained competencies at the end of schooling. This is especially true for children and youth with migration backgrounds, as they are often underprivilged, not well integrated, and even discriminated against in German schools (cf. Bos 2003). But is the relatively high number of immigrant children the most important reason for the PISA place of Germany? If that were correct, then one would immediately have to enquire about the corresponding percentage in classical immigration countries such as Canada, and compare its own PISA standing. Countries with comparable or much higher proportions of migrant children are far ahead of Germany (Canada, Australia, England etc.).

One must consider that, for example, many migrants in Canada and other classic immigration countries mostly speak the (English) language of the receiving society right from the beginning of their immigration. Thus they have, perhaps, less integration problems than immigrants in Germany. But one must also consider that it is not first and foremost a matter of the volume of migrants and their offspring, but more or less a matter of successful strategies for integrating immigrants into their respective societies and educational systems (cf. Baumert 2001: 12).

The PISA-Rankings of the Czech Republic, Poland, Russia, and other Eastern European Countries (former socialistic countries) are – of course – only comparable under certain conditions. The Czech Republic stands here at 19th, 18th, and 11th in the above mentioned competence areas. Poland's standing was also not impressive (24th, 24th, 21st), and Russia placed 27th, 22th, and 27th.

As in Germany, parts of the Czech population see the growing number of immigrants as a burden for the country — at least economically. In the Czech Republic dismissive attitudes are voiced particularly in connection with the ethnic group of the Roma. They constitute a great social, educational and organizational challenge to the country. For various reasons, the Roma have the greatest problems integrating into this society. They were the victims of discrimination over long periods of time, were persecuted under totalitarian regimes and for the most part segregated because of their specific way of life and cultural traditions. The disadvantaged status of the Roma in Czech society is still evident today in their educational levels. In 1991 only 80% of this group reported having an elementary education, about 10% had no formal education whatsoever, and only 1% had a university education. Estimates show that between 50% and 80% of the children of this minority are transferred to special schools. This decision is justified by pointing to the results of psychological tests indicating readiness for school and intelligence quota, but these tests are designed for the children of the majority culture and in no way take into consideration the special socio-cultural world of the Roma. It is easy to imagine the high unemployment rate among adult Roma—estimated at 70% (cf. Kubecek 2003). The often heard, but very superficial argument which claims that minority groups, and particulary the Roma, misuse the social system, which was circulated by extremist movements in the 1990s. The overall aversion of the majority population to the Roma has partly led to acts of open discrimination which have even aroused international criticism against the Czech state. It is a fact that there were attempts (end even real actions) taken against the Roma in the city of Usti nad Labem. In one part of the city the Czech majority built a wall in the middle of a district, in order to separate themselves from the Roma and keep them out, because of their specific cultural characteristics. The Canadians (the Canadian Government) were the harshest critics, internationally, of this situation. So parts of the Czech society, e.g. border police at the check points, took their revenge and temporarily did not allow Canadians to enter the country without a visa. This is – of course- not to be generalized.

Aside from some instances of racist tendencies, one could consider the situation of migrants and ethnic minorities in the Czech Republic to be generally satisfying. There is, for example, the implementation of the international „Step by Step" program, established in 1994 by the „Soros Foundations Network and Children's Resource International" (Washington, D.C.). This program is of great importance for the integration of the Roma and their children, as well as of other minority groups into Czech society and the existing educational system. This alternative pedagogical project concentrates on pre-school and elementary school children and their families as well as on teacher training. The principal goals are to focus attention on the interests and needs of each pupil, the strengths and weaknesses, to respect the domestic culture of the family, and to develop strategies and activities that do justice to these cultural differences. Individualized learning in an appropriate environment should ensure each child the chance to develop his or her own personality. Because of such cultural traditions, the cooperative work between teachers and the families of Roma children is of crucial importance. (cf. Rydl 2001, Kargerova / Krejcova 2001, Kubecek 2003).

As one could see, the PISA-Results of Poland were not impressive either. But here it has very little to do with the relatively small proportion of newcomers and people from different cultures. The search for a new orientation of minority groups in *Polish* society in the 1990's has in no way been free of problems and remains unfinished today. However, one can discern in contemporary Poland a stronger presence of minorities and their organizations in the struggle to preserve and develop native cultural traditions, as well as greater participation in the social life of the mainstream.

At the same time, one cannot overlook the fact that Polish accomplishments — particularly in the area of intercultural education — have been rather modest (cf. Porozynski 2001). Assimilative and integrative approaches to dealing with minorities seemed to be equally at work in Poland, whereas in the Czech Republic, for example — here in step with the Western European tendency — the scale seems to tilt more strongly in the direction of integration. The assimilative expectations toward migrants and ethnic minorities cherished on the part of the majority population, as well as by some politicians and social scientists who do not appear very progressive when measured against the greater experience of classical and newer immigration countries.

Among educational scientists, discussion of the goals, contents and forms of intercultural education has intensified — obviously spurred by the impending integration of Poland into the European Union. In dealing with minorities and developing a corresponding policy for intercultural education, two goals are discussed. First of all, it is a matter of ensuring an equal chance to whatever group it may be in the pursuit of social life, yet taking care to preserve this group's right to pass on its particular language and culture. Secondly, contacts must be made possible between the members of various ethnic groups. It is not only a matter of compensating for social and educational deficits in the sense of a „special pedagogy" for minorities, but also of familiarizing the dominant group with other cultures, and of helping restore respect on the part of dominant groups toward the cultures of minorities.

Polish educational scientists also remind us to take well into consideration the proportional balance between prudent integration into Western culture on the one hand, and preservation of a national cultural identity on the other (cf. Porozynski 2001, Zebrowski 2001, Mazurek 2004).

References:

Allemann-Ghionda, C. (1995): Interkulturelle Bildung zwischen Universalität und Partikularität ... In: Tertium comparationis 1(1995), S. 96-112

Auernheimer, G. (1989): Kulturelle Identität - ein gegenaufklärischer Mythos. In: Das Argument 175: 381-394.

Balint, M. (1972): Angstlust und Regression. Beitrag zur psychologischen Typenlehre. Reinbek.

Bos, W. u.a. (2003): Erste Ergebnisse aus IGLU. Schulleistungen am Ende der vierten Jahrgangsstufe im internationalen Vergleich. Münster / New York.

Cropley, A.J./Lüthke (1994), F.: Psychologische Aspekte der Adaptation von Zuwanderern. In: Probleme der Zuwanderung. Bd. 1. Göttingen/Stuttgart, S. 19-32.

Demorgon, J. (1999): Erziehung und Globalisierung. Für eine Kultur der Kulturen. In: Globalisierung: Perspektiven-Paradoxien-Verwerfungen. Jahrbuch für Bildungs- und Erziehungsphilosophie 2: Schneider Verlag Hohengehren: 9-25.

Education and Globalization (2004). Materials of Baikal International Conference, September 8-10, 2004. Ed.: Malanov, I.A. Ulan-Ude: Buryat State University Publishing House.

Faist, T. (1995): Sociological theories of international sought to north migration... Zentrum für Sozialpolitik, Universität Bremen, Arbeitspapier Nr. 17.

Golz, R. (2004): Probleme und Chancen der Integration russisch-jüdischer Migranten. In: Golz, R. / Ostrovskij, A. (Hrsg.): Probleme und Wege der Integration jüdischer Immigranten. Magdeburg: Otto-von-Guericke-Universität: 103-116; 221-234.

Janssen, S. (1997): Vom Zarenreich in den amerikanischen Westen: Deutsche in Russland und Russlanddeutsche in den USA 1871-1928.

Kargerova, J. / Krejcova, V. (2001): The Romany Minority and their Education in the Chech Republic. In: Humanisierung der Bildung. Jahrbuch 2001. Frankfurt a.M. (u.a.): 58-71.

Kubeček, M. (2003): Die Problematik der nationalen und ethnischen Minderheiten in der Tschechischen Republik (http://tucnak.fsv.cuni.cz/~kmv/pubCZE-minderheiten.doc).

Masschelein, J. (1995): Wo wohnen Weltenwanderer? (...). In: Koch, L. / Marotzki, W. / Peukert, H. (Hrsg): Erziehung und Demokratie. Weinheim: 117-122.

Mazurek, K. (2004): Polish Education Students´ View on Political Developments in the Former Soviet Union and Germany: A Longitudinal Study. In: Gumanizacija Obrazovanija. Moscow/Sochi: 100-112.

26

Nieke, W. (1995): Interkulturelle Bildung und Erziehung. Wertorientierungen im Alltag. Opladen.

Nieke, W. (1995): Interkulturelle Erziehung und Bildung (...). Opladen.

Porozynski, H. (2001): Polykulturalität im Polen der Zwischenkriegszeit und heute – eine pädagogische Herausforderung. In: Humanisierung der Bildung. Jahrbuch 2001. Frankfurt a.M. (u.a.): Lang: 37-45.

Rau, J. (2000): "Ohne Angst und ohne Träumereien: Gemeinsam in Deutschland leben" (http:www.bundespraesident.de/reden/rau/de/00_0512.htm [entnommen am 26.06.00]).

Rau, J. (2000): „Ohne Angst und ohne Träumereien: Gemeinsam in Deutschland leben" (http:www.bundespraesident.de/reden/rau/de/00_0512.htm [26.06.00]).

Retter, H. (1998): Das Phänomen der Migration (...) In: Das multikulturelle Europa. Akten der XXIV Internation. Tagung deutsch-italienischer Studien. Merano (Manuskript) 1998.

Rydl, K. (2001): Die Tschechische Republik und die Bildung ethnischer Minderheiten. In: Humanisierung der Bildung. Jahrbuch 2001. Frankfurt a.M. (u.a.): Lang: 46-57

Sassen, S. (1996): Migranten, Siedler, Flüchtlinge (...) Frankfurt a.M.

Suárez-Orozco, M.M. / Quin-Hilliard, D.B. (Hg.) (2004): Globalization. Culture and Education in the New Millennium. Berkeley / Los Angeles / London.

Wenning, N. (1993): Migration und Ethnizität in pädagogischen Theorien. Münster/New York

Wenning, N. (2004): Heterogenität als neue Leitidee der Erziehungswissenschaft? In: Zeitschrift für Pädagogik, Heft 4: 565-582.

Zebrowski, J. (2001): Multicultural Education in Modern Societies. In: Humanisierung der Bildung. Jahrbuch 2001. Frankfurt a.M. (u.a.): 13-19.

Oleg Zajakin (Pädagogische Universität Bijsk, Russland)

Russische Sprache und Kultur in historischen und aktuellen Prozessen der Binnenmigration und Transformation im Vielvölkerstaat Russland

Abstract
The history of Russian language and culture is characterized by a balance within the Russian system, which calls for one official language and common valuesas well as autonomy of ethnic groups living within the system - that claim for the sustainment of the own language and culture. Between these two contradictions is an educational system that has to be consistent with political goals of the epoch and talso has to consider the character of the several groups at the same time. The "multicultural phenomenon" has been a challenge for every political system in this area and in times of globalization and increasing migration this ongoing process steps into a new dimension with new challenges. Russian language again plays a key role in educating the next generations.

Das heutige Russland ist ein Vielvölkerstaat, der in seiner nationalen und staatlichen Zusammensetzung in der Welt keine Entsprechung hat. Die nichtrussische Bevölkerung in ihm beträgt insgesamt 20%, sie umfasst etwa 120 Ethnien. Unter den 89 Subjekten der Föderation, haben 32 den Status der nationalen Territorien.

Im Kontext der ökonomischen Globalisierung findet auch eine kulturelle Globalisierung statt. Letztere ist vor allem mit einer stürmischen Entwicklung auf dem Informationssektor verknüpft. Sie hilft, Kontakte zwischen Völkern und deren Kulturen rascher zu entwickeln. Hier ist nicht die Rede von einer Verwischung spezifischer Unterschiede zwischen Nationen und Nationalitäten, sondern von einer wechselseitigen Durchdringung unter Wahrung des Toleranzprinzips. Diese Idee ist weder außergewöhnlich noch neu. Bereits im 20. Jahrhundert drückte der bekannte russische Pädagoge P.F. Kapterev das so aus:

"Nationalität ist nicht von ewigem Bestand. Nicht nur deshalb, weil Völker nach einander von der Bühne der Geschichte abtreten, sondern weil sich mit der Zeit die internationalen Unterschiede und Grenzen verwischen und aufweichen. Die Völker werden sich ähnlicher, entlehnen von einander, treten in immer engere Beziehungen. Die Völker streben immer mehr nach Nähe und Vereinigung, sie streben danach, sich zu vereinen und nicht sich zu trennen. Heute sind die nationalen Besonderheiten noch deutlich sichtbar, die nationalen Interessen gehen häufig auseinander, es gibt noch viel nationale Feindschaft; doch das Werk geht hin zur Versöhnung und Vereinigung der Nationalitäten und nicht zur Teilung. Unter den Kulturvölkern gibt es so viel Gemeinsames, dass die wahrhaft gebildeten Menschen, zu welcher Nation sie auch gehören mögen, eine Gesellschaft bilden, und das Ideal des kulturellen Strebens ist eine freundschaftliche, einige Menschheit und nicht die Separierung der Nationalität. Ja, es wird eine einheitliche Herde und einen Hirten geben" (Kapterev 1915, S. 566-577).

Wenn wir von der Originalität eines Volkes sprechen, so haben wir vorrangig seine Kultur und seine Sprache als ein gemeinsames Ganzes im Blick. So war die Sachlage im Russischen Reich, später in der Sowjetunion und darauf im postsowjetischen Russland. Die Geschichte der Sowjetunion war im Bildungsbereich der nationalen Minderheiten durch eine stürmische Blüte der Schule mit einem Unterricht aller oder einem Teil der Fächer in der Muttersprache gekennzeichnet. "Diese Schulen wurden als Elemente des Aufbaus des Sozialismus betrachtet. Die offizielle sowjetische Doktrin ging von der Vorstellung der bevorstehenden Vereinigung der Nationen und der Homogenität einer künftigen klassenlosen Gesellschaft aus" (Kuzmin 1999, S. 645). Dieser Idee hing auch im bestimmten Grade der bekannte Wissenschaftler S.I. Hessen an.

Er ist überzeugt, dass der muttersprachliche Vorschulunterricht ein notwendiges Werkzeug für die Schüler ist. Unstrittig bleibt für ihn auch, dass die Staatssprache Unterrichtsfach ist. Nach seiner Meinung muss der gesamte Unterricht nur dann in der Muttersprache geführt werden, wenn die Qualität des Unterrichts, "der ein Bildungsziel verfolgt, die Schüler an eine weltumfassende, allgemeinmenschliche Kultur heranzuführen" nicht beeinträchtigt wird. Er ist entschieden gegen einen totalen Unterricht in der Muttersprache, wenn dieser "infolge der Unfertigkeit der Sprache, des Mangels an Literatur und an einer gebildeten Lehrerschaft nur fähig ist, die Unterrichtsqualität zu mindern, und Barrieren bei der Heranführung der Schüler an den Strom der heutigen Kultur errichtet" (Hessen 1995, S. 356-357).

Im Laufe einer verhältnismäßig langen Zeit ist die russische Sprache auch für die Russen selbst ein origineller Akkumulator der Weltkultur, die durch Übersetzungen vieler Werke sowohl ausländischer als auch jener Schriftsteller, die im Russischen Reich und später in der Sowjetunion lebten und in ihrer Muttersprache schrieben, in die russische Kultur eindrangen. Beispiele dafür sind der Kirgise Dshingis Ajtmatov, der Dagestaner Rasul Gamzatov, der Weißrusse Vasil Bykov und andere. Mittels des Russischen lernten alle Völker, die unsere Heimat bevölkern, ihre Werken kennen.

Unter Peter I. war die deutsche Sprache ein originelles "Fenster" in die Weltkultur, unter Katharina II. löste die französische Sprache die deutsche ab. Das war nicht nur der Mode geschuldet. "Das war eine zwingende Notwendigkeit, weil damals die französische Sprache den Zugang zur großartigen französischen Kultur, einschließlich der Wissenschaft möglich machte, was besonders in dieser Epoche wichtig war, da das Lateinische allmählich die Position der universellen Gelehrtensprache verlor" (Mironov 2002). In der ersten Hälfte des 19. Jahrhunderts wurde das Russische für die Völker Russlands Akkumulator der Weltkultur. Diese Rolle spielten und spielen für andere Völker die französische, portugiesische, spanische und schließlich die englische Sprache.

Die wunderbare Losung von der Gleichberechtigung aller Völker, von der Notwendigkeit, allen Völkern das Recht auf Selbstbestimmung – auch im Sprachgebrauch - einzuräumen, kollidiert mit der objektiven Realität unseres Lebens, die viele Völker zur Zweisprachigkeit zwingt. Doch bei näherer Betrachtung dieses Problems, zieht das nicht zwangsläufig die Assimilation eines bestimmten Volkes, dessen Sprache und Kultur nach sich, sondern rettet es in der Mehrheit der Fälle vor einer kulturellen Segregation.

Die geopolitischen Interessen des Staates bewirkten zu Beginn des 16. Jahrhunderts eine Missionsbewegung ähnlich der in den Kolonien der westlichen Staaten. Die "Sammlung" des Imperiums durch gewaltsame territoriale Eroberung konnte nicht das notwendige Ergebnis bringen, weil sich in diesem Fall das angeschlossene Volk bald von einem äußeren zu einem inneren Feind wandeln konnte. Davon ausgehend, war die Taktik und Strategie bezüglich der nichtrussischen Völker vor allem auf ihre allmähliche und freiwillige Integration in das Russische Reich und in die russische Kultur gerichtet. Zur Erreichung des gewünschten Ergebnisses war es notwendig, sich um die Bildung zu kümmern. Gegenstand der Sorge sollte, nach Meinung vieler, vor allem der Unterricht in der Muttersprache sein. Die Ausbildung einer nationalen Elite würde danach die notwendigen Voraussetzungen für die Christianisierung der nichtrussischen Bevölkerung und für die atmosphärische Kultivierung eines starken "russischen Reiches" sein. Besonders erfolgreich verlief eine analoge Bildungsarbeit im Wolgagebiet und in Sibirien. Jedoch ging der Ausweitungsprozess des Imperiums bei weitem nicht ungetrübt vonstatten. Beispielsweise wurden der Nordkaukasus, Nordasien und Polen durch Eroberungen angeschlossen. Deshalb "empfanden viele Völker Russlands nicht nur einen fruchtbaren Einfluss der russischen Kultur, sondern die gewaltsame Christianisierung und die Russifizierung" (Gračev 2002, S. 75). In den Unruheregionen wurde der Schwerpunkt auf die Erweiterung der weltlichen

Bildung, auf die sphärische Ausweitung der russischen Sprache und zum Nutzen Russlands auf die Veränderung der geopolitischen Orientierung gelegt. Auf diese Weise sammelte Russland über Jahrhunderte einmalige historische Erfahrungen bei der Errichtung eines komplizierten Systems interethnischer und interkonfessioneller Beziehungen, die objektiv durch Bildungswege die Neutralisation eines potentiellen und realen Separatismus beförderte. Im Ergebnis der Verwirklichung der Bildungspolitik, die auf der Nutzung der Muttersprache beruhte und ethnopsychologische, soziale und alltägliche Besonderheiten der Völker berücksichtigte, konnte das Russische Reich seine Position in den fremden Regionen festigen. Das geschah größtenteils dadurch, dass die orthodoxe Missionierung starken Einfluss auf die Formung eines positiven Bildes des Russischen Staates in der nichtrussischen Bevölkerung nahm (vgl. ebd.).

Jedoch befürchteten einige Staatsmänner, dass eine liberale Politik des Staates hinsichtlich der nationalen Bildung sich auch auf die politische Sphäre auswirken und die Gefährdung des territorialen Werts und der Einheit des Russischen Imperiums zur Folge haben könne.

Zu Beginn der Sowjetmacht im Jahre 1917 führte die neue Regierung des Landes beständig das Wort von der Unterrichtung aller oder der Mehrzahl der Schulfächer in der Muttersprache. Diese Bildungspolitik der 20er Jahre des vergangenen Jahrhunderts kollidierte mit einer Reihe von objektiven Umständen, vor allem dem Fehlen einer Schriftsprache bei vielen kleinen, im Land lebenden Völkern.

Die Bildungs- und Kulturpolitik auf Grundlage der Muttersprache könnte man als Fortsetzung der zaristischen Politik betrachten. Jedoch bei genauerem Hinsehen wird deutlich, dass erstens der christlich-religiöse Ursprung, der allmählich in das Bewusstsein der nichtrussischen Völker eindrang, durch die Ideologie der Bolschewiki ersetzt wurde, die nicht den nötigen Widerhall fand. Zweitens lief die Konzeption der übernationalen Erziehung den politischen Losungen vom nationalen Selbstbewusstsein und von der nationalen Identifikation zuwider.

Die Bildung in der UdSSR im Jahre 1922 und ihre folgende Erweiterung verlief praktisch in den Grenzen des ehemaligen Russischen Reichs. Die sowjetische Regierung traf auf die gleichen Probleme eines Vielvölkerstaates, mit denen es die zaristischen Herrscher zu tun hatten. In der Stalinzeit begann man die russische Sprache als internationales Verständigungsmittel zu betrachten. So kann man, wenn man sich diesem Begriff nähert, die russische Sprache formal als Instrumentarium zur Ausübung einfacher kommunikativer Funktionen betrachten, wie es hinsichtlich des Englischen möglich ist, wenn z.B. sich ein Spanier und ein Schwede verständigen. Doch eine solche Betrachtung der Rolle der russischen Sprache würde sie auf ein "Alltagsniveau" reduzieren. Tatsächlich spielte und spielt die russische Sprache (bei allen politischen und ideologischen Umständen) eine wesentlich bedeutendere Rolle im Leben eines solchen Vielvölkerstaat wie Russland.

Die Binnenkultur der nichtrussischen Nationalitäten blieb in der Zarenzeit hinlänglich erhalten. Ursache dafür war die sesshafte Lebensweise ihrer Träger. Doch viele zu Ende der 20er Jahre in die Kulturrevolution einbezogene Nationalitäten konnten jene Grenze nicht schnell überwinden, die die Völker mit einem patriarchalischen System von denen trennte, die bereits in den Industrialisierungsprozess geraten waren. Die Entwicklung des sozialistischen Staates in Richtung Industrialisierung und Kollektivierung der Landwirtschaft, d.h. jene Fundamente des gesellschaftlichen Lebens, die objektiv vom Bildungsniveau der Bevölkerung abhängig sind, führten dazu, dass am Ende der 30er Jahre die russische Sprache für den Unterricht obligatorisch wurde.

Das Wachsen der Industrie brachte den Urbanisierungsprozess in Bewegung. Jedoch lebte bis in die Mitte der 50er Jahre der größte Teil der Bevölkerung auf dem Lande. In dieser Zeit erhielt die Bevölkerung des Landes die Möglichkeit einer größeren Freizügigkeit. Die Abwanderung von Vertretern kleiner Völker aus ihren Diasporen führte allmählich dazu, dass sie die Bindung an ihre angestammte Kultur und Sprache verloren. Sie waren objektiv gezwungen, sich mit der russischsprachigen Kultur zu "vereinen" und die russische Sprache zu beherrschen. In jener Zeit migrierten Vertreter des russischen Volkes in die Republiken der Sowjetunion, wo sie danach im Verlaufe von vier Jahrzehnten lebten.

Der Zerfall der Sowjetunion war mit vielen Problemen verbunden, die nur in schönen Träumen einfach zu lösen sind. Mit der Gewinnung der Unabhängigkeit und der damit verbundenen Staatlichkeit standen die neuen Länder vor der politischen, nationalen und ideologischen Wahl der Staatssprache. Logisch betrachtet, sollte das die Sprache der Titelnationalität sein. In der Mehrzahl der Fälle fiel die erste Entscheidung so aus. Doch die Lebensrealität, die auf historischen Ereignissen und Prozessen beruht, brachte ihre Korrekturen. Die Jahrhunderte während gemeinsame Geschichte der nebeneinander lebenden Völker zeigte deutlich jene Schwierigkeiten, mit denen das Land im Bereich der nationalen Bildung kollidierte.

In Abhängigkeit vom Vorhandensein national-territorialer Formationen unterscheidet man gegenwärtig unter den ethnischen Gruppen einige Typen:

1. Gruppen, die ihre national-territoriale Formationen haben, die aber außerhalb deren Grenzen leben (z.b. Tataren in Baschkirien, Tschuwaschen in den Nachbargebieten von Tschuwaschien);
2. Gruppen, die ihre Staatlichkeit außerhalb der Grenzen der Russischen Föderation haben (Deutsche, Griechen, Juden) sowie Ethnien der ehemaligen Republiken der Sowjetunion (z.B. Ukrainer, Weißrußen, Georgier, Armenier u.a.);
3. Gruppen die keine eigene Staatlichkeit, aber viele Diasporen außerhalb der Russischen Föderation haben (z.B. Kurden, Sinti und Roma, Eskimos);
4. Gruppen, die keine eigene Staatlichkeit haben und vorrangig auf dem Territorium der Russischen Föderation sind (z.B. Wepsen, sibirische Tataren usw.)

(vgl. Matveev 1998, S. 635)

Die Nationalitäten, innerhalb Russlands leben, z.b. Baschkiren, Tschuwaschen u.a. vermieden zwei Extreme – die Assimilation und Segregation. Die russische Sprache ist für sie kein "Reizfaktor", was man am Beispiel anderer ehemaliger Republiken der Sowjetunion beobachten kann.

Gruppen, die keine eigene Staatlichkeit haben, "reagierten" unterschiedlich auf die russische Sprache und Kultur. Einige von ihnen existieren frei in einem bilingualen Raum und bewahren ihre eigenständige Kultur, viele andere assimilierten sich fast völlig.

Am Beispiel der Russlanddeutschen kann man den Prozess eines teilweisen oder völligen Verlusts der nationalen Kultur beobachten, der relativ schnell in der zweiten Hälfte des 20. Jahrhunderts verlief. Ende des 17. Jahrhunderts begannen Deutsche in Russland einzutreffen und dort zu siedeln, vor allem in dessen zentralen Teilen. Unter Katharina II. entstanden deutsche Kolonien im Wolgagebiet und in Neurussland, im 19. Jahrhundert im Kaukasus und im Südural, im Altaj sowie in ganz Sibirien. Nach Verlassen ihrer historischen Heimat setzten die Übersiedler ihre Traditionen fort, pflegten ihre Sprache und Kultur. Doch nach Ausbruch des Zweiten Weltkriegs, im August 1941, wurden die Deutschen auf Befehl der Regierung der UdSSR nach Kasachstan und nach Westsibirien deportiert. Damit wurde die Geschlossenheit ihrer Lebensweise gestört. Objektive und subjektive Faktoren trugen zur Zerstörung der Traditionen und zum Verlust der Muttersprache bei. Die Massenausreise der Russlanddeutschen in den 90er Jahren des vergangen Jahrhunderts in ihre historische Heimat zeigte, dass die in den 40er und 50er Jahren geborene Generation ihre innere Kultur und Muttersprache praktisch verloren hat. An ihre Stelle traten als Ausdrucksform die russische Sprache und russischsprachige Kultur. Und in der Folge ging eine Veränderung der Mentalität jener einher, die sich zur deutschen Nationalität zählen. Mit dieser kulturellen Mentalität behaftet kommen sie in ein Land, in dem für sie angefangen von der Sprache bis hin zu den Traditionen, Feiertage zu begehen, alles fremd ist. Es stellt sich die ahistorische Frage, was wäre wohl mit den deutschen Kolonien geschehen, wenn es keine Massendeportation gegeben hätte. Möglich ist, sie hätten die Sprache ihrer Vorfahren bewahrt, die nur noch in bestimmten Teilen Deutschlands gesprochen wird. Es ist auch möglich, sie hätten sich allmählich in der russischsprachigen Kultur "verloren". Ein analoges Beispiel liefern die Bewohner des Böhmischen Dorfs in Berlin, die in der deutschen Kultur völlig aufgegangen sind.

Dasselbe kann man hinsichtlich der russischen Juden sagen, deren Mehrheit nicht Jiddisch spricht und die Traditionen nicht genau befolgt, die ihre Vorfahren im Russischen Reich pflegten.

Die Migrationsprozesse sind mit vielen Faktoren verknüpft. Von denen spielen Sprache und Kultur eine wichtige Rolle. Die Mehrheit der 11 Millionen Menschen, die von 1989 bis 2002 nach Russland einwanderten, taten das aus Furcht vor Segregation im sprachlichen und geistlich-kulturellen Bereich und in der Folge in allen Bereichen des gesellschaftlichen Lebens in ihrer früheren Wahlheimat.

Fazit:
Die russische Sprache war für die Völker, die Russland besiedelten, ein origineller Akkumulator der Weltkultur. Die russische Sprache war und ist ein Mittel der interkulturellen Kommunikation in einem großen multinationalen Staat, sie spielte bei der Lösung staatlich-nationaler Probleme die Rolle des "über dem Wasserspiegel liegenden Teils eines Eisbergs".

Literatur:

Гессен, С.И. (1995): Основы педагогики. Введение в прикладную философию. Москва: Школа-Пресс.

Грачев, С.В. (2002): Образование нерусских народов Российской империи в геополитическом контексте. В: Советская педагогика (7): 72 – 80.

Каптерев, П.Ф. (1915): История русской педагогию Петроград: Книжный склад «Земля».

Кузьмин, М.Н. (1998): Этнопедагогика. В: Давыдов, В.В. (Ред.): Российская педагогическая энциклопедия. Москва: Большая Российская энциклопедия: 644 – 646.

Матвеев, К.П. (1998): Этнические группы. В: Давыдов, В.В. (Ред.): Российская педагогическая энциклопедия. Москва: Большая Российская энциклопедия: 635 – 637.

Миронов, Ю.В. (2002): Русский язык. В: www.left.ru/2002/26/mironov76.html

Irina. I. Caunenko and Lucia Gasper (University of the Republic of Moldova)

The Formation of Ethnic Youth Identities and the Problem of Tolerance

Abstract

The unique situation of the Republic of Moldova is that all age groups face the crisis of social identity. Our experimental research on the problem of formation of adolescents' and young people's ethnic identity revealed potential for the formation of positive ethnic identity. Summarizing our research and practical experience in the given field, we can underline the following aspects: the practical work on ethnic tolerance formation is necessary to carry out with an adolescent's social environment such as his or her parents, teachers, and peer groups. The difficulties in communication which an adolescent face, are largely caused by lack of "place of gathering", inadequate communication in the family, as well as little interaction with different ethnic groups. For Moldova, which is a multiethnic country, the problem of ethnocultural competence and intercultural dialogue is one of the burning issues of the day.

At present the unique situation of the Republic of Moldova is that all age groups face the crisis of social identity. For youth the problem is choosing the social group through which they can identify themselves. For the elderly it is the loss of identity, which is linked with a feeling of a senselessly spent life (Andreeva 2000). For the middle-aged it is a changing attitude towards their self-determination and what is going on in the changing world.

Our experimental research on the formation of adolescents' and young people's ethnic identity (Caunenco 2000, 2001; Caunenco/Miron-Gasper 2001) revealed the difficult and contradictory process of ethnic identity formation, and the presence of the potential for the formation of positive ethnic identity in both ethnic groups (titular and ethnic minorities, united in our research by the "Russian-speaking" group). The continuation of the empirical research on ethnic identity was searching for ways to develop adolescents' and young people's ethnic tolerance. Summarizing our research and practical experience in the given field (2001-2003), we can underline the following:

Practical work on ethnic tolerance formation is necessary to carry out with an adolescent's social environment such as his or her parents, teachers, and peer groups.

At the beginning of our work we included in the training programs only adolescents and young people. The implementation of the program, "The Development of Adolescents' Ethnic Identity" (with the assistance of Soros Foundation in

Moldova – 2001) identified a number of difficulties typical for the majority of the participants of the Program. The following problems were referred as general difficulties: interpersonal and interethnic communication, self-reflection and self-knowledge, and inadequate communication with parents.

The difficulties in communication, which an adolescent faces, are largely caused by lack of "place of gathering", inadequate communication in the family, as well as little interaction with different ethnic groups. For example, the adolescents taking part in our research in Chisinau knew little or nothing about the Gagauz people, who live in the south of Moldova.

Our research identified a rather distant position of national schools, which obviously impoverishes the experience of interethnic communication and makes it difficult to establish an intercultural dialogue. The Program resulted in the necessity to include both teachers and parents, because they themselves sometimes are ethnically prejudiced and need both informational and psychological support.

We have come to the conclusion that the basis of an effective work on interethnic tolerance formation must be family – school – peer group relationships.

While working with an adolescent's social environment, it is necessity to provide psychological support and broaden ethno-cultural knowledge.

At the next step of our research we included parents and teachers as well as adolescents in the Program of tolerance (the Project "Development of Tolerance – the Basis of Intercultural Dialogue of the Young People" – with the assistance of Moldova Soros Foundation 2002). It was teenagers who insisted on such a project. ("We are talking about tolerance, but the parents don't understand us. Do work with them and let them know about it"). On their own initiative, they began working on tolerance with younger classes.

The Program took two directions. The first was on the positive image "I" (self-appraisal) and behavior reaction, and the second was the work at intergroup level. We proceeded from the fact that positive ethnical contact increases the positivity of ethnical images. The joint activity changes the images of different groups in a positive way (Lebedeva/Luneva/Stefanenko/Martynova 2003) and contributes to moral reflection, world ethnical cultural variation, and ethnic knowledge.

The main goals of the program were as follows: development of ethno cultural sensitivity, communication skills, strengthening social relations, development of skill in establishing intercultural dialogue, and psychological support.

We used the following forms of work: socio-psychological training, conversations, and discussions. Adolescents between 14 and 19 years of age, and parents and teachers between ages 25-55 were enrolled in the study. The number of participants varied from 8 to 14 people. Participation of various ethnic groups living in the same district was obligatory. Therefore, the participants involved were students attending both Russian and Romanian schools.

The work on self-knowledge was the most interesting, yet also the most difficult. The following statements were common: "We got used to the fact that our main responsibilities are the work and the family and there is no time to think about ourselves and to have a heart-to-heart talk with somebody".

While doing the exercise "I can be proud of myself because…" often there were such answers from teenagers. "I'd better say that everything is bad with me, because we were told so by our teachers and parents. I know about this" ,and from adults, "It is impossible to answer at once. We live in such times that have forgotten to think about good things. If only we could survive. We must think about it".

The most frequent response the adolescents gave to the question "My best day of the year" was either the day of a parent's return (who earned money abroad) or a day spent with their family. Nowadays, the family is support for a teenager and a "silent harbour" where one can hide from social difficulties. This was also proven by empirical data from many authors whose research supports these health and development issues of Moldova youth (The Project "Health and Development of Moldova Youth", the leader of the project Galina Lesco, UNICEF Moldova, 2003. Representative selection – 2170 teenagers and young people). Our research indicated that for youth, the leading values were a happy family life, health, good and faithful friends, and love. At the same time, these values (which transcended region, gender, and age) were also the most problematic. Prevalence of subjective importance of these life spheres over accessibility leads to fear and anxiety.

While analyzing the participants' self-knowledge, we identified adults' tiredness in their struggle for "survival", instability of the present and unpredictability of the future (especially anxiety about the future of their children). For children, loneliness was caused either by inadequate communication with their parents or the parents' long absence due to their work abroad. Therefore, we can say that there grows a whole generation which episodically interacts with their parents. At the same time practically all the participants in the program took part with a sincere interest.

In our time the psychologist's task is to help "ordinary man to find himself in a new changed society, to become proficient in new roles dictated by new times, and to correlate more exactly his notion about the world with the real one" (Andreeva 2000, p.197).

The work with teachers was the most difficult. The influence of the authoritarian educational system is still strong; moreover, there are plenty of personal problems which do not "fit in with" the educational activity. The overall teachers' tiredness is also noteworthy, which demonstrates their need for psychological support and attention.

The analysis of cultural stereotypes and the emotional experience of the ethnic group was one of the most difficult. One of the participants of our program, a teacher, declared: "Other people know that they are Ukrainians or Gagauz. They have their holidays to celebrate together. But I hold Byelorussian nationality after my father and Russian nationality after my mother. I know neither traditional customs of Byelorussians, nor their language. Everybody goes with their people but I am with nobody".

While analyzing cultural stereotypes and intercultural perception, we identified young people's aspiration to understand the modern world, interest in how to establish relations with people of another culture, and desire to analyze the current changes in their own ethnic group: "We, the Gagauz people, were friendlier in the past. My grandfather used to tell me that if they had milled corn flour, they did it all together and very friendly. But nowadays people are selfish. Everything has changed". The work at intergroup level indicated a low intercultural communication level and sometimes poor knowledge of one's own culture. For example, in the exercise "Analysis of Sayings" (when the participants of training were divided according to ethnicity) even the process of choosing the defining qualities of an ethnicity and demonstrating cultural situations of the ethnic group caused difficulties. In our research we used the general "we" to mean common purpose and interdependency. We proceeded from the assumptions that overlap between categories results in blurring the intergroup borders, along with them all the negative social purposes. (Stefanenko 2003, p.199). We asked the participants to write their thoughts on the themes of "Moldova is...", "My future", "Moldova is a country of small tourism" and others. While working with parents, we found ethnic tolerance through family history and tolerant attitudes in the family. Our research identified an acute problem of resocialization of family members who were away from home for a long time due to their work abroad. We observed the following: "It's difficult for my son to communicate with his father. My husband feels hurt when our children turn to me if they have any problems. As if they have no father." This leads to family tension and sometimes misunderstanding.

The Program identified that it is necessary to acquire knowledge about interethnic relationships and to understand the psychology of ethnic identity as being important components in the formation of your own cultural identity.

In conclusion, for Moldova, which is a multiethnic country, the problem of ethnocultural competence and intercultural dialogue is one of the burning issues of the day. Neglecting this problem would lead to segregation and marginalization of the different ethnic groups in Moldova (Lebedeva 2003, pp. 248-249).

References

Andreeva, G.M. (2000): The psychology of social cognition. M.: Aspect

Caunenco, I.I.: On the problem of formation of ethnical identity of teen-agers. (On the material of Moldova). In: Journal of Applied Psychology. M., 2000: No. 2: p. 58-61

Lebedeva, N.M.: Social identity in the Former Soviet Union space. From the search of self-respect to the search of sence. In: Journal of Psychology, 1999: No 3: p. 48-58

Lebedeva, N.M./Luneva, O.V./Stefanenco, T.G./Martynova, M.I. (2003): The intercultural dialogue: Training of ethnical cultural competence. M.

Stefanenco, T.G. (2003): Ethnical conflicts: The reasons of their appearance and the methods of their regulation. In: Martynova, M.I./Tishkova, V.A./Lebedeva.,N.M. (Ed.): Intercultural dialogue: Training of ethnical cultural competence. M.

Stefanenco, T.G. (2002): Social psychology in the cultural-historical perspective. In: Andreeva, G.M./Dontsov., A.I. (Ed.): Social psychology in the contemporary world. Aspect Press,

Lebedeva, N.M./Tatarko, A.N. (Ed.)(2002): Ethnical tolerance in the polycultural regions of Russia. M.: Publishing House PYDH

Caunenco, I./Miron-Gasper, L.: Ethnical identity. In: Journal of Psychology, 2001: Vol. 47, No. 3-4: pp. 279-287

Laurie Walker (University of Lethbridge, Canada)

Political Tensions and Resistance in the Reform of Teacher Training in Kosovo, 2001-2004

Abstract

This paper is concerned with a project to transform part of the shattered education system of Kosovo. It presents a case study of some of the factors that were impediments to the formation of a reformed system for training new teachers as part of the attempt by international agencies to assist Kosovo in modernizing its schools, curriculum, and teaching and learning. Although internationally funded projects were generous and well meaning, responses by stakeholder groups were not always positive. Transformative change was a threat to some vested interests and opposition and resistance had to be factored into attempts to re-build and reform institutions. This paper focuses on the education of new teachers which was one of many educational reform projects underway in Kosovo in the post-war period, 2000-2003, many of which still continue. It attempts to analyze the resistance and political tensions that this project encountered.

Introduction

In 2001 the Canadian International Development Agency [CIDA] approved funding for a three-year project to assist Kosovo in re-building and reforming its programs for training teachers. The amount provided was $8 million Canadian dollars, or about 12 million Deutschmarks, the currency used in Kosovo until January 2002 when the Euro was adopted. At the current exchange rate, the allocation would have been about 4.9 million euros. In 2003 CIDA approved a three-year extension until 2007 with additional funding.

Following the war of 1999, which ended by the NATO bombing in Serbia and Kosovo, the United Nations took over the administration of Kosovo. Security was provided by NATO military forces and by a large international contingent of police officers. Education was administered by the Department of Education and Science staffed by United Nations appointed officials paired with local Kosovars. The Head of the Department of Education and Science [DES] also had considerable authority over the University of Pristina.

Re-building

The Department had an enormous task to rebuild a functioning education system at the elementary, secondary and post-secondary levels. Since the 1980's the Serbian authorities had undermined education for the majority of the population of ethnic Albanians. Albanian speaking professors had been dismissed and expelled The university, which had been established in 1971, became a Serb language institution. Albanian public schools suffered the same fate. The Albanians, showing great resilience in the 1990's, established underground education systems using funds from expatriates living in other European countries and in North America. Classes were offered in garages and private homes. Teachers and professors taught heroically for little or no salary in a remarkable response to state oppression. However, the system had its dark side. Learning resources were scarce and poor so that achievement levels were low. The flow of funds from the voluntary taxation was difficult to control and corruption flourished. Thus the legacy, which post-1999 Kosovo inherited, was one of heroism but on the other hand, low standards and misuse of resources resulted.

Reform
The task was not simply to restore programs of teacher training; fundamental reform was also needed. The preparation of new teachers for Kosovo's schools was the responsibility of the University of Pristina. In 2000 pre-primary and primary programs (up to grade 9) were offered by five units of the University. Four of these were higher pedagogical schools in Pristina, Gjilan, Prizren and Gjakove. The fifth was a relatively new faculty of teaching. Programs in the HPS's were two years in length; the faculty of teaching's programs were 4 years in length, like most programs offered by the University. The preparation of higher secondary teachers (grades 10-12) was in the hands of the academic faculties of the University. These single subject programs were also four years in length.

The vision for a post-war Kosovo established by the United Nations was of a peaceful transition to a pluralistic democracy and a market economy. Success would depend upon development of the skills, talents and knowledge of the population (the youngest in Europe), and upon broad acceptance of the values of equality, tolerance, respect for difference, human rights, and justice. Clearly education had a vital role in this transformation of Kosovo society. However, all aspects of education – curriculum, facilities, resources, governance, funding and teaching – had themselves to be transformed before children graduating from the public schools could make any contribution to the economic, political and social agenda. This paper deals with the planned transformation of teacher training as one part of the overall reform of public education.

The higher pedagogical schools and the faculty of teaching were very weak. Their buildings were in poor repair; teaching facilities were bleak; library resources old fashioned and inadequate. Teaching methods were mostly lecture; learning was usually a matter of memorizing verbatim information. Professors were mostly elderly; texts books, except those written by professors and published by the university press, were in many cases over twenty years old. Examinations were usually oral, and students often claimed that corruption was rife. Professors were authoritarian in their approach to students.

Practice teaching was of short duration (two weeks in total). It was not directed by explicit policies and requirements. The roles of the professor and of the mentor teacher were not articulated as formal policy and requirements. One form of practice teaching was for the student teacher to teach a lesson in a school with the other members of the methods class watching with the professor. Such a system did not allow students to teach many classes nor to develop confidence in their professional work.

The programs for training high school students were mostly intensive four-year studies of a single subject such as biology or mathematics. Included in the programs designated as teacher preparation and operated autonomously by academic departments were usually a course in psychology and a methods, or didactics, course in the single subject. Practice teaching might be offered as part of the methods course, but this was left to the initiative of the instructor. Some students completed their program without any teaching experience or guided practice teaching. Subject competence was the only criterion in learning to be a high school teacher.

In all programs of teacher preparation (17 units of the University in total) had their own independent programs), the typical pattern of enrolment was very large classes in first year with heavy attrition rates reducing second year enrollment by as much as 50 per cent. One popular department, English studies, would typically have 400 students enrolling in first year, but only ten students would graduate four years later. One consequence of this attrition was that most teaching resources in the University went into courses for first-year students, many of whom did not return for the subsequent years of study. Students paid very little in the way of fees.

Goals of the Teacher Training Project
As defined in the memorandum of agreement signed by CIDA and the Ministry of Education and Science in 2001, KEDP's goals were to bring about reform in the training of teachers. One branch was to develop in-service programs for current teachers and the other branch to develop a reformed system of pre-service training. The work of the second branch is the focus of this paper. Broadly the

goal of the pre-service branch was to help Kosovars raise the standard of pre-service teacher preparation to the level of countries in western Europe, a somewhat nebulous target. The first operational goal was to replace the existing system of multiple small departments and higher pedagogical schools with a single, integrated faculty of education responsible, initially, for the preparation of all new teachers for Kosovo's schools. Eventually, the expectation was that the faculty would become a comprehensive institution for the education of teachers, both pre-service and in-service, for research into education and for graduate studies. As the DES Head said, the faculty would be a "beacon" for education in Kosovo. The creation of a single Faculty of Education was seen as a prerequisite for the total work of the Project. Otherwise the current systems of training teachers would remain un-coordinated and incoherent, incapable of embarking on the major changes needed. A single Faculty of Education was expected to provide a more powerful voice for teacher training in the University, to lead the process of reform in teacher education, and to be able to attract more external funding resources.

The second operational goal was to create reformed and up-dated programs, offered in cooperation with academic departments which would be responsible for the academic, or subject matter training, leaving the Faculty of Education with responsibility for the professional component (pedagogy, didactics, foundations, etc.), and for a refurbished practice teaching which was to be the focusing centre of the program reforms..

The third operational goal was to provide professional development for professors to re-orient them to the new programs and to modern approaches to curriculum and teaching so that students would be learning and observing effective teaching on the campus and practicing these professional skills as student teachers in the schools.

Graduates of the Faculty's programs, taught by professors using modern techniques and Who were confident in their professional expertise, would be able to teach the new curriculum. Their pupils would have the skills, knowledge and attributes needed by the new Kosovo.

The purpose of this third goal was not to outlaw or denigrate the lecture form of teaching. However it was obvious that the lecture form had fallen into disrepute in Kosovo's teacher training and in broader University studies. Restoration of effective lecturing involves paying attention to the necessary qualities of effective direct teaching: engagement of students, linking previous knowledge with new information, and provision of practice and application of the ideas presented (Joyce 2000). In addition, this goal included showing professors how to use other proven teaching models or approaches such as group investigation, inductive teaching, concept attainment, and advance organizers. In other words, the goal was to help professors increase their teaching repertoires.

Summary of Progress, 2001-2003

1. After nearly a full year of negotiation, lobbying, political set-backs, procrastination and debate, in May, 2002, the newly appointed Minister of Education, Science and Technology [MEST] and the Rector of the University of Pristina agreed to set up a Joint Steering Board]JSB]to recommend policies, design, structure and programs of a new faculty of education. The Minister set out some major parameters for the Board's work. Programs were to be four years in length. Initially the faculty's programs would be limited to pre-primary and primary teacher preparation with a maximum of 320 students admitted. The higher pedagogical schools were to cease admission of pre-primary and primary candidates to their programs in the fall of 2002. They would become regional centers of the new faculty of education. The Minister decreed that if the faculty were successful in its first year of operation, it could then plan to introduce new programs for the preparation of lower secondary teachers (grades 6-9) in the fall of 2003.

2. The JSB began its work immediately and by September 2002 it had logged over 40 meetings. Chaired by the Director of KEDP, which also provided expert advice as well as a stipend for each of the local members for each meeting attended, the ten-member JSB brought forward in July a comprehensive plan for the new faculty. This plan was immediately accepted by the Minister and Rector, and, after considerable debate and delay, it was finally approved by the university Senate in September of 2002.

3. With the new Faculty of Education approved and an interim dean appointed, admission examinations for applicants were held, For the 320 positions available, over 1200 applications were received. Faculty members were appointed and classes began in October, 2002, which was one month later than the official beginning of classes in the University.

4. Workshops and seminars were held for professors on planning courses, evaluation of students' work, teaching methods and, most importantly, on a new conception of practice teaching. This professional development work was carried out by KEDP staff and by experts from Albania, Slovenia and Denmark.

5. Practice teaching was the core of the reform of pre-service teacher preparation. Students were to spend a total of 22 weeks in full-time practice in schools, fol-

lowing a developmental model of the formation of the skilled and professional teacher. In order to ensure a successful first practicum in April of 2003, much detailed planning, led by KEDP, began in the preceding October. Orientation meetings for mentor teacher-volunteers took place in each of the faculty's centers; detailed handbooks were written, field tested and translated; professors attended workshops on their roles as mentors and supervisors; students themselves were given detailed orientation to their roles in schools. The first two-week practicum was a resounding success. All participants – students, teachers and professors – spoke highly of the experience.

6. In January, 2003, the Minister announced that he was satisfied with the faculty's first semester of operation and that the JSB should proceed with phase 2 planning for the inclusion of lower secondary teacher training (grades 6-9) in the faculty's responsibilities, effective October, 2003. It was not just a matter of handing programs offered by the HPS's over to the new faculty. Kosovo's new Curriculum Framework approved in 2001 proposed major changes in the school curriculum at all levels, and it was obviously necessary to build a pre-service training program that would prepare new teachers to implement the new curriculum. The Kosovo tradition of preparing lower secondary teachers to work with two subject areas was continued. In addition a coherent professional component was developed and the same amount of practice teaching as in the pre-primary and primary programs prescribed. Another Kosovo tradition was followed whereby all courses and components of the lower secondary programs were offered by the faculty of education instead of working in cooperation with other faculties in the provision of the academic, or subject courses.

7. Senate approval for the new set of lower secondary programs was very late with the result that classes for the first cohort of lower secondary students began late in the year 2003 and, in some cases, classes did not begin until the following February. The Interim Dean (now Dean) had enormous difficulty in finding professors to teach the new courses in each of the centers. In addition to the lower secondary cohort, the 2003-2004 academic year brought in new first year cohorts for pre-primary and primary as well as year 2 classes for those programs. Total enrolments for all faculty programs went from 320 in year 1 to 900 in year 2. The number of full-time faculty members went from 14 in the first year of operations to nearly 50 in year 2.

8. By the end of 2004, the consensus was that the new faculty was a success but that it was still a very fragile institution: lacking its own space in Pristina and operating in difficult circumstances with respect to instructors and faculty members; inadequate resources for students; and a thin administrative system.

Resistance

The project began in 2001 in a spirit of naïve optimism on the part of the Canadians in the project. We understood that a six-week study of the needs of teacher education in Kosovo had been concluded and that a plan and design for a new faculty of education had been approved by a majority of Kosovo stakeholders. There was an assumption that, as far as the Faculty of Education was concerned, the task was to implement what had been planned and endorsed. We were ready to work with colleagues from Kosovo to use generous resources from Canadian tax payers to help remedy problems in education and teacher education. It seemed as though Kosovars were eager for us to get started. Of course this simple view of the task was a naïve delusion.

No one seemed to have considered the scale of operations even if programs for high school teachers were not included. The new faculty would have to take over multiple programs that needed massive changes. It would have to plan for admission of at least 1,000 students to the first of four years of study, leading to a potential enrolment of 3000 to 4,000 within four years for programs to train teachers for pre-primary to grade 9. Also required would be the appointment of a large number of professors from a pool that contained few younger candidates and almost none who had any exposure to modern approaches to teacher education.

Once the Canadians were on the ground in Kosovo (June, 2001) it was clear that not all stakeholders supported the ambitious and grandiose plan for a new Faculty of Education. The deans and directors of the large number of existing faculties, departments and schools providing programs to train teachers quickly moved to protect their own interests in the education of teachers.

Resistance from the Academic Faculties

The Deans of the Faculties of Science and Mathematics, Philology, Social Sciences, Physical Education, and Fine Arts made it clear that, although they welcomed reform of teacher education and the possible resources that would be available, they were not willing to give up their role as providers of programs for the preparation of high school teachers. They did not mind that the higher pedagogical schools would be replaced by a single Faculty of Education, provided the academic faculties were untouched. They claimed to have only vague recollections of the consultations that had led to the preparation of the Canadian plan. With all the international agencies who were in Kosovo proffering assistance in education, it was quite likely that the deans were having difficulty sorting out who was who in the business of education reform. They certainly had not understood the massive nature of the changes, nor had they realized the impact of these changes on their faculties.

One argument that the Deans raised was that in 2001 their faculties were working through the Bologna Accord reforms of their programs and that Deans and professors were exhausted by the planning needed to reduce four-year degrees to three-year programs. These major reforms were approved by Senate in September 2001. The Deans were emphatic that their faculties would not be willing to embark on a second set of major changes on top of new programs to be implemented in the 2001-2002 academic year. This was a rational and reasonable point of view. We were puzzled why the Canadian Plan designers had not referred to this major, university-wide change as part of the context in which the new Faculty of Education was to be implemented.

The Deans were also worried that if their teacher training programs were handed over to a new faculty, their enrollments would plummet. Given the context of University study in Kosovo, this anxiety was very real. The tradition in Kosovo was that students enrolled in specialist, single-subject programs within academic faculties. A student, for example, could choose biology in the Faculty of Science and Mathematics. The full four years of study would be in the one department and the graduate would be an "expert" in the single subject of biology, albeit not necessarily an expert in modern biology. A student would also choose between the regular program in biology to be trained as a biologist, or the teacher training program to prepare to be a biology teacher. Each department in the academic faculties managed its own program. Given the economy of Kosovo and the massive unemployment, the teacher education programs seemed to provide a better chance of employment so a large proportion of students at the University of Pristina were, nominally at least, enrolled in teacher education programs

The tradition did not place much value on professional and practical courses in education as a field of study. Apart from a course in didactics and a course in psychology, there was little preparation for prospective high school teachers in foundations, pedagogy, learning, curriculum, evaluation, or the social context of education. Practice teaching in the schools, while formally required, seemed to be left to the professors teaching the didactics course. For the academic Deans, the teacher education programs were cheap to operate. Since the traditional concept of a high school teacher was someone who was an expert in a subject and who disdained professional knowledge and expertise, there was little local cause for the Deans and department heads to feel ashamed about the inadequacy of their teacher training programs for the needs of schools and teachers in post-war Kosovo.

The lines quickly became drawn. The professors, department heads and Deans insisted that the training of new high school teachers must not be included in the mandate of the new Faculty of Education. They were not interested in cooperation with the new faculty whereby the academic faculties would offer the courses in the subject disciplines while the Faculty of Education would be in charge of the professional courses and practice teaching. The Canadians tried to explain the three essential and inter-related components of modern teacher education: academic learning, professional knowledge, and practice skills. The Deans seemed to find this analysis very difficult to grasp and certainly beyond trust. Reform was welcome but not in their programs. They stuck to their guns on this issue so that to date they still remain in sole charge of teacher training for the high school level. There have been some overtures from the academic faculties to Education seeking assistance with the internal reform of their teaching.

Resistance from Higher Pedagogical Schools and the Faculty of Teaching
Three out of the four directors of the HPS's and the Dean of the Faculty of Teaching welcomed the idea of reform as long as it did not affect their programs. The Faculty of Teaching had been established in 1997 by the Rector of the University as step one in the elimination of the HPS's. However, the addition of one new player in teacher education for pre-primary and primary teachers was not followed by step 2, the elimination of the old fashioned HPS's. When it comes to programs, universities, by their nature, always find it easier to add than to subtract.

The HPS's were under the nominal but not very active supervision of the Rector and Pro-Rectors and they had strong representation on the Senate of the university. They offered, until 2001, two-year programs for teachers who would be licensed to teach up to the end of compulsory schooling (grade 9). There were three sets of these programs: pre-primary, primary, and lower secondary. Lower secondary programs were two-subject preparations, for example, geography and history. The primary programs prepared class teachers, that is teachers who generally taught all subjects in grades 1 to 5. Pre-primary prepared educators to work with children from age 3 years until the beginning of primary education at age 7.

The HPS's were not highly regarded by the rest of the university, although they did have their strategic allies among the professors who were able to earn extra income from teaching courses in the two-year programs. They were looked down on as inferior academic units, staffed with weak instructors. This status issue was a major theme for the HPS's: most of their positions on reform were based in their ambitions to win academic respect for their individual units. For example, their lower secondary programs seemed to be designed to imitate the courses offered in the university proper, with a heavy emphasis on academic courses and, as a result, weak professional and practice teaching components. It looked as though the HPS directors were trying to achieve in two years what the academic faculties did in four.

Secondly, very significant for the Canadian project to establish a single Faculty of Fducation, was the fact that the HPS's were included in the Bologna Accord reforms of 2001. In other words, they were required to revise their two-year programs to the new norm of three years, leading to a degree, or diploma. The HPS's saw this as a boost to their status; their programs were now to be of the same duration of the faculties' and they were now providing diplomas. Shouldn't they now be fully-fledged faculties? Bologna became a kind of touchstone of their own appeal for faculty status.

In October, 2001, in the midst of planning for the new faculty, three of the four HPS's embarked on a coordinated campaign to advance the claim that each of the four HPS's was de facto a separate Faculty of Education. They welcomed, they said, the new, proposed faculty of education as one of six faculties of education in Kosovo, all faculties within the University of Pristina: four former HPS's, the faculty of teaching, and the new comer Faculty of Education proposed by the Canadians. On two HPS campuses signs went up proclaiming the new status as "faculties of education". One HPS published leather-bound notebooks for its staff embossed with "Faculty of Education, Prizren". The faculty of teaching's position was that it should be the core of the new Faculty of Education. No one else took this claim seriously.

The International Head of DES made strong statements in writing and in meetings with the Directors about the hopelessness of their cause. However, they did not accept his orders to plan for the incorporation of their institutions into the new faculty. In the fall of 2001, the Directors of the HPS's realized that the International Head of DES was soon to hand over power to the new Kosovar Ministry of Education, Science and Technology. They campaigned vigorously for the status of individual faculties. Their staff members wrote letters to the press, spoke on television, recruited political allies in their local communities, and contacted key members of the new Kosovo government, including President Rugova and the Prime Minister. There was evidence of some ferment in the university community. When KEDP organized information meeting with the HPS staffs, agendas were hijacked by set speeches about the traditions of the HPS's, about the quality of their work, and the glorious future that the Bologna reforms promised them as individual Faculties of Education.

One factor that contributed to the opposition was that there was no serious attempt to involve HPS's staffs in shaping the reforms and re-building. The DES, the Rectorate, and, later, the Minister of Education refused to consider the inclusion of HPS staff members in the planning process on the grounds of incompetence. KEDP pointed out that research is clear on the obvious principle that change requires buy-in on the part of those who will be affected by reforms and who will be involved in their implementation. This exclusion was a serious flaw in the planning for the new faculty. However, given the authoritarian tradition in Kosovo, it was likely that such participation by the HPS staffs would have been little more than a token gesture.

Resistance from Professors

One fundamental factor affecting the stance of professors toward reform involved low salaries. Although a Kosovar professor enjoys high status in society and especially in the extended family which is so important to all Kosovars. His/her salary is very low by European standards, although on a par with regional standards. In 2000-2001 the DES salary scale for teachers and professors provided a monthly salary of DM 420 for full professors, secondary school teachers DM 318; and primary teachers DM 291. (OECD Centre for Cooperation with Non-Members 2001, p. 24) There are no retirement pensions for professors. To augment their meager salaries, most taught in more than one faculty or school; some traveled to Tetova in Macedonia to teach courses at the Albanian university. Friday was a poor day for meetings because that was the day professors were on the road to Tetova.

Their economic condition affected the motivation of many professors to take seriously the task of upgrading and learning new ways to teach and conduct their classroom work. At workshops and seminars we would hear complaints that it was not worth their while to learn new things when the economic rewards were so low. One administrator told me he arrived at work at 9.00 a.m. and at 2.00 p.m. he went home to get ready for his private classes in English that he taught in his home. He said he was not willing to consider anything that would add to the time he spent at his official work.

When KEDP scheduled training workshops for professors, we would have complaints that they could not attend for full days because they had other jobs that paid better than their professorial positions. Some international organizations paid professors to attend workshops and seminars. KEDP paid for meals for participants and for accommodation and travel for events held outside the capital, Pristina. It was said that the Department of English at the University lost several professors and students who found lucrative employment as translators with international organizations in Kosovo.

Another way of dealing with the idea of change in teaching was to claim that they already used modern techniques. Their belief seemed to be that the main element of reform in teaching was to have students work in small groups, a technique which some claimed to be using already. They saw group work as a simple technical teaching method that anyone could learn to use easily. While group work is an important part of modern pedagogy, its success requires fundamental changes in the relationship between professor and students and deep differences in classroom management.

For example, I was able to observe the teaching of several Kosovo professors The traditional relationship between student and professor in Kosovo lecture rooms was strictly authoritarian. Students were, for the most part, silent. If called upon to answer or to raise a question, the student would stand at his/her desk waiting for the professor's permission to speak. This was a management technique that kept all power over classroom discourse in the hands of the professor. Standing to attention seemed to be part of some military tradition. Modern pedagogy requires some sharing of power between professor and students. A certain amount of free talk by students is essential for social forms of classroom learning such as group exploration of concepts, concept development and problem solving. Learner-centred instruction where students are actively engaged in their own learning does not work if the questions and answers are all pre-ordained by the professor.

Classroom management was based on the authority of the professor who would reprimand students for unauthorized talk. I was told that students could be asked to leave the room if they asked critical questions or challenged the professor's ideas. My impression from about a dozen lectures that I had videotaped of volunteer professors was that instructors relied on a kind of charisma in their teaching; a lecture was a kind of performance as though on the stage. The professor would move energetically around in the space in front of the class. Vigorous hand movements, facial mobility and high volume delivery seemed to have a kind of mesmerizing effect on students who would sit very still, eyes fixed on the professor performing in front of them. Some would make the occasional note in their book, but many did not have paper or pen in front of them.

In one videotaped lecture the professor charged about the classroom waving and gesticulating with a large wooden pointer. The performance was so highly charged that the students could have experienced it as an intimidating encounter. I spoke to this professor one day to tell him I had viewed his videotape. His response was "let me know if you want another lesson videotaped; I can give you an even more spectacular lesson than the first one." Indeed professors seemed to be providing "spectacles" in their classrooms. A huge pedagogical distance has to be traversed if professors are to abandon the authoritarian lecture and charismatic delivery in favour of interactive learning. I think they realized the real nature of the changes required, and, in many cases, they realized they did not have enough working years ahead to make these changes successfully.

A more democratic pedagogy also requires students to make changes in their classroom behaviour. Young Kosovars, who as prospective teachers, knew what the general direction of the proposed reforms, and they looked forward to learning about them when the new Faculty of Education was in place. However, democratic, engaged learning makes different demands on them too. In teaching two sections of a course myself with a colleague and translation in the spring semester of 2003, I ran into difficulties when we tacitly lifted the traditional sanctions on talking. Everyone wanted to talk at once. To pose a question to the class was to invite a crescendo of arm waving and shouting. To have the tables and chairs moved into clusters for group work in crowded rooms with concrete floors was another form of pandemonium. The lesson was that students have to be trained in their roles if pedagogical reforms can take place. Rules related to attendance, punctuality, speaking, listening, contributing, cooperating have to be negotiated, articulated, accepted and followed if this transformation is to be successful.

Professors knew the depth of the changes to be made. Given the poverty of resources and the relative absence of up-to-date teaching materials, they realized they were being asked to re-order their universe of teaching. For many this was too much to ask of older men who earned only a pittance in salary. So many of them resisted the proposed changes.

Political Tensions

The project to establish the new faculty was further slowed down by tensions between the Department of Education and Science, whose authority was derived from the United Nations' Interim Mission in Kosovo [UNMIK], and the Rectorate of the University. The International Head of DES,was the main champion of the new Faculty of Education as the sole teacher education unit in Kosovo. There was resentment in the Rectorate and among the professors that the International Head of DES was pushing hard on reform of university operations. Resistance to the Faculty of Education project within the University and its faculties and HPS's put pressure on the Rectorate not to cooperate with the Head in bringing forward a plan for the new faculty.

In September, 2001, the International Head of DES announced that he was setting up a Board to draw up recommendations for the establishment of a new comprehensive Faculty of Education. The Board was to be chaired by a member of the Canadian project [KEDP]. The membership consisted of the four Directors of the Higher Pedagogical Schools, three Deans (Faculty of Teaching; Philology; and Science and Mathematics) and two professors from the Department of Pedagogy, a department within the Faculty of Philosophy.

The mandate was to bring forward a plan and design for the new faculty with a four-week deadline. The Board met for 5 half days, KEDP providing a stipend and travel reimbursement for each local member.

Meeting protocols were different than those followed by Canadians. No one would move acceptance of agendas or minutes; no one would move motions to be voted on. Some members made the same set speech at each meeting. The Academic Deans supported the concepts of a new faculty provided it was only responsible for teacher training up to the end of grade 9. The Dean of the Faculty of Teaching supported the idea, provided his faculty was the core of the new faculty. Three of the four Directors were adamant that their Higher Pedagogical Schools had each to be a Faculty of Education. Nevertheless a report was prepared for the Director in early October 2001.

It recommended that a new faculty be established whose mandate for the first year of operation was to be the preparation of teachers up to the end of grade 9. Further study would be needed in order to add to this mandate the preparation of high school teachers in year 2. The Higher Pedagogical Schools were to become regional centers of the Faculty of Education, with the Pristina HPS subsuming the Faculty of Teaching. Voting never achieved unanimity, but the various political alignments in the Board allowed these recommendations to go forward with narrow majorities.

The DES Director rejected the Board's recommendations. He was not willing to compromise with a two-step implementation; his position was that the new faculty had to be responsible from the beginning for the preparation of all teachers, pre-primary through grade 12. If implementation were to be a two-step process, we would never get to step two. Inspite of wide-spread opposition within the higher education community, unilateral revisions were made in the recommendations by KEDP which had the effect of restoring the faculty's immediate mandate to include preparation of all teachers. This was not a popular decision. Opposition showed up at all information meetings we held for stakeholders. Given the magnitude and complexity of the changes, and the short time-line for implementation (October, 2002) as well as the resistance within the University, it was a daunting task.

Nevertheless the International Head of DES, in his capacity as International Administrator of the University, took the plan to the Senate and it was passed on December 23, 2001. But it was clear that the matter was not resolved simply by formal motion of the Senate. The Rector was under a lot of pressure from professors and deans to prevent the formation of the new faculty. The response of the Rector and Vice-Rector was passive resistance. No planning was possible without the support of the University Administration.

A new element entered the politics of the situation in Kosovo in the fall of 2001. There was a democratic election for membership of the new Kosovar Legislative Assembly and a new Kosovar Government. Under an interim constitution, a democratically elected Kosovar Government was formed with responsibility for a number of portfolios, including education. It meant the creation of a Kosovar Minister of Education and the gradual handing over of administrative positions to local Kosovar officials. Since the new government was a coalition, ministerial appointments took several months of arguments about the composition of the new government, including the naming of the new Minster of Education, Science and Technology.

It was clear by January, 2002 that the Department of Education and Science was preparing for hand over of authority over education to Kosovars. The UNMIK DES Head was obviously losing power as international officials in the Department began to focus on planning for the new regime, and as several resigned. The Faculty of Education Project had lost its main advocate in the weakened International Head of DES; and without a new Minister yet being appointed, the Ministry could not provide any support.

The initiative on the Faculty of Education project shifted from the DES to the University. The Rector wanted a compromise that would leave the preparation of high school teachers in the hands of the academic faculties, and that would place the higher pedagogical schools under the authority of the new faculty. The Head of DES agreed to this in February, and the compromise was approved by Senate, despite vigorous opposition from the HPS members. The University now set in motion the process of appointing an interim dean for the Faculty of Education. This appointment was made and approved within the University.

However, the faculty planning came to a sudden stop when the new Minister of Education, appointed by the Prime Minister, announced that he was canceling all decisions made by the University regarding the Faculty of Education, including the plan approved by Senate, and the appointment of the interim Dean. There was a political dimension to this sudden action. First of all, the Minister was a member of the LDK political party, whereas the leadership of the University in the Rectorate and decanal offices was mostly PDK. The Vice-Rector was an elected PDK member of the Legislative Assembly. These two parties dominated the governing coalition. The Minister made it clear he was not happy with the university's political coloration. He was prepared to take on the University for these political reasons and to reform the institution, especially with respect to alleged corruption. The Minister announced that he would require the University to bring forward a new Statute to replace the interim statute drawn up with assistance from the European Union in 2000. He indicated his intention to make sure that the revised statute would have to allow him as Minister wide powers over the university, especially regarding the preparation of teachers. In other words, he was challenging the concepts of university autonomy and academic freedom.

For a few months in the early past of 2002 it felt as though the Ministry of Education and the University were at war with each other. It was as though the new Minister, who had been a DES official and an outspoken critic of the DES head, had now inherited the conflict with the University.

However, the Minister moved quickly in May 2002 to re-start the planning of the new Faculty under a new vision. His position was that the previous plan had been too ambitious in its initial scope. He wanted a more modest start with a first entry cohort of 300 students to be admitted in fall, 2002. Only the programs for pre-primary and primary would be offered in the first year. Lower secondary programs would begin in 2003 provided the faculty's first year was successful. He agreed that all programs should be 4 years of study with a large component of formal, developmental practice teaching. In addition he mandated the incorporation of the higher pedagogical schools into the Faculty of Education as regional centers.

To develop detailed plans for the new faculty and to advise the Minister and Rector on policy issues, the Minister and the University cooperated in setting up a Joint Steering Board [JSB]. The Board had two members appointed by the Minister, including his political advisor for higher education. Two other members were appointed by the Rector. An international member was appointed by the Minister, as well as a representative of the HPS's. KEDP provided the chairperson of the Board and two advisors. When a new interim dean was appointed, he joined the Board too. KEDP urged the Minister to include in the planning process consultatiom with the staffs on the HPS's. He dismissed this suggestion saying these professors would have nothing useful to add. He, as the Minster, was in charge. Probably he was right: the process needed a strong person willing to take tough decisions and set out the main parameters for the work of the JSB.

The JSB was a very hard-working group, logging 40 meetings in the period May through September, 2002. It drew up a detailed program with courses descriptions. It advised the Minister and Rector on matters related to appointment of faculty members, admission of students, and the gradual incorporation of the HPS's into the faculty.

The hard work carried out by the JSB and the new Dean of Education, with consistent support from the Minister, led to the successful establishment of the Faculty of Education. The new institution is nearing the end of its second year of providing pre-service training for teachers in Kosovo. The enrolment at the end of year two approaches 1,000 students in four regional centres. If the current admission policy continues, the number of students active in courses will be about 1,500 in October, 2004 and 2,100 in 2005. The faculty is very fragile: professors are not yet skilled in newer teaching methods and no clear plan exists to find a remedy for that deficit, especially urgent because of inevitable forthcoming retirements; facilities are still primitive; the University does not provide enough financial support for a special faculty's needs for more administrative staff to manage its more complex operations, such as practice teaching.

Lessons Learned

1.   Transformation of educational systems and institutions is complex because people's lives and careers are at risk. The creation of a new Faculty of Education within an established University community and involving re-allocation of functions takes time. Granting agencies are always impatient for outcomes and results to be achieved within years or quarters. In institution building, negotiating, planning, re-training, and implementing take several years.

2.   The members of institutions place higher priority on survival of the familiar and the known than on the mission (if there is such a thing) and needs of the clients and society. The University of Pristina has no experience in looking out to Kosovo society and asking the question: what is the role of the University in meeting the changing needs of that society? Decisions are for the benefit of professors, not students. Appeals to the moral high ground by internationals has no value to the debates.

3.   Careful planning requires a deep and sophisticated understanding of the risks involved in an international project, not to assess whether or not a project should be undertaken but to understand the level of real support and real opposition among the key stakeholders. In this project the preliminary report, lasting only 6 weeks, badly over-estimated support for the Faculty of Education project and failed to anticipate the vigour with which opponents of the project could impede the process.

4.   An international agency has no decision-making authority; it can only advise and facilitate. Its influence is based only on its expertise and the resources it can make available. Consequently a project needs strong local support from a legitimate source. In the first year of this project strong leadership was provided by the International Head of DES. He was the legal Head of Education authorized by UNMIK to make decisions. He was willing to make tough decisions in order to advance the cause of the project which he supported vigorously. This individual was able to champion the project effectively until the end of 2001. By then it was clear that Kosovo would have an elected government and a new Ministry of Education, and the Head became a lame duck official. In the immediate absence of a leadership alternative, the project foundered for several months. The University could not provide the leadership because the Rector and Vice-Rector could not push the project hard enough, given the consensus model of decision-making in Universities. It was not until a new Minister of Education was appointed in 2002 that the project once again had a powerful champion. As a local Kosovar,

the Minister had more credibility than the former Head, and he was able to take charge of the planning process and pressure the University to provide reluctant approval of plans, programs and appointments. At first the Minister was successful in forcing the University to cooperate, but he was not able to get his own way on matters such as hiring qualifications for professors in the new Faculty of Education for he was seen to be intruding too heavily into the academic freedom of the University. The Minister's tough support for the project was crucial to the progress that it was able to make.

5.   Change that involves a University presents particular challenges. Claims for autonomy and academic freedom require that reforms have to be accepted and approved by majorities of departments, faculty and senate. Attempts to impose changes from outside or even from the Rector's office can be opposed and blocked, formally and informally, by the professoriate. It makes no difference if the changes are intended to modernize or get rid of corruption. Vested interests in universities can be nearly untouchable. Effective and strong leadership can, of course, make a difference; in its absence little can be done and progress is painfully slow. It might have been more effective in the case of Kosovo to have created a new teacher training institution, independent of the University. Such a college or professional school with a clear mission could have been created by the Minister. It could have started with small numbers with care taken to appoint the best professors available. International agencies would likely have been willing to steer their funding in support of such an institution. It would have provided competition for the University, and it would have been able to attract the best students. In retrospect, I think it would have been a good idea to have studied this option carefully before rushing into the plan for a new faculty within the university.

6.   Finally, interesting issues arise when so-called experts from other countries are brought in to advise and guide the process of transformation. Language is one huge issue where translation of oral and written communications is slow and ponderous (even with excellent translators). There are also cultural differences that are slowly revealed to internationals. For example, it took me too long to realize that in the Albanian culture it was important to go visit professors in their offices, even when there was no particular matter to be discussed. The excuse of pressure of work was not acceptable. Berit Backer, in her excellent anthropological study of one Kosovo village, described how the women in the village would chide her for not visiting them. If she pleaded that she had been too busy, they would retort: "does that mean your work is more important than we are?" It was very easy to miss key understandings. Kosovars were used to their method of operation within a University; internationals brought in their own as-

sumptions with the result that there was the risk of invisible issues. Both sides could believe that their assumptions represented the norm for how things worked in Universities. For example, KEDP recommended that professors be required to be more explicit and open about their courses. Rules were set up requiring that professors provide a standard course outline to be filed with the Dean's office and distributed to students in a class. The rationale was that students would have a better understanding of the course content and the requirements they had to meet. The rules also said that the professor should indicate to students how their work would be evaluated for a final grade; professors were encouraged to include on-going evaluation instead of just relying upon a single final examination, which was current practice. I did not realize, and no one pointed out, that this regulation could potentially cause a lot of difficulty. Under traditional regulations, students who failed a course had the right to try again by taking the examination in the next examination period. In the two classes I taught a total of 26 students in both sections failed to pass the course in June based on essays, tests, attendance and final examination. All of them applied to re-take the examination in September. However, the class did not meet again after June. The regulations did not state what could be counted in the re-examination. Did their essay marks and attendance points count or did everything have to rely on the final examination? The students, reasonably enough, asked what the policy was. It was an important question to them because they would have to prepare for the re-examination without help from the instructor. Besides if they failed on the second attempt, they could take the final examination over and over again. Who would set and mark these retakes if I, as instructor, were no longer in Kosovo.? This anecdote contains two lessons: (1) make sure that policies are developed with a full understanding of the knock-on effects of a policy introduction and try to get both sides to interrogate policy proposals so that buried assumptions are revealed; (2) it is a good idea for foreign advisors to have experiences in the front line classrooms as a test of their understandings.

References

Backer, B. (2003): Behind Stone Walls. Peja: Dukagjini Publishing House

Centre for Co-operation with Non-members of the OECD in Cooperation with the Stability Pact for South Eastern Europe. Thematic Review of Education. 2001: Kosovo *(44 pages, available on the OECD Website)*.

Joyce, B./Weil, M. (2000): Models of Teaching. Boston: Allyn and Bacon: 6th Edition.

Nicolas Robert Hurst (University of Porto, Portugal)

Migration Patterns in Portugal

Abstract
*This paper describes the shifting focus of migration in Portugal and the conse-
quent related social and educational issues. The historical position of Portugal is
of being a net exporter of labour, predominantly to France and Germany, but
also to other European countries and North America. However, this position has
recently become inverted so that large numbers of migrants are now arriving
from countries with no obvious connection to Portugal. Previously, immigrants
came mainly from former Portuguese colonies in Africa and South America
benefiting from a special status, in legal terms, and also often sharing the same
language, religion and other cultural ties. Currently, large numbers of immigrants are arriving from Eastern Europe, in particular, the Ukraine.*

Migration Patterns in Portugal

This article will seek to describe the shifting focus of migration in the context of
recent developments in Portugal. The historical position of Portugal was of being
a net exporter of labour, predominantly to France and Germany, but also to North
America (e.g. Toronto, Canada and Newark, USA.). This pattern has recently become inverted so that large numbers of migrants are now arriving from countries
with no obvious connection to Portugal. Prior to the beginning of this century,
immigrants came mainly from former Portuguese colonies in Africa and South
America benefiting from a special status, in legal terms, and also often sharing
the same language, religion and other cultural ties. Recently, large numbers of
immigrants have been arriving from Eastern Europe, in particular, the Ukraine.
Portugal is in many ways unique in its relationship with Europe. Since the 15th
century Portugal has looked outwards from the Iberian peninsular, across the Atlantic Ocean and beyond, with a rich tradition of maritime exploration and dis-
covery. The empire which resulted from this period left many legacies, including
around 200 million speakers of Portuguese around the globe today. In addition,
in the 20th century, the dictatorship established by Salazar adopted an isolationist
stance with respect to European relations (for example, Portugal was neutral during World War Two). Foreign policy concentrated on retaining its grip on the
remaining Portuguese colonies, mainly in Africa. Portugal was the last of the
European imperial powers to recognise the rights of its colonial populations and
this regime and policy focus was only ended in April 1974 with the "Revolution
of the Carnations". Only when Portugal became a member of the European Union in 1986 can it be said that the country reoriented its gaze. Portugal has a
population of approximately 10 million people with an estimated per capita an-

nual income of around 11,000 US dollars (http://news.bbc.co.uk/1/hi/world/
europe/country_profiles/994099.stm).
One of the results of the pre-1974 political situation was that Portugal developed
economically at a much slower rate than the rest of Europe during the 1950s and
60s. As a result many Portuguese nationals emigrated in search of better wages
and higher spending power. A figure of 100,000 workers per year has been estimated for the late 1960s. No other EU country has proportionally produced so
many emigrants. Currently there are thought to be around 1 million Portuguese
living outside Portugal within the European Union, with France being the most
preferred destination. The world total is thought to be more than 4 million. These
figures are quoted in a recent report on immigration in Portugal (cf. Falção
2002). One often quoted EU example is that 40% of the residents of Luxembourg
have Portuguese origins. It could be said that there is an emigratory tradition in
Portugal which bears a heavy significance in Portuguese people's attitudes towards immigrants: the statistics indicate that there can be few Portuguese families which do not have members who have lived in a migratory context themselves.

A readily identifiable turning point was is January 2001 when the Portuguese
government embodied the need to legislate for an increasing trend of immigration by passing a law specifically aimed at attempting to regulate the flow of
people. This is perhaps a reasonable time span after the fall of the Berlin wall in
1989, the effects of opening up of eastern Europe to have impinged on economies on opposite sides of Europe. Immigrants previously working illegally were
now supposed to obtain a one-year temporary residence permit which was then
renewable for up to five years continuously, at which stage residence would become permanent automatically. The scale of numbers of people involved and the
notoriety of employer/employee abuses were perhaps the main impulses for this
governmental reaction. The motivation behind this turning of the migratory tide
has been identified in a succinct manner by the BBC journalist Alison Roberts:
"Labour shortages, a booming construction sector and the authorities' reputation
for turning a blind eye to illegal employment have accelerated the process, at-
tracting tens of thousands of migrants from eastern Europe. They travel across
Europe on tourist visas and are placed by local agents, mainly in construction."
(http://news.bbc.co.uk/1/low/world/asia-pacific/1510471.stm) While this was not
the first attempt by the government to regulate the situation, it was certainly the
largest with more than 127,000 aliens without legal status being granted temporary residence permits in less than two years (cf. ECRI report 2002, paragraph
48.) The ECRI report emphasises the linkage between obtaining a contract of

employment and qualifying for the residence permit, a concern which has been given prominence by other organisations as well.

The European Industrial Relations Observatory (online edition) at http://www.eiro.eurofound.eu.int/index.html made reference to a figure 40,000 workers being present in Portugal without legal status as at June 2000. It is difficult to believe that this figure has not increased on a scale similar to the growth in official statistics for legal migrant workers. However, it is not only the relationship with the host state which is relevant: at a more individual level any immigrant is at the mercy of the prevailing conditions and practices of the labour market. The EIRO has consistently insisted that migrant workers should be granted the same rights as locally born workers. The jobs available to migrant workers are generally not attractive to educated, qualified young people from the local population. Recent arrivals from eastern Europe may also be well-educated and have filled positions requiring qualifications in their own domestic labour market. Research by João Peixoto of the Institute of Economics and Management (ISEG) from Lisbon Technical University (UTL) points to an average of about 30% of immigrants also being "highly qualified": 33% in 1999 and 22.3% in 2000 (cf. O Público 2004, p. 27). However, the language barrier may initially be an impediment which serves to downgrade these newcomers' employment prospects in Portugal. Indeed, there is an increasing awareness that some form of provision of language training could be a highly productive means of assisting integration. The Faculty of Letters of the University of Porto provides several different types of course for people wishing to learn the Portuguese language (http://www.letras.up.pt/deper/). The annual course of 2003/2004 was attended by a total of 448 people. However, 63.2% of these people were EU 15 countries and only 6.7% of the people were of eastern European origin (Russia, Romania, Ukraine, Moldova). Cost may be a conditioning factor here as each semester entails the payment of a fee of 250 euros. Another local Porto initiative organised by Joana Vasconcelos at the Garcia de Orta secondary school involved Portuguese language training at no cost. The course started with 23 participants, 34.8% were of eastern European origin (Russia, Ukraine, Poland, Hungary and Lithuania), but not all the students were able to complete the course due to changes in their professional lives (all the students were adult learners).

Furthermore, the Portuguese labour market was already comfortable with the concept of employing workers with no legal documentation as a result of the previous influx of migrant workers, largely from African former colonies. Several non-governmental organisations (such as *SOS Racismo* and *Olho Vivo*) have stressed that the limited rights attributed to migrant workers with temporary residence permits tends towards the creation of a kind of underclass who cannot join trade unions, who cannot be candidates for university places, who cannot obtain consumer credit, who cannot live with their families and who receive lower wages than they should. "Exploitation and fear" are also two of main elements of the immigrant experience as described in interviews conducted by H. Dieux as part of his extensive article in *"Le Monde Diplomatique"* (http://mondediplo.com/2002/08/07portugal). These concerns are also voiced by the ECRI: "One of the most significant problems concerns the insecurity in which these people find themselves, as a result of which they may accept working conditions that Portuguese nationals would refuse, since failing to obtain work or losing a job would cause the residence permit to be withdrawn. Numerous abuses have been reported, ... Moreover, although aliens with temporary resident status enjoy the same right to health care as Portuguese workers, ... this right is not always effective since certain administrative services refuse to recognise the validity of temporary residence permits. ... the situation of aliens ... remains insecure, largely because they face insuperable obstacles when applying for bank loans." (ECRI Report 2002, paragraph 50).

The UNHCR provides figures for Portugal in the year 2001 regarding a total 135,000 persons who received temporary residence visas . The percentage breakdown of that total is as follows: Eastern European countries with 51.8%; former Portuguese colonies in Africa with 23.7%; Brazil with 17.3%; and "Others" with 20.2%. The Ukraine is alone responsible for 35% of the total figure. Even after endorsing a special bilateral agreement, under which as many as 31,000 Brazilian immigrants applied for legal residence status in September 2003, the Portuguese government has responded to the continuing flow of migrant workers by launching a new period of registration and legalisation procedures for foreigners who entered Portugal before March 12th 2003. This new opening, based on a new law passed on April 26th 2004, closed on June 14th 2004. Illegal immigrants may conduct the form filling procedures in person at any branch of the Portuguese Post Office. Provisional figures, reported in the local press, point to a number in excess of 40,000 people taking advantage of this new opportunity (cf. O Público, 2004, p. 30). This recent development may also be seen as a response to the difficulties that the Portuguese Aliens and Frontiers Service (SEF) was experiencing in dealing with the bureaucracy associated with the granting of temporary residence permits. According to ECRI: "Since the 1980s, the foreign population in Portugal has increased sevenfold (from 50,000 to 350,000 persons). ... ECRI is seriously concerned about the excessive amount of time taken by SEF (*Aliens and Frontiers Service*) to reply to applications and issue documents." (ECRI Report 2002, paragraph 54). The Portuguese government has recently opened support centres for immigrants in Lisbon and Porto where various procedures, relating to different administrative departments may all be dealt with under one roof. Clearly when dealing with immigration on the scale of which is presently the case in Portugal the government has every motivation for attempting to bring this sector of the working population within the state sponsored system of social security (to gain both the employer and employee contributions) and taxation (to gain both the corporate and individual payments). Indeed, ACIME (The High Commission for Immigrants and Ethnic Minorities) in a report on 2001 calculated that there was a net positive balance of 323,605,900 euros generated, in terms of the benefit to the Portuguese economy arising from the presence of immigrant workers. This figure was arrived at by offsetting costs such as schooling, health care and so on against receipts from taxation, fines and so on (www.oi.acime.gov.pt; Corrêa D'Almeida A 2003). A local newspaper, *Jornal de Notícias*, reported that research carried out by the Lisbon Autonomous University (UAL) had found that immigrants produced approximately 5% of the Portuguese Gross Domestic Product in 2001, equating this with the concept of "national wealth". Looking at the figures by employment sector, the figures were 14.8% in construction, 11.7% in hotels/restaurants and 9.6% in business services. The research also estimates the working immigrant population to be in the order of 233,000 people (cf. JN 2004, p. 18). This economic aspect is high on the agenda of another website closely associated immigrants with the former African colonies. *Africa Hoje* provides a forum for many issues, among which a recent article, making use of statistics provided by ACIME, highlighted both the benefits for Portugal, as "host" country and also the benefits for the "home" countries of origin, in terms of the remittances sent each month: for example, 148 million euros to the Ukraine, 40 million euros to Brazil and 16 million euros to Angola (http://africa.sapo.pt/1GO8/3777522.html) for the year 2001. Thus, in economic terms, it is difficult to see who is NOT benefiting from this phenomenon.

The geographical distribution of the most recent immigrants has also proven distinct from that of the previous generations. Currently there is a much more even distribution around Portugal, outside Lisbon. In terms of residency permits granted by the regional departments of SEF, the figures are: the North with 16%, the Centre with 15%, The Algarve with 14%, Madeira and the Açores with 3% and Lisbon and the Tagus valley with 52% (www.sef.pt/statisticas.htm). Although the predominance of Lisbon is still an important feature other areas of Portugal are also receiving large numbers of immigrants (these statistics for 2001 contemplate a universe of about 120,000 people). Today, immigrants can be found working not only all around the country but also in a variety of industrial sectors: 40% in construction, 16% in financial and business activities, 14.6% in manufacturing industries, 11.4% in hotels and the like as well as smaller figures for other areas, such as agriculture with 3.7%. Immigration may also be seen in terms of gender distribution: in 2001 males accounted for 77.1 % of the totals and females for 22.9% (cf. Falção 2002, p. 10). It may well be that this is classic migration pattern, where the male went abroad in search of work before calling his partner to join him, is being repeated in the context of Portuguese immigration.

Since Portuguese legislation envisages a temporary period of five years of permit renewals before allowing for permanent status to be applied for, then it is perhaps only after 2004 that the longer term nature of the current pattern of immigration may become clear. For example, it may be correct to assume that only after gaining permanent status that many immigrants would consider constituting their family life in Portugal and therefore, perhaps, create greater demands on the local educational system. For 1999/2000 it was estimated that there were approximately 52,000 non-Portuguese students in primary and secondary schools, equivalent to 3.7% of the total school population (cf. Corrêa 2003, p. 16). However no distinction is made in terms of origin and many of these schoolchildren may well be of a Portuguese speaking background (from Brazil or Angola, for example). It could be that only after such a 5 year period has elapsed since the surge in immigration at the turn of the century that any major impact on the local education systems is felt outside Lisbon. In the north of Portugal, in the area administered by the Northern Area Educational Directorate (DREN), a preliminary study of the student population of schools who do not have Portuguese as their mother tongue has been carried out. In the schools that provided the requested information, the report states that there are 777 students from 54 different nationalities. The Ukraine (124 students/16%), Russia (46 students/5.9%), Romania (39 students/5.0%), Bulgaria (16 students/2.1%) and Moldova (14 students/1.8%) account for 30.8% of the students referred to as not having Portuguese as their mother tongue. There is also a sprinkling of students from other eastern European nations such as Poland (5) and Byelorussia (4). Studies of the age profile of the non-Portuguese (NPP) and Portuguese populations (PP) provide some evidence to support the notion of immigrant communities essentially focussed on simply working rather than on settling: whether in terms of elderly people (over 65 years old: NPP 4.8% compared to PP 16.4%) or in terms of people in the prime of their working lives (between 15 and 34 years old: NPP 47% and PP 29.5%) these strong contrasts were already apparent in 2001 (cf. Valente et al 2003, p. 45). In many cases immigration constitutes a new experience and a new challenge for the majority of the Portuguese population, outside of Lisbon and the Tagus valley, where the tradition is very much of a mono-lingual, mono-cultural, mono-religious working and living environment. ECRI also brings this aspect to the fore in its recommendations: "ECRI urges the Portuguese authorities to take action against "two-speed" immigration ... to ensure that no immigrant community is disadvantaged in comparison with any other. ... it recommends that the authorities raise public awareness in order to combat stereotyping and prejudice ... increasing emphasis on the notion of Portugal as a multicultural society..." (ECRI Report, paragraph 59). The notion of cultural distance is also significant here as while there may be little in the way of historical connection between eastern Europe and Portugal and while there is certainly a great geographical separation, it should also be noted that the countries of origin referred to include Romania, Moldova and some southern regions of the Ukraine which share a Christian heritage, a Romance language background as well as a similar racial typology. Hence the cultural distance in question may not as great as initially imagined. This indeed what may be inferred from the ECRI reference to two speed immigration or taking the notion on from there, two speed integration. This point is taken up by the journalist Hervé Dieux: "Everyone recognises that the East Europeans are willing and dedicated workers, and judging by their comments, many Portuguese feel sympathy for them. This may explain why the East Europeans have not had to contend with the anti-foreigner attacks against the African and Gypsy communities. By some accounts, the East Europeans may even be experiencing positive discrimination, which will only fuel the resentment felt by the children of Portugal's African immigrants. Struggling to overcome the exploitation their parents faced, this second generation feels cheated, with true integration a distant dream." (Dieux 2002, p. 4)

What may be developing is more complex than a straight-forward binary distinction between native and non-native communities inside Portugal. "Viagens de Ulisses – efeitoes da imigração na economia portuguesa" (Sousa et al 2003) is a study which highlights this very issue and has been commented on recently in the local press. For example, in a recent edition of the weekly newspaper "Expresso", the journalist Nicolau Santos uses as the headline for his article the phrase "Racial tensions inevitable" and develops his commentary to include the idea that employers are laying off African origin workers in order to hire eastern Europeans since the latter are better educated and more productive. Low rates of unemployment among this community point towards strongly economic motives for leaving their countries of origin. For example, an unemployment rate of 1% for migrant workers from the Ukraine, Moldova and Romania is quoted. This figure rises to 11% for Angola and Mozambique: a contrast which may also be behind the affirmation that "serious social tensions" are likely to occur between immigrant communities within two years (cf. Expresso, Economic and International supplement 2004, p. 3). The report also makes references to the lack of any totally reliable statistics since various government agencies provide differing data. However, a total of 300,000 people is put forward as a consensus figure with respect to the period 1998/2002 with the strongest levels of increase being attributed to immigrants of non-EU, Asian or Brazilian origin.

When considering to what extent it is possible to talk of integration with any particular community, generally, several factors are considered fundamental in the process of creating a sense of belonging: place of birth/nationality, bloodline/ancestry, appearance and linguistic capacity. With respect to immigrant populations and the first factor, the "host" country cannot alter in any way the facts of matter, but it can contribute to positive perceptions being associated with a particular place or country, for example, by supporting consciousness raising activities in the fields of the arts, sports and so on which may well have an echo in the local media, the crucial agents in terms of forming public perceptions. Indeed, recent research has been undertaken which explores the development of "new" stereotypes for immigrants from Eastern Europe in the Portuguese press (cf. Solovova 2004). The importance of factor of language remains difficult to determine. For example, in the context of Germany, it has been reported that "The locally born children of *gastarbeiter* (guest workers) are seen as Turks, Greeks, etc, rather than as Germans – no matter how fluent their command of the language, no matter if they have never set foot outside the *Bundesrepublik*. Legal status does not appear to influence this perception: even German-born children of immigrants who have become citizens seem to be classified as foreigners." (Forsythe 1989, p. 144) Integration in Portugal may then only function in this light through the resolution of the ambiguities and contradictions inherent in multiple social identities over a time span which covers many generations.

Some form of cultural universalism would need to apply in Portugal so that all cultures were associated with equally valid values. Without such fundamental starting point of mutual respect and acceptance, it is difficult to effectively combat intercultural conflict, racism and xenophobia. The contrast between notions of "integration" and "assimilation" has yet to be fully played out in terms of concrete consequences in Portugal. Can or should further immigration be controlled or ended is also a question without an answer. However, one cornerstone is already in place: the positive role of current population of migrant workers in the economic development of Portugal.

References

Corrêa, D'Almeida A. (2003): Impacto da imigrção em Portugal nas contas do estado. Lisboa: ACIME.

Dias, F. R.: Mais de 40 mil imigrants já requereram legalização. In: O Público, 08.06.2004.

Dieux, H: Sleepwalkers of Portugal. In: Le Monde Diplomatique, MondeDiplo.com, August 2002.

European Commission against Racism and Intolerance. The Council of Europe: Second Report on Portugal. Adopted on 20 March 2002.

Falção, L. (2002) : Immigration in Portugal. Report presented by Delta Consultores under the Socrates Program – Immigrant Language Learning. Lisboa.

Forsythe, D. (1989): German Identity and the Problem of History. In: Tonkin, E./McDonald, M./Chapman, M. (Ed.): History and Ethnicity. (ASA Monographs 27), London: Routledge.

Leira, I.: Quase um terço dos imigrantes com profissões altamente qualificadas. In: O Público, 18.04.2004: p. 27.

Santos, N.: Tensões racias inevitáveis. In: Expresso, 22.05.2004: Economia p. 3.

Solovova, O.: A new stereotype in the making: imigrantes de Leste. In: The University of Coimbra.

Unattributed author: Imigrants produzem 5% da riquesa nacional. In: Jornal de Notícias, 20.05.2004

Valente, R.MJ./Seabra, H./Santos, T. (2003): Contributos dos Imigrantes na demografia portuguesa. Lisboa: ACIME.

Antonio Bueno-Gonzales/ Nieves Pascual-Soler/ Salvador Valera-Hernandez
(University of Jaen, Spain)

Education for Immigrants in Andalusia : A special form of Interculturality

Abstract
While a social fact for some time, immigration is becoming an issue in Spain only recently, or at least so is it felt by a large part of the population and, to some extent, by governmental agencies. This paper focuses on immigration in Andalusia and how the regional and state agencies are approaching education for immigrants. Updated figures of the evolution of immigration and of the integration of immigrants into the educational system are reviewed. The essential educational tools are described to highlight the strengths and weaknesses of the management of immigrant education by the authorities.

Emigration is still the tendency in Spain. Even though there are still more Spaniards living abroad than foreigners in Spain, the 1990's witnessed a noticeable increase in immigration, mainly by North Africans (Morocco, Ghana, Sierra Leone, and Senegal), and South Americans (Ecuadorians, Colombians, and Dominicans making up 57% of the Latin American community), followed by Eastern Europeans (Romania), Russians, and Asians (figure 1).

Figure 1. Number of immigrants with work permit per province, 12/2003 (source: Ministry of Interior).

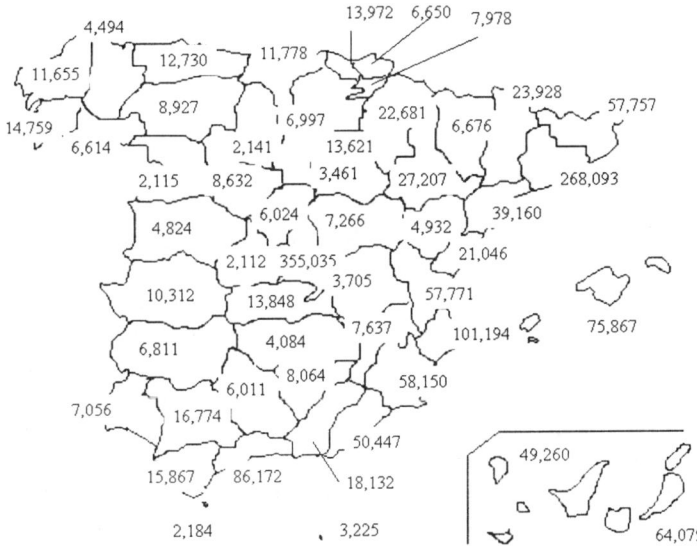

72

A key element in Spain's migratory situation is feminization. Although along history women have always been present in migratory flows, traveling to meet their partners, in the last ten years they have often traveled by themselves, setting off the migratory chain, to which men have incorporated later. Most of them come from Europe. Latin Americans, Africans, and Asians come second, third, and fourth (figure 2).

Figure 2. Number of immigrants with residence permit by continent, December 2003. 126 cases not recorded (source: Ministry of Interior —Government Agency for Foreigners and Immigrants, *Delegación del Gobierno para la Extranjería y la Inmigración*, 2004, p. 7).

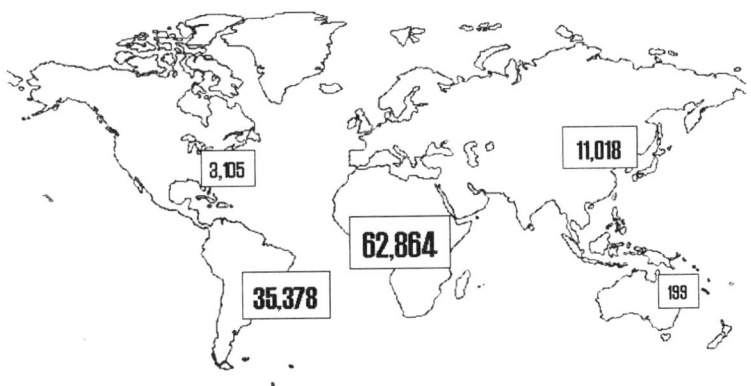

1. Immigration Laws and the overall Situation in Spain

In the year 2000, the Spanish Government centralized immigration issues under the competence of the Ministry of Interior. That same year, Organic Law 4/2000 on the rights and integration of foreigners came into effect (although we will be using the terms "immigrants" and "foreigners" indiscriminately, the word "immigrant" —"inmigrante"— is often used for people from underprivileged countries. The word "foreigner" —"extranjero"— is used to refer to outsiders from the so-called developed countries). Residence, health care and social security were thereby regulated. Article #9 granted immigrants under eighteen the same rights as Spanish nationals in education and study grants. Eleven months later the law was modified to accommodate the targets agreed upon at Tampere, i.e., control of illegal immigration, support of social integration, and fight against xenophobia.

In 2001 the Spanish Government signed formal agreements with Ecuador, Colombia and Morocco to prevent clandestine immigration and hinder exploitation of foreign workers. The Global Program for the Regulation and Coordination of Foreigners and Immigrants (GRECO Program) was put into action. In 2003 the program was assigned 261 million €, which meant a 3.81% increase over the preceding year. On September 29, 2003 Organic Law 4/2000 was modified again to help ensure security and integration of foreigners. The eradication of domestic violence was another of its goals.

In November 20, 2003, a new Organic Law came into effect to regulate the betterment of the juridical status of aliens in Spain and endorse the taxes approved by the European Union in matters of visa expeditions, transportation and expulsion. Agreements were signed with Bulgaria, Morocco, Mauritania, Guinea Bissau, and Switzerland. Three new offices were opened in Ecuador, Poland and Romania, strengthening the network of branches in charge of transacting work and residence permits already extant outside Spain. The results of these efforts are reflected in the increasing number of visas expedited to foreigners during the years 2003 and 2004, and the amount of money invested in programs designed to attend and protect immigrants in vulnerable conditions.

In fact, according to the data published by the Ministry of Interior, in October 2003 the number of foreigners with health insurance was 619,598. The increase was 9.26% with respect to January the same year. During the academic year 2002-03, 303,827 foreign students registered in primary and secondary education, totaling 4.10% of the students registered. Significantly, the number of immigrant students is also increasing at the universities. In 2003, 18,416 students attended first and second cycle courses, while 11,106 applied for PhD courses. That meant 1.2% and 16.18% respectively out of the total number of nationals officially registered.

However, and despite the efforts made to normalize this state of multiplicity following the dictates of the European Commission against Racism and Intolerance (ECRI), xenophobia is intensifying in places of cultural contact as well as where the presence of immigrants is minimal, even more so when difference is made visible in the flesh. In both sides the knowledge of the other is shaped by myths rather than by direct experience. As a result, and because the model citizen is identified with the city centre, the unwanted and unfamiliar are expelled to the outskirts out of fear of physical and spiritual contamination. As William A. Cohen (2003) makes explicit in "Deep Skin," racial edges invariably become dermal boundaries. The gipsy population, though native residents, is likewise considered abject, and is therefore relegated to the same "zones of uninhabitability" (since they are not immigrants, this minority falls beyond the scope of this paper). Butler (1993, p. 3) eloquently points out that:

"The abject designates here precisely those `unlivable´ and `uninhabitable´ zones of social life which are nevertheless densely populated by those who do not enjoy the status of the subject, but whose living under the sign of the `unlivable´ is required to circumscribe the domain of the subject. This zone of uninhabitability will constitute that site of dreaded identification against which —and by virtue of which— the domain of the subject will circumscribe its own claim to autonomy and to life. In this sense, then, the subject is constituted through the force of exclusion and abjection, one which produces a constitutive outside to the subject, an abjected outside, which is, after all, `inside´ the subject as its own founding repudiation."

An outside that is inside, because in Spain we are all immigrants and have for decades been exporting labour. Unfortunately, we tend to forget it.

Besides, Spain has not been immune to the sort of Islamophobia that has spread in Europe since the September 11 attacks. Less than two years ago Spaniards rampaged through a Moroccan neighbourhood in the town of El Ejido after a mentally disabled immigrant killed a young woman. The train bombing in Madrid in March 2004, the release of a videotape by a man calling himself a military spokesman of Al Qaeda, and the arrest of three Moroccans have left Spain's Muslim population in a state of profound unease.

The increscent fear and hatred of aliens has forced immigrants to organize themselves. Whereas in the 1990's they were organized by trade unions (like CCOO, *Comisiones Obreras,* Workers' Committees) and Catholic institutions, at the end of the decade they started to coordinate themselves either within direct democratic organizations, such as GGT, or by themselves. Prominent among these is the Association for Moroccan Workers in Spain (Atime), headed by Mustapha El-Mrabet, who has put a great effort into disarticulating subterranean traffic networks. Yet, illegal aliens continue to die in droves on the daily treacherous journey from Africa to Europe in rafts. In January 2004 sixteen would-be immigrants died when their boat capsized off Fuerteventura. In April 2004 at least 14 suspected immigrants drowned at sea off the coast of Spain's Canary Islands. According to Spanish trade union UGT (*Unión General de Trabajadores,* Workers' General Union) between half a million and 800,000 illegal immigrants live in this country. It could be more. They refuse prescribed paths and live on the edge of society. They cannot get apartments or legal employment. They work for virtually no money in unskilled agriculture or construction sites. Often they clean houses. They live in deserted houses or unused greenhouses and loiter on village squares. It is just recently that for the first time the International Association for

Migration has set up a new mechanism to facilitate the voluntary return of foreigners unable to integrate into the Spanish work market and lacking the resources to come back to their native lands. Incidentally, during 2003 the repatriated foreigners were mainly Romanians, Moroccans, Bulgarians and Ecuadorians.

2. The situation in Andalusia

In Andalusia, a region of about 33,700 sq miles located in the South of Spain, the flow of immigration appears to be bigger than anywhere else in the country, as attested by a work recently published by *Andalucía Acoge* (Andalusia Welcomes, a non-governmental organization). The research was financed by the *Consejería de Gobernación de la Junta de Andalucía* (Andalusia Government Council). Out of 1,647,011 immigrants in Spain, 208,523 reside in Andalusia.

Figure 3. Immigrants with residence permit by province. December 2003 (source: Ministry of Interior —Government Agency for Foreigners and Immigrants, *Delegación del Gobierno para la Extranjería y la Inmigración*, 2004, p. 6).

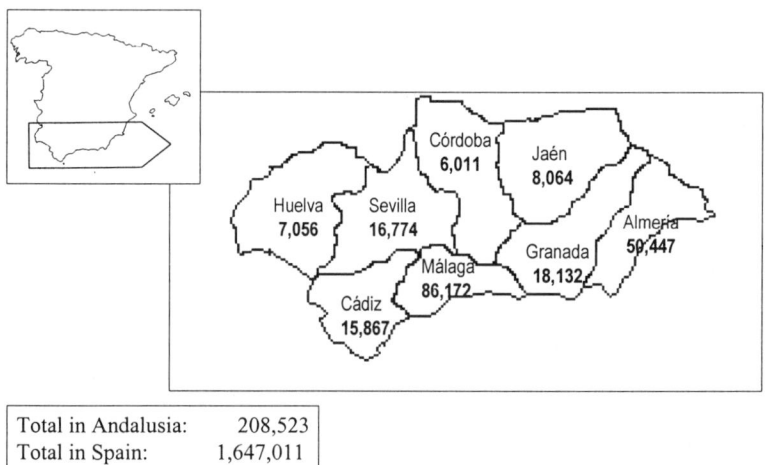

Total in Andalusia:	208,523
Total in Spain:	1,647,011

The region, in fact, has a great demand of unskilled labour due to the prominence of agriculture and fishery as means of subsistence (as seen in the table, the highest number of immigrants with residence permit is located in Málaga and Almería). Its geographical location on the Mediterranean and the Atlantic also favours the incoming of outsiders. However, soon after landing, guests discover

76

that the condition of indigence suffered by part of the native population in the area makes of immigration a particularly cumbersome "problem," because most Andalusians think that the newcomers will deprive them of their means to earn a living. As a result, incomers often live in conditions of socio-economic privation. Delinquency is on the increase, and becomes associated with immigration in the people's minds.

3. Education for Immigrants in Andalusia
In the belief that translation and understanding of cultures is eased through knowledge and training, the Andalusian Regional Government (*Junta de Andalucía*) has since 2001 concentrated attention on the education of the children of immigrant families and the formation of adults. Schools are deemed to be ideal settings for teaching how to live with tolerance and solidarity, and eradicate discrimination. But to achieve success all social and teaching institutions — whatever ethnic diversity in their districts— must be involved in permanent interdisciplinary programs, collaborative networks and research.
Success appears to be making way. The number of students registered in Andalusian schools has increased noticeably (approximately eightfold) since 1995 (figure 4).

Figure 4. Immigrant students registered in Andalusian schools 1995-96 to 2002-03 (source: Andalusian Regional Government —General Office for Participation and Solidarity in Education, *Dirección General de Participación y Solidaridad en la Educación*, http://www.juntadeandalucia.es/educacionyciencia/dgoes/scripts/INTERES/INMIGRANTES/E STADIST.htm, 25/07/04).

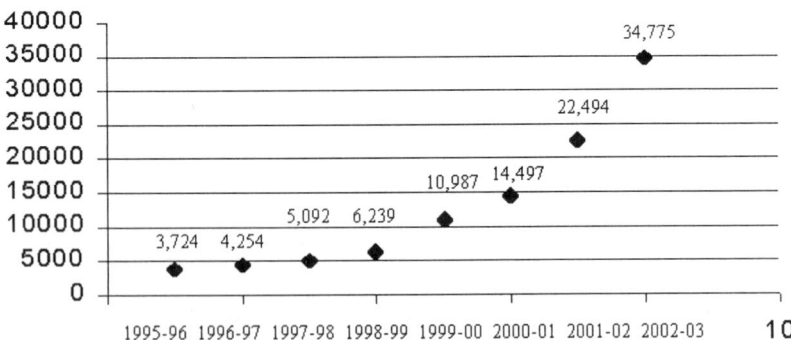

51.42% of immigrant students attend Primary Schools, and less than half register in Secondary Education institutions (figure 5).

Figure 5. Immigrant students by studies for the academic year 2002-03 (total: 34,775) (source: Andalusian Regional Government —General Office for Participation and Solidarity in Education, *Dirección General de Participación y Solidaridad en la Educación*, http://www.juntadeandalucia.es/educacionyciencia/dgoes/scripts/INTERES/INMIGRANTES/E STADIST.htm, 25/07/04)

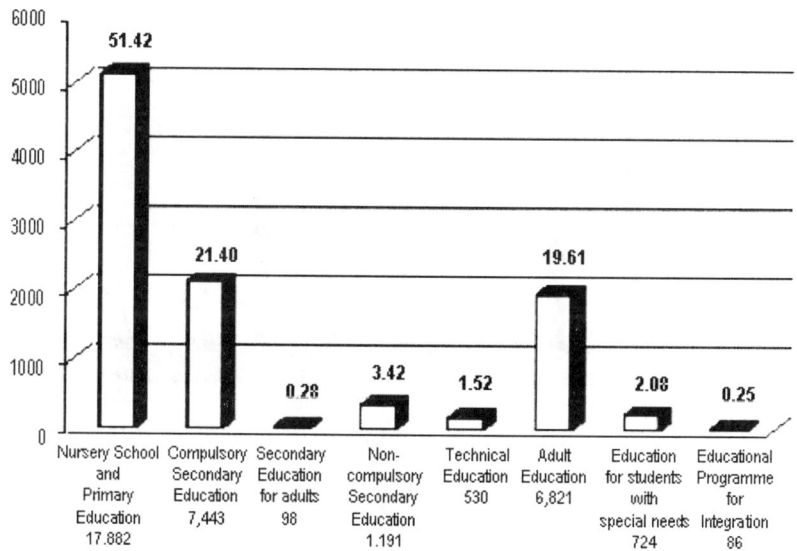

Their profile is, in broad lines, relatively easy to draw: most of them come from Africa, Latin American and the European Union (figure 6), prefer state free centres over costly private institutions (figure 7), and, despite the process of feminization referred to above, the majority of students registered are male (figure 8).

78

Figure 6. Provenance of immigrant students for the academic year 2002-03 (total: 34,775) (source: Andalusian Regional Government —General Office for Participation and Solidarity in Education, *Dirección General de Participación y Solidaridad en la Educación*, http://www.juntadeandalucia.es/educacionyciencia/dgoes/scripts/INTERES/INMIGRANTES/E STADIST.htm, 25/07/04).

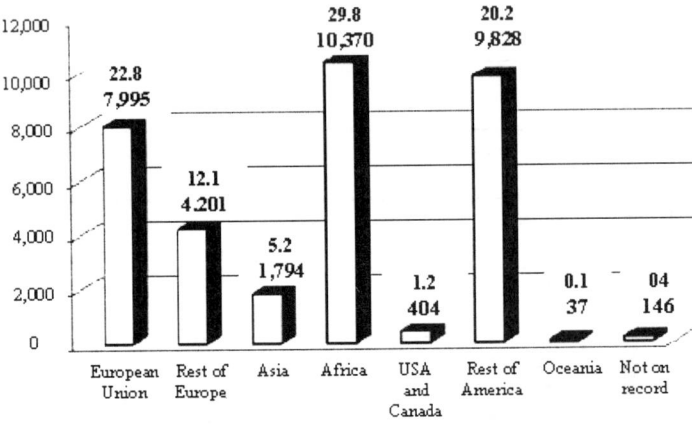

Figure 7. Immigrant students in private (in white) and state (in black) schools by province (2,892 students, i.e., 8.3% vs. 31,883 students, i.e., 91.7%, respectively) for the academic year 2002-03 (source: Andalusian Regional Government —General Office for Participation and Solidarity in Education, *Dirección General de Participación y Solidaridad en la Educación*, http://www.juntadeandalucia.es/educacionyciencia/dgoes/scripts/INTERES/INMIGRANTES/E STADIST.htm, 25/07/04).

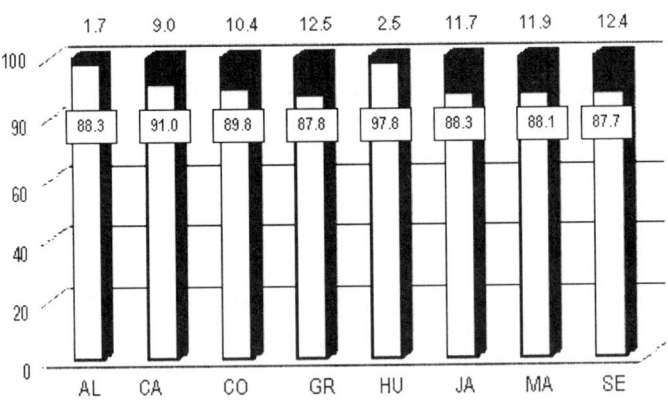

Key to the provinces in the X axis: AL = Almería; CA = Cádiz; CO = Córdoba; GR = Granada; HU = Huelva; JA = Jaén; MA = Málaga; SE = Sevilla.

Figure 8. Male (in white) vs. female (in black) immigrant students by province (19,099 students, i.e., 54.9% vs. 15,676 students, i.e., 45.1%, respectively) for the academic year 2002-03 (source: Andalusian Regional Government —General Office for Participation and Solidarity in Education, *Dirección General de Participación y Solidaridad en la Educación*, http://www.juntadeandalucia.es/educacionyciencia/dgoes/scripts/INTERES/INMIGRANTES/E STADIST.htm, 25/07/04).

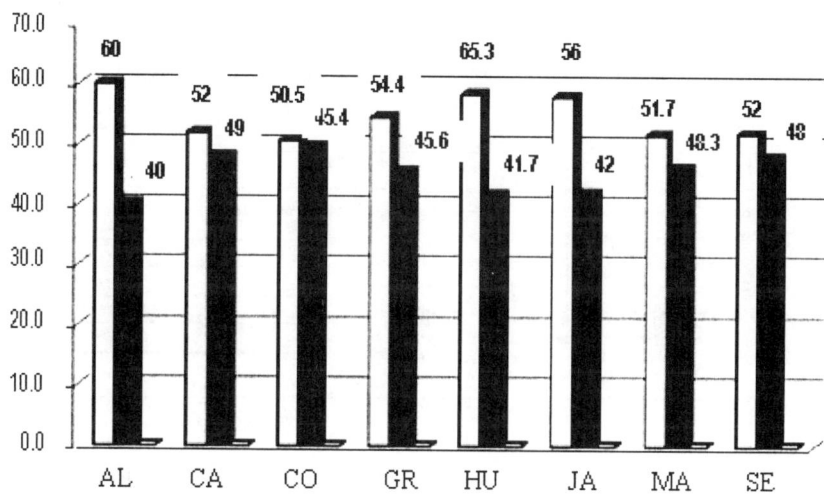

Key to the provinces in the X axis: AL = Almería; CA = Cádiz; CO = Córdoba; GR = Granada; HU = Huelva; JA = Jaén; MA = Málaga; SE = Sevilla.

As it happens, immigrant cultures have a poor economy and are highly patriarchal. Males are considered the heads of the family and therefore the depositaries of knowledge and education. Paradoxically, women are in charge of transmitting these chauvinistic values.

The Europe-Canada Mobility Project will transfer 16 students from Jaén to three different Canadian institutions in Vancouver, Lethbridge, and Regina in two academic years starting September 2004. The aim is to deepen the understanding of the cultural and social environments of foreign teaching institutions in matters of migration in order to develop teacher training curricula courses on cross-cultural approaches to learning and helping to learn. Out of 208,532 immigrants residing in Andalusia, 8,064 live in Jaén. 860 foreign students are registered in 310 schools out of 452 extant in the province (figure 9).

80

Figure 9. Immigrant students in pre-university studies in Jaén for the academic year 2002-03 (860 students in 310 schools, out of a total of 452 schools) (source: Jaén Local Education Authority —*Delegación Provincial de Educación de Jaén*).

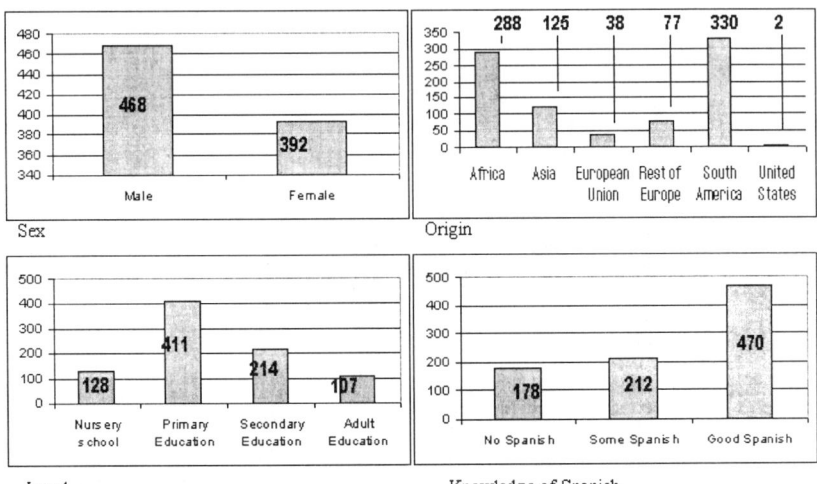

Of these, 411 are enrolled in Primary Education schools. Only half of them move to Secondary institutions. A small minority makes its way into the university. Sciences are preferred over the study of literature, philosophy and the arts. Since a good part of them (330, i.e., 80.29%) come from South America, they encounter no language problems. In the understanding that command of the language of the recipient country paves the way to adaptation, increases self-esteem and controls anxiety, support classes are provided for adults and older children in need of language help. These are usually itinerant, and always temporary —students are expected to shift to normal teaching once they know the basic vocabulary and structures to find their way in the school. Classes are mixed in respect of age, sex, first language and educational level, and they normally take from 10 to 12 students, yet they may vary in number and distribution according to needs and availability. Small children, though, are immersed in classrooms with nationals from the beginning. The mother tongue is at all costs maintained. There were two temporary Spanish Language Support Classes (*Aulas temporales de adaptación lingüística*) in Jaén during the academic year 2001-02. It increased twofold the following year, but a need for a bigger effort is felt in high schools hosting immigrant students.

The Plan for the Education of Immigrants designed by the Andalusian Regional Government is based on a broad definition of culture as the way of behaviour of the community. The sum of beliefs, arts, ethics, rights, customs, capabilities and habits acquired by the individual conforms his or herself. On such a view, in the reproduction of culture individuals get their identity. Ultimately, however, this perspective leaves no room for selfhood, liquidates individuality and dissolves the "I".

Conterminously, this document decomposes the range of possible attitudes towards the immigrant reality, i.e., indifference, marginalization, assimilation, multiculturalism, and interculturality. According to Fernández Bote *et al.* (2002), indifference maintains differences and prolongs the initial disadvantage of the newcomer. Marginalization sustains a monologic version of history and promotes the use of different times and spaces, whereas assimilation implies the loss of native identities, languages, food habits and religions, and often results in a clash between first and second generation immigrants, because the latter lose memory and aggregate into mainstream society, trying to become as Spanish as they can. Multiculturalism does not eliminate social differences, as it has been argued, rather —according to this governmental document— it leads to variants of racism. Although it fosters contact, it also furthers persistence of clichés and stasis. On arriving, immigrants set up exclusive ghettos that imitate what they leave behind, or rather exceed in imitation. Since immigration implies loss of continuity over temporal, spatial, and familial links (cf. Grinberg/Grinberg 1989, p. 20), these first immigrants tend to overcompensate the loss by making old rules heavier than before, even when they are no longer hegemonic in their countries of origin. Simply put, they reinvent their cultures as a form of self-preservation. All of these positions are consequently ruled out as subterranean forms of xenophobia. Nowadays, our regional government advocates for *interculturality*, a novel term that subscribes cultural interaction as a teaching model.

Interculturality, as defined by the Andalusian Regional Government, shares with multiculturalism the interest in minorities, but, by contrast, promotes cultural sharing, exchange, interaction, and cooperation within the same spatial and temporal axes. It fosters knowledge of cultural differences —accepted as positive valences— and similarities. It raises awareness of the need to eliminate social and economic barriers, avoids the clash of multiple cultures, multiple languages, multiple ways of thinking the world, and relates minorities to majorities. Besides, it sustains —say Essomba Gelabert *et al.* (1999)— a dynamic view of identity, advocates for the fusion of horizons, and refuses cultural distance so as to enable students to take identities on and off, so that they can be different persons in different situations. In the ingenious words of Franco/Shimabukuro (1992, p. 4) "[I]ntercultural education fosters an understanding of tightly integrated relations between language, communication, and culture. Intercultural curricula focus on how individuals are shaped by the norms, values, beliefs, and the language of their culture."

Nevertheless, the governmental approach to intercultural education presents, in our view, four important drawbacks. First, it is written by a majority trying to discipline a body of minorities into normalized identities. It invariably shows condescension. Second, by refusing to hold cultures at a distance, it runs the risk of obliterating the particular cultural matrices that conform uniqueness. Third, it fails to take into account other theoretical approaches more attuned to the modern realities of internationalization and globalization. According to Pickert (1992, p. 20), international education "[...] includes the study of relations among nations, particular regions of the world foreign languages and cultural, comparative and intercultural approaches to particular disciplines, and the examination of issues affecting more than one country." How to educate people in ecological sustainability, global interdependence, human rights and social justice at the cognitive, emotional and active levels, in sum, how to become competitive skilled-citizens for the global marketplace is, likewise, discarded. Fourth, there is no staff prepared for teaching the students how to get healthy intercultural, international, and global identities.

4. Underachievements

The socio-economic status of students has been proved to be an influence on their academic achievement. Although every effort is being done in Spain to fully integrate immigrants in the education system, it goes without saying that the situation affecting their families (frequently without a home and a job, and awaiting official recognition) influences their academic life, and results in school underachievement.

More often than not, underachievement derives from absenteeism (a phenomenon also quite common in the gipsy population in Spain, and particularly in Andalusia). Parents are normally worried about issues they consider vital, such as getting a job or official documents, that either consciously or unconsciously pay less attention to their children's academic achievement.

Other reasons which may account for low results at school (though this is not always the case) are related to the absence of a real future job or university prospects (an aspect which also affects Spanish teenagers themselves). Few immigrants think of the possibility of university education, although some exceptions may be quoted, such as the increasing presence of people from other countries studying at the University of Jaén (a particular worth-mentioning example is that of Iranian students in the Doctorate program of our English Department).

Some immigrants —though by no means all— are also affected by the need to leave school too young in order to work and help their families (if they are lucky, to find a —frequently illegal— job). Other times they fail to attend school and involve themselves in petty crime. We may say that this same situation is applicable not only to immigrants but also to Spaniards of low social classes living in the outskirts of big cities, affected by other problems such as drug addiction and delinquency.

One other factor which may also explain underachievement in some immigrants in Andalusia (especially in the first months of their stay here) is the language barrier. For those who do not speak Spanish (obviously this is not a problem in the case of the considerable amount of immigrants coming from South America), this is an added difficulty. The Andalusian Regional Government is trying to do its best by means of the temporary Spanish Language Support Classes (which have already been referred to in this paper) in order to bridge the language gap. Anyway, it is just fair to recognise that immigrants strive to overcome this difficulty as soon as possible (in some cases surprisingly fast, as is the case of children coming from The Sahara or from other European countries to Spain to spend the summer), perhaps because they possess a really high degree of both integrative and instrumental motivation.

In several educational experiences in Spain (some of them carried out in a few schools in Jaén) English acts as a sort of "lingua franca" since some subjects such as History and Natural Sciences are taught in English. This facilitates academic achievement to immigrants speaking English either as their mother tongue, second or foreign language. Anyway, it is also true that these experiences (highly related to what has been termed "Content-Based Instruction" —CBI—) are usually implemented in private schools attended by students from upper-class families, which means that immigrants rarely gain access to them.

5. Proposals in Education

It has been customary to say that the final goal of language teaching has to do with the achievement of "communicative competence." This expands the Chomskyan idea of "linguistic competence" as the abstract system underlying the concrete behaviour or "performance," and which can be defined as a more general communicative ability concerning language "usage" (our knowledge of the formal system of a language) as well as "use" (using the formal system of a language to achieve some kind of communicative purpose) within the sociocultural context in which language interaction takes place. Communicative competence has been said to include four "subcompetences": grammatical, discursive, strategic and sociolinguistic (cf. Canale/Swain 1980; Canale 1983).

The concept of "sociolinguistic competence" starts from the idea that language occurs in a social context which promotes interaction and in which aspects such as setting, participants, goals, illocutionary force of speech acts, register and appropriateness are crucial for communication to develop satisfactorily. The social context is closely related to the cultural aspects of the people involved in conversation and this has led to the notion of "sociocultural or cultural competence" (cf. Bueno González 1996, pp. 345-373), which has to do with the social and cultural aspects of the people who speak a given language and of the country or countries in which that language is spoken. This means that linguistic proficiency is not enough to master a language, it is also essential to be familiar with cultural aspects.

When people from different nationalities get in contact (and this is the case of immigrants all over the world) not only two different languages but also two different cultures are at issue. Trying to assimilate the new language and culture without losing their mother tongue and culture forces them to develop what has been termed "intercultural communicative competence," which implies effective interaction and the establishment and maintenance of relationships among people from different cultures. In this respect, intercultural competence surpasses communicative competence (cf. Guilherme 2000; Byram 1997).

In the case of immigrants both sociocultural and intercultural competences have to be taken into account in any education proposal. Syllabus design and methodology have to be sensitive to this new reality (and in fact this is happening in Andalusia, where special intercultural education programs are increasingly being designed for immigrants). The importance of cultural values both from the immigrants' native country and the host country is taken for granted and cannot be underestimated. Even linguistic development closely depends on this cultural component (together with grammar, vocabulary, pronunciation, discourse and strategic behaviour). The new situation in Andalusia (and partly in the rest of Spain), where more and more immigrants from different parts of the world are coming, demands the inclusion of intercultural objectives, contents and activities in any syllabus design (cf. Byram/Gribkova/Starkey 2002, p. 9; Byram *et al.* 1994, pp. 51-52; Stern 1992, pp. 223-232; Byram 1994, pp. 41-60). The writers of teaching materials also have to bear this intercultural component in mind.

Some of the arguments for an (inter)cultural syllabus are related the obvious benefits of fostering international understanding and preventing negative stereotypes and other prejudices. The comparison between both cultures is always fruitful and helps learners to appreciate their own culture. In addition, the inclusion of an intercultural component motivates learners and helps to integrate the language course in an interdisciplinary curriculum (cf. Adaskou/Britten/Fahsi 1990).

The contents of an intercultural syllabus transcend and complement those of a cultural one. It is not only a question of including information about the foreign country in aspects such as places, individual persons and way of life, people and society in general, history, institutions, art, music, literature, daily routine, food, drinks, festivities, etc. It is rather a question of integration of both cultures and the development of a new competence, the intercultural one, in which, on the basis of reciprocal respect and mutual understanding and valuing, a sort of hybrid enriching knowledge develops. The achievement of this type of interculturality has evident linguistic, social and human advantages and favours the cohabitation of different cultures. This is the reason why the development of intercultural competence is included in *The Common European Framework of Reference for Languages* (2001, pp. 103-107). In the official education documents for Primary and Secondary Education both in Spain (national level) and in Andalusia (regional level) the intercultural component is considered (e.g. *Real Decreto 117/2004 de 23 de enero para Bachillerato* —Compulsory Secondary Education—, in which several objectives and contents are related to (inter)cultural aspects).

From the methodological point of view, teachers should face this new situation by first of all creating an authentic classroom environment (posters exemplifying some cultural aspects, realia, a classroom library including cultural aspects, magazines, etc.). Cultural aspects may be provided by means of "culture asides"

—items of culture presented in the course of language work— "culture capsules" —an isolated item of cultural information— and "culture clusters" —two or more capsules— (cf. Stern 1992, pp. 223-232). Techniques should also be developed to overcome "culture shock" by drama tasks. Readings of informative and descriptive texts, folk tales and literary pieces, cultural visits, lectures, discussions and debates are also recommendable.

The following activities can be proposed: listening to/reading a text and extracting any cultural facts appearing in it, creating cultural expectations before reading/listening to a text, information-gap activities in pairs and in groups concerning cultural aspects, contrasting cultural aspects between both countries, viewing and performing sketches about daily-life matters, identifying monuments and public buildings from both countries, cultural questionnaires, games related to cultural aspects, and project work.

References

Adaskou, K./Britten, D./Fahsi, B.: Design decisions on the cultural content of a secondary English course for Morocco. In: ELT Journal (1990) 44/1: 3-10.

Bueno González, A. (1996): Sociolinguistic and sociocultural competence. In: McLaren, N./Madrid, D. (Eds.): A Handbook for TEFL. Alcoy: Marfil.

Byram, M. (1997): Teaching and Assessing Intercultural Communicative Competence. Clevedon: Multilingual Matters.

Byram, M. et al. (1994): Teaching-and-Learning Language-and-Culture. Clevedon: Multilingual Matters.

Byram, M./Gribkova, B./Starkey, H. (2002): Developing the Intercultural Dimension in Language Teaching. A Practical Introduction for Teachers. Strasbourg: Council of Europe.

Butler, J. (1993): Bodies that Matter: On the Discursive Limits of "Sex." New York: Routledge.

Canale, M. (1983): From communicative competence to communicative language pedagogy. In: Richards, J.C./Schmidt, R. (Eds.): Language and Communication. Harlow, Essex: Longman.

Canale, M./Swain, M.: Theoretical bases of communicative approaches to second language teaching and testing. In: Applied Linguistics (1980) 1: 1-47.

Council of Europe (2001): Common European Framework of Reference for Language: Learning, Teaching, Assessment. Cambridge: Cambridge University Press.

Cohen, W. A. (2003): Deep Skin. In: Cohen, J.J./Weiss, G. (Eds.): Thinking the Limits of the Body. Albany: State University of New York Press.

Essomba G., Miguel Á. et al. (1999): Construir la escuela intercultural: reflexiones y propuestas para trabajar la diversidad étnica y cultural. Barcelona: GRAO.

Fernández Bote, F. et al. (2002): Acogida y atención del alumnado inmigrante. Guía para la tutoría. Sevilla: Consejería de Educación y Ciencia.

Franco, R.W./Shimabukuro, J.N. (Eds.) (1992): Beyond the Classroom: International Education and the Community College. Honolulu, HI: Hawaii University.

Guilherme, M. (2000): Intercultural competence. In: Byram, M. (Ed.): Routledge Encyclopaedia of Language Teaching and Learning. London: Routledge.

Grinberg, L./Grinberg, R. (1989): Psychoanalytic Perspectives on Migration and Exile. New Haven: Yale University Press.

Junta de Andalucía (2001): Plan para la atención educativa del alumnado inmigrante en la comunidad autónoma andaluza. Sevilla: Consejería de Educación y Ciencia.

Ministerio del Interior (2003): Balance 2003. Madrid: Delegación del Gobierno para la Extranjería y la Inmigración, Oficina de Relaciones Informativas y Sociales, Ministerio del Interior.

Pickert, S. M. (1992): Preparing for a Global Community: Achieving an International Perspective in Higher Education. Washington, DC: School of Education and Human Development, the George Washington University.

Stern, H. H. (1992): Issues and Options in Language Teaching. Oxford: Oxford University Press.

Nailia Skrynnikova (Universität Magdeburg, Deutschland)

Bilingualität als Problem und Chance in Integrationsprozessen von Migranten. Aspekte eines studentischen Forschungsprojekts

Abstract:
Die Globalisierungseffekte, die Auswirkungen der europäischen Einigung und die Migrationsprozesse bewirken und verstärken die Multikulturalität der deutschen Gesellschaft. Damit verbinden sich verschiedene Herausforderungen für die Integration von ausländischen Kindern in Deutschland. Am Beispiel der Auswanderer aus Gebieten der ehemaligen Sowjetunion soll dargestellt werden, was Vertreter der deutschen Majoritätskultur unter Interkultureller Bildung verstehen, und inwieweit Bilingualität sowohl von Angehörigen der deutschen Mehrheitskultur als auch von Migranten nicht nur als Problem sondern auch als Chance betrachtet wird.

1. Problemlage

Obwohl Deutschland schon seit langem ein Einwanderungsland geworden ist (vgl. Schmalz-Jacobsen 1994, S.1), hat man mit den damit verbundenen Herausforderungen noch sehr wenig Erfahrung. Integration ist ein zweiseitiger Prozess, die Migranten müssen sich integrieren, die Möglichkeit und Chance zur Integration muss ihnen jedoch von dem Einwanderungsland geboten werden. Die Integrationsbemühungen in Deutschland wurden jedoch bisher nicht dementsprechend verstärkt. In der Realität sind die Integrationsmöglichkeiten für Ausländer in Deutschland leider immer noch sehr begrenzt.

Ein zeitlich geringes und nicht nach Leistungen differenziertes Programm von Sprachkursen für neuangekommene Migranten ist offensichtlich nicht ausreichend für das neue Leben. Die Folge ist zwangsläufig eine fehlende bzw. zu geringe deutsche Sprachkompetenz bei vielen Ausländern. Ohne eine hinreichende deutsche Sprachkompetenz ist eine Integration jedoch nahezu unmöglich. So ist die geringe deutsche Sprachkompetenz bei vielen Ausländern eine Ursache, dass Ausländer statistisch gesehen wesentlich stärker von der Arbeitslosigkeit betroffen sind als Deutsche. Ausländer sind wesentlich öfter und wesentlich länger arbeitslos. Es findet hierdurch zwangsläufig eine zusätzliche Trennung zwischen Einheimischen und Ausländern statt.

Bis jetzt hat sich in Deutschland das Bewusstsein, ein Einwanderungsland zu sein, noch nicht durchgesetzt. Dies zeigt sich deutlich an der sogenannten „Greencard-Regelung", die einen zeitlich begrenzten Zuzug von Spezialisten ermöglicht, sowie an den langwierigen Verhandlungen im Bundestag über ein Einwanderungsgesetz. Schon allein aus demographischen Gründen ist Deutschland auf eine kontinuierliche Einwanderung angewiesen. Für eine konstante Bevölkerung werden je Familie 2,1 Kinder benötigt. In Deutschland liegt die Anzahl der Kinder pro Familie jedoch nur bei 1,4. Dies bedeutet, dass die nächste Generation um ca. 1/3 kleiner sein wird als die heutige. Dies führt zwangsläufig zu Problemen auf dem Arbeitsmarkt (Arbeitskräftemangel) sowie bei den Sozialsystemen. Es ist daher erforderlich, dass sich das Migrationsverständnis in der deutschen Gesellschaft neu definiert. In der Zukunft muss man in Deutschland Ausländer als Teil der Gesellschaft und als Chance betrachten. Die Gesellschaft in Deutschland und auch in Europa wird zwangsläufig zunehmend multikulturell geprägt sein.

2. Allgemeine Sprachsituation und Integrationsmöglichkeiten von Auswanderer in Deutschland

Bei der Integration von Ausländern ist oft das größte Problem die fehlende deutsche Sprachkompetenz. Ohne Beherrschung der deutschen Sprache sind die Chancen auf dem Arbeitsmarkt sehr schlecht. Die ohnehin minimalen Erwerbschancen beschränken wiederum oft die allgemeinen Kommunikationsmöglichkeiten. Die Konsequenz ist damit häufig eine erzwungene dauerhafte Isolation.

Selbst bei einer groben Beherrschung der deutschen Sprache werden Immigranten oft nur gering qualifizierte Tätigkeiten angeboten (vgl. Rapithwin 2001, S. 13-17). Meist wird nicht versucht, sie basierend auf ihrem bisherigen beruflichen Werdegang für eine entsprechende Tätigkeit auf dem deutschen Arbeitsmarkt zu qualifizieren. Dies führt leicht zu einem Gefühl der Herabwürdigung und erschwert den Prozess der Integration.

Die qualifizierte Vermittlung der deutschen Sprache ist daher von grundlegender Bedeutung für eine erfolgreiche Integration. Auf vier Monate reduzierte Sprachkurse für neu angekommene Migranten sind für viele nicht ausreichend. Zusätzlich sind die Lehrkräfte oft nicht entsprechend zielgerichtet qualifiziert. Es werden häufig Deutschlehrer ohne entsprechende Vorbereitung eingesetzt. Ein weiteres Problem bei den Sprachkursen ist, dass das Angebot für den „Durchschnittseinwanderer" gedacht ist bzw. sich oft sogar an den leistungsschwächsten orientiert. Dies hat zur Folge, dass es insbesondere für Akademiker sehr schwierig ist, eine entsprechende deutsche Sprachkompetenz zu erwerben. Einen zusätzlichen Sprachkurs können sich neuangekommene Migranten in der ersten Zeit in der Regel nicht leisten.

Für eine erfolgreiche Integration sind daher ausbildungs- und fähigkeitsadäquate Integrationsmaßnahmen, wie Sprachkurse und Förderung der Einwanderer, sehr wichtig.

3. Allgemeine Situation der Kinder von Migranten in deutschen Schulen (am Beispiel der Auswanderer aus der ehemaligen Sowjetunion)
Die Kinder von Migranten haben bessere Chancen als ihre Eltern, da sie zusammen mit deutschen muttersprachlichen Kindern die gleiche Schule besuchen. Außerdem ist im Kindesalter bzw. in der Jugend die Lernfähigkeit von Sprachen höher als im Alter. Trotzdem zeigt es sich in der Praxis oft, dass auch Kinder viele Probleme beim Erlernen der deutschen Sprache haben (vgl. Klemm 1987; Keck 2001, S. 152).[1] Es zeigen sich unterschiedliche Problematiken.

In vielen Großstädten ist, bedingt durch den Ausländeranteil und die größere Anzahl von Kindern je Familie, die Anzahl ausländischer Kinder sehr hoch. Hierdurch ist in Städten, wie Frankfurt, Hamburg oder Berlin, in einzelnen Stadtteilen in den Schulklassen der Anteil der Kinder sehr hoch, die Deutsch nicht als Muttersprache sprechen. In Extremfällen liegt dieser Anteil bei über 50 %. So gibt es in einem Stadtteil Frankfurts Klassen, in denen der Anteil von Ausländerkindern bei 80 % liegt (vgl. Schmoll 2004). Die Lehrer sind auf diese Herausforderung oft nicht entsprechend vorbereitet bzw. es fehlen ihnen die Möglichkeiten (vgl. Keck 2001, S.153). Die Gefahr eines hohen Anteils von Nichtmuttersprachlern ist, dass die ausländischen Kinder wegen der fehlenden Notwendigkeit nicht genügend motiviert sind, Deutsch zu lernen und in den Pausen bzw. außerhalb der Schule zu sprechen. Ein möglicher Grund dafür ist meines Erachtens, dass die gesamte Umgebung und auch die Schule den Kindern nicht das Gefühl vermittelt, dass Mehrsprachigkeit bzw. gleichzeitiges Aufwachsen in zwei Kulturen ein großer Vorteil ist.
Ein weiterer Aspekt ist, dass die Förderung leistungsstarker Kinder in Klassen mit großem Ausländeranteil oft sehr problematisch ist. Die Lehrer müssen zwangsläufig mehr Zeit und teilweise andere Lehrmethoden verwenden, um allen Kindern den Lernstoff auf Deutsch zu vermitteln. Um ein entsprechendes Unterrichtsniveau ihrer Kinder abzusichern, versuchen viele deutschsprachige Eltern daher in diesen Fällen, die Schule zu wechseln. Dies hat zur Folge, dass häufig in diesen Klassen nur die leistungsschwächeren deutschen Kinder und ausländische Kinder mit schlechten Sprachkenntnissen bleiben. Die späteren Chancen der Kinder sind dadurch oft reduziert. So wurde in einem Bericht der FAZ über die Integration ausländischer Kinder erwähnt, dass an einer Frankfurter Gesamtschule an einem der sozialen Brennpunkte in der Abschlussklasse von 18 Schulabgängern 16 keine Lehrstelle oder auch keinen Abschluss bekommen haben (vgl. Schmoll 2004).

---

[1] Klemm berichtet 1987 von zwei Tendenzen der Bildungsbenachteiligung ausländischer Schüler: der Normalisierung und der Hierarchisierung.

Die Problematik bei der Schul- und Bildungspolitik ist in der Statistik deutlich erkennbar. „Laut Migrationbericht für Hessen aus dem Jahr 2002 werden Migrantenkinder im Vergleich zu deutschen mehr als doppelt so häufig vom Schulbesuch zurückgestellt. Sie wiederholen drei- bis viermal so oft eine Klasse, fast ein Viertel von ihnen bleibt ohne Hauptschulabschluss, und nur elf Prozent erreichen das Abitur." (ebd.) Ein Lösungsansatz für dieses Problem ist ein verstärktes Bemühen der Schule, Einwandererkindern Kenntnisse der deutschen Sprache zu vermitteln. Hierzu läuft derzeit in Hessen an drei Schulen in Frankfurt mit einem hohen Ausländeranteil ein Modellprojekt. Erstklässler mit schlechten Deutschkenntnissen werden in Deutsch und Mathematik in Fördergruppen täglich zwei Stunden parallel zum Klassenverband unterrichtet. Dieses Modellprojekt wird wissenschaftlich begleitet.

Ein anderer Lösungsansatz wendet sich bewusst an Einwandererfamilien. An einigen Schulen in Frankfurt a.M. werden Sprachkurse für die Eltern angeboten. Die Vermittlung deutscher Sprachkenntnis an die Eltern bietet einen doppelten Vorteil: die Integration der Familien in ihr Umfeld wird erleichtert und die Eltern können ihren Kindern bei den Schulaufgaben besser helfen.

In vielen Mittel- und Kleinstädten zeigt sich demgegenüber eine vollkommen andere Problematik. Der Anteil von nicht muttersprachlichen deutschen Kindern in der Schule ist ziemlich gering. Die ausländischen Kinder lernen daher gut deutsch und sind gut integriert. Es besteht jedoch die Gefahr, dass die Kinder ihre Muttersprache verlernen bzw. nicht mehr richtig erlernen. Teilweise reden die ausländischen Kinder sogar im Familienkreis nur deutsch. Die Kinder verlieren hierdurch die Chance, mehrsprachig aufzuwachsen und sich bewusst zweisprachig in zwei gleichwertigen Kulturen zu entwickeln.

Bei der Betrachtung der Bildungsmöglichkeiten von Zuwandererkindern sollte man neben dem Ausländeranteil an Schulen natürlich auch andere wichtige Aspekte berücksichtigen. So verstehen verschiedene kulturelle Gruppen (Nationalitäten) aus mehreren Gründen (kulturell, religiös, historisch, mental usw.) den Integrationsprozess selbst und die Notwendigkeit der Integration oft unterschiedlich. Daher sind die Integrationsbemühungen und der Integrationserfolg sehr oft unterschiedlich.

Es gibt mehrere statistische Untersuchungen zu den schulischen Leistungen und dem Bildungserfolg bei Einwanderern unterschiedlicher kultureller Gruppen. So zeigt Keck (vgl. Keck 2001), dass es zwischen den Nationalitäten der Einwanderer hinsichtlich des Bildungserfolgs große Unterschiede gibt.[2] In einer anderen

---

[2] Keck (2001) stellt in Anlehnung an einen Bericht des Beauftragten der Bundesregierung für Ausländerfragen (1997) deutliche Unterschiede zwischen den Nationalitäten fest: „Spanische Jugendliche haben den höchsten Anteil an Realschulen und Gymnasien und den Auszubildenden in der Berufsschule. Griechische Jugendliche sind selten in einer Ausbildung, aber sehr häufig in der Sekundarstufe II, (...). Italienische Jugendliche sind hingegen besonderes selten an Gymnasien zu finden und türkische Jugendliche

Studie wurde gezeigt (vgl. Beuchling 2003), dass z.B. bei vietnamesischen Familien die Eltern auf den schulischen Erfolg der Kinder einen sehr großen Wert legen und sie entsprechend fördern. Dies führt dazu, dass die Kinder dieser kulturellen Minderheit sehr schnell deutsch lernen und häufig überdurchschnittliche Leistungen bringen.

Aber auch bei Einwanderern aus dem gleichen Land gibt es unterschiedlich motivierte Gruppen. Meiner Meinung nach ist der entscheidende Faktor für die Motivation der Eltern ihr sozialer, beruflicher und kultureller Hintergrund.

Ein interessantes Beispiel sind die Einwanderer aus der ehemaligen Sowjetunion. Es gibt hier zwei große Gruppen von Einwanderern: Russlanddeutsche und jüdische Kontingentflüchtlinge. Ein großer Teil der Russlanddeutschen kommt aus den ländlichen Gegenden Kasachstans. Die andere Gruppe, jüdische Kontingentsflüchtlinge, kommt primär aus den Städten. Der Anteil von Akademikern ist in dieser Gruppe sehr groß. Diese beiden Gruppen haben ein vollkommen unterschiedliches Bewusstsein:

Die alte Generation der Russlanddeutschen kommt mit der Erwartungshaltung, in ihre alte Heimat zurückzukehren. Die junge Generation teilt diese Haltung jedoch meistens nicht. Sie sehen sich eher als Russen und grenzen sich oft gegenüber den Deutschen ab. Es kommt hierdurch leicht zu einer Gruppenbildung verbunden mit einer Abkapslung und einer alleinigen Gebrauch des Russischen in der Freizeit. (vgl. Zimprich 2004) Dies wird verstärkt durch die ländliche Herkunft und das dadurch sehr stark geprägte kollektive Zusammengehörigkeitsgefühl. Die Folge ist sehr oft eine eher geringe deutsche Sprachkompetenz und schlechte schulische Leistungen. Diese Misserfolgserlebnisse verstärken wiederum leicht die Abgrenzungstendenzen.

Im Gegensatz dazu ist bei den jüdischen Kontingentsflüchtlingen bei der alten und bei der jungen Generation das Gefühl vorhanden, in der Fremde zu sein und sich von vorne alles neu aufbauen zu müssen. Dies führt zu einem verstärkten Integrationsbemühen, einer hohen sprachlichen Kompetenz und guten schulischen Erfolgen. Die Kinder dieser Einwanderergruppe bringen oft schon nach kurzer Zeit die gleichen Leistungen, die sie auch in ihrer Heimat gebracht hätten. Durch die städtische Herkunft ist bei dieser Gruppe in der Regel der Individualismus stärker ausgeprägt als bei den Russlanddeutschen. Bei dieser Gruppe zeigt sich jedoch oft der Nachteil, dass die Kinder durch den intensiven Kontakt mit der deutschen Kultur ihre eigene Muttersprache immer weniger verwenden und leicht vergessen. Um dies zu vermeiden, versuchen die Eltern in der Freizeit, die Russischkenntnisse der Kinder zu fördern.

---

haben insgesamt relativ schlechtesten schulischen Voraussetzungen: keinen Schulabschluss oder nur den Hauptschulabschluss sowie niedrige Ausbildungsquoten." (S. 153)

Die Beispiele zeigen, dass für eine erfolgreiche Integration von Einwanderern die verschiedenen Gruppen unterschiedlich zu fördern sind.

4. Interkulturelle Bildung / Befragung

Die Entwicklung unserer Gesellschaft hin zu mehr Multikulturalität ist unvermeidlich. Multikulturalität entsteht nicht nur durch Einwanderung, sondern auch durch die Globalisierung und durch die europäische Einigung. Eine mehrsprachige Sprachkompetenz wird zunehmend zu einem Schlüsselkriterium unserer heutigen Gesellschaft. Die Kenntnis und das Verständnis fremder Kulturen werden immer wichtiger. Interkulturelle Bildung ist daher auch für die Deutschen von großer Bedeutung.

Die Frage ist, ob sich diese Erkenntnis und die daraus ergebenden Folgerungen in der Gesellschaft schon entsprechend verbreitet haben. Aufgrund der Bedeutung der Schulerziehung habe ich hierfür an der Internationalen Grundschule Pierre Trudeau in Magdeburg die Eltern befragt. Die Internationale Grundschule in Magdeburg ist eine bilinguale Schule, die im August 2000 gegründet wurde. Der Unterricht findet auf deutsch und französisch durch muttersprachliche Lehrer statt. Ich habe mich für diese Schule entschieden, da ich hier ein stärkeres Bewusstsein für die Bedeutung der Multikulturalität erwarte als an einer normalen Grundschule.

Die Mehrzahl der Kinder hat deutsch als Muttersprache, vgl. Abb. 1 und 2.

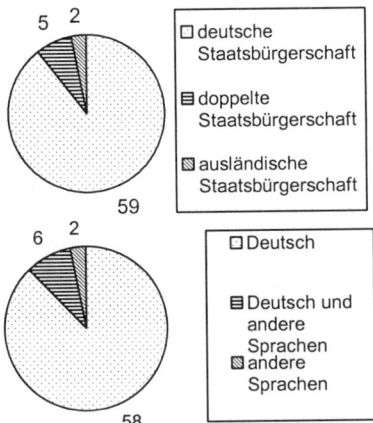

Abb. 1: Staatsangehörigkeit der Kinder   Abb. 2: Muttersprache der Kinder

Ungefähr ein Drittel der Kinder (20 von 66 Kindern) hat schon vor dem Besuch der Grundschule Erfahrungen mit Fremdsprachen gemacht. Zehn Kinder haben schon Englisch und sechs Kinder Französisch kennen gelernt.

Die meisten Kinder kommen aus Familien, in denen die Eltern mehrere Fremdsprachen beherrschen. Abb. 3 zeigt die Anzahl der Fremdsprachen. In ungefähr
der Hälfte der Familien (44%) können die Eltern Französisch.

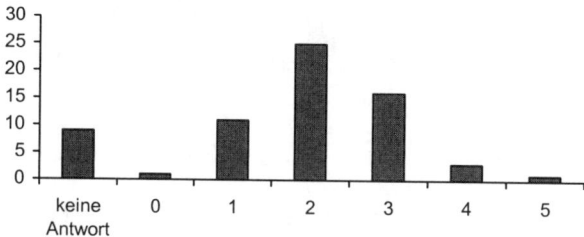

Abb. 3: Anzahl der in den Familien beherrschten Fremdsprachen

Auffallend ist, dass sich ca. ¾ der Eltern schon längerfristig für eine bilinguale
Erziehung ihrer Kinder entschieden haben. Die Entscheidung, die Kinder bilingual zu erziehen bzw. mit einer Fremdsprache von Anfang an vertraut zu machen, ist also eine bewusste Entscheidung. Alle Eltern haben als Grund für die
Schulwahl die bilinguale Erziehung angegeben.

Die Motivation der Eltern, die Kinder bilingual zu erziehen, basiert auf zwei
Punkten:

- spätere berufliche Vorteile für die Kinder und
- Vermittlung der französischen Kultur und Verbundenheit mit Frankreich.

Interessant sind außerdem die Freitextantworten einiger Eltern:

- „Förderung des Gedankens der Völkerverständigung"
- „Interessen für andere Kulturen wecken"
- „Aufgeschlossenheit gegenüber anderen Kulturen"
- „Einzige Schule dieser Art in Magdeburg"

Viele der Eltern haben sich aktiv an der Gründung der internationalen Grundschule beteiligt. Nahezu alle Eltern wünschen sich ein weitergehendes bilinguales Schulangebot. Ab Schuljahr 2004-2005 wird das bilinguale Unterrichtsange-
bot (mit mathematisch-wirtschaftlichen Profil) an dem Internationalen Gymnasi-
um Pierre Trudeau fortgesetzt.

Interessant ist, dass sich die meisten Eltern einen möglichst frühen Beginn der
bilingualen Erziehung wünschen. Es besteht ein reges Interesse an einer bilingualen Erziehung ab Geburt des Kindes (75%) bzw. ab dem Kindergarten (25%),
(vgl. Abb. 4).

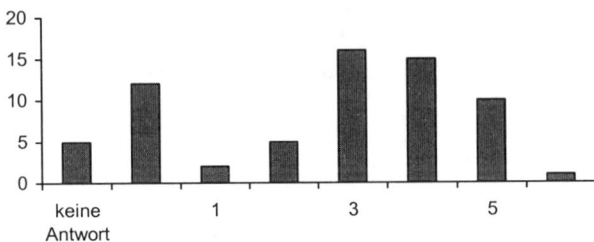

Abb. 4: Bevorzugtes Alter für den Beginn einer bilingualen Erziehung

Auffallend ist, dass sehr viele Eltern sich nicht primär für eine deutsch-französische bilinguale Erziehung sondern für die bilinguale Erziehung an sich entschieden haben. Mehr als die Hälfte aller Eltern haben als Kriterium für die Auswahl der Sprache (Französisch) „einzige angebotene Fremdsprache" genannt. Die Hälfte von diesen Eltern hätte eine deutsch-englische bilinguale Erziehung bevorzugt (als bevorzugte Sprache wurde nur englisch genannt), die andere Hälfte hätte keine andere Sprache bevorzugt. Die Sprache an sich war für diese Gruppe daher weniger wichtig.

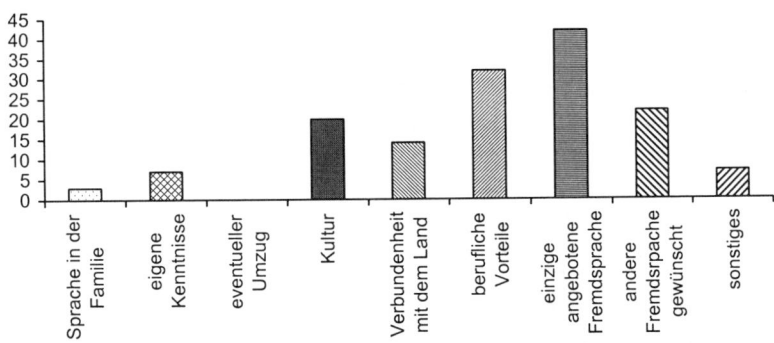

Abb. 5: Antworten auf die Frage „Nach welche Kriterien haben Sie die Sprache ausgesucht"

Die Befragung hat gezeigt, dass die Eltern an einer vielfältigen Erziehung der Kinder interessiert sind. Sie haben sich bewusst für eine bilinguale Schulbildung entschieden. Zusätzlich besucht ein sehr großer Teil der Kinder in der Freizeit die Musikschule oder macht Sport, (vgl. Abb. 6).

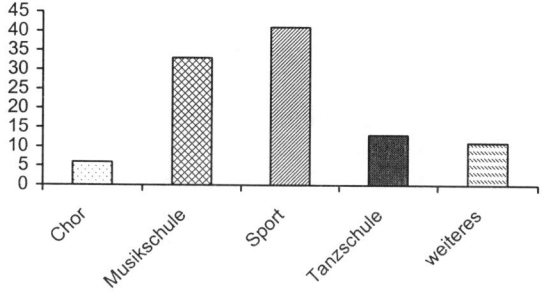

Abb. 6: Außerschulische Aktivitäten der Kinder

Die Eltern sind also hoch motiviert und fördern ihre Kinder in allen Bereichen. Hierbei spiegeln sich die zwei Aspekte der bilingualen Erziehung:

- kulturelle Bereicherung und
- berufliche Vorteile

in der Motivation der Eltern wieder.

Die Befragung hat gezeigt, dass die Vorteile und Möglichkeiten der bilingualen Erziehung bei einem interessierten Elternkreis (Eltern von Schulkindern der Internationalen Grundschule Pierre Trudeau) gesehen werden. Im Rahmen weiterer Arbeiten ist geplant, eine ähnliche Befragung an einer nicht bilingualen Grundschule durchzuführen.

In Deutschland befindet sich die bilinguale Erziehung noch im Anfangsstadium. Die Internationale Grundschule in Magdeburg stellt noch eine Ausnahme dar. Erst in den letzten zwei bis drei Jahren wurde verstärkt damit begonnen, ein bilinguales bzw. internationales Schulbildungsangebot einzurichten.

5. Schlussfolgerung

Deutschland ist schon seit langem ein Einwanderungsland geworden. In der Vergangenheit war die Einwanderung unauffällig, Integration war kein Thema. Heute ist jedoch die Anzahl der Einwanderer und der damit verbundenen Integrationsprobleme in Deutschland so groß und offensichtlich geworden, dass eine öffentliche Diskussion dieses Themas unvermeidlich ist. Die Gesellschaft in Deutschland und in Europa wird zwangsläufig zunehmend multikulturell geprägt sein. Es ist daher erforderlich, dass ein Bewusstsein „ein Einwanderungsland zu sein" bzw. „eine offene Gesellschaft zu sein" in der deutschen Gesellschaft entsteht. Gleichzeitig sind die schon seit Jahrzehnten in Deutschland lebenden Ausländer als Teil der deutschen Gesellschaft anzuerkennen.

Für eine erfolgreiche Integration der Einwanderer sind ausbildungs- und fähig-keitsadäquate Integrationsmaßnahmen, wie Sprachkursen und Förderung der Einwanderer, sehr wichtig. Die verschiedenen Einwanderergruppen benötigen eine unterschiedliche Förderung. Lange Zeit hat es hier an entsprechend geeigneten Lehrkräften, einer wissenschaftlichen Begleitung und einer Forschung und Analyse von Migrationsproblemen gefehlt.

In deutschen Schulen fehlt ausländischen Kindern sehr oft die Motivation die beiden Sprachen (Deutsch und die Muttersprache) gleich gut zu lernen. Den ausländischen Kindern sollte bewusst gemacht werden, dass eine zweisprachige Entwicklung in zwei gleichwertigen Kulturen eine sehr große Chance ist. Dies kann am besten durch die Schule vermittelt werden.

Internationale bzw. bilinguale Schulen bieten deutschen Kindern die Möglich-keit, ebenfalls zweisprachig in zwei Kulturen aufzuwachsen. Die Kinder können frühzeitig auf die Möglichkeiten gegenseitiger kultureller Bereicherung aufmerk-sam gemacht werden und Toleranz lernen– nicht gegeneinander stehen, sondern sich sinnvoll ergänzen. Gleichzeitig bietet die Förderung der Fremdsprachen-kenntnisse für die berufliche Perspektive Vorteile. Das Verständnis für die Be-deutung einer internationalen bzw. bilingualen Erziehung setzt sich in Deutsch-land zunehmend durch und es wurden in verschiedenen Städten entsprechende Schulen gegründet. Die hierbei gewonnenen Erfahrungen sind in der Zukunft noch wissenschaftlich auszuwerten.

Literaturverzeichnis

Bauman, Zygmunt (1992): Moderne und Ambivalenz – Das Ende der Eindeutig-keit, Hamburg, Junius Verlag

Bericht des Beauftragten der Bundesregierung für Ausländerfragen über die Lage der Ausländer der Bundesrepublik Deutschland. (1997): Bonn

Beuchling, Olaf (2002): Kulturelle und religiöse Vielfalt in der Bundesrepublik Deutschland. In: Bekker, Cok / Beuchling, Olaf Griffioen, Karin (Hrsg.): Kul-turelle Vielfalt und Religionsunterricht. Münster – Hamburg – London: Lit Verlag: 60-67

Beuchling, Olaf (2003): Vom Bootsflüchtling zum Bundesbürger. Migration, Integration und schulischer Erfolg in einer vietnamesischen Exilgemeinschaft. Münster: Waxmann Verlag

Daten und Fakten zur Ausländersituation (1999): Hrsg. von den Beauftragtender Bundesregierung für Ausländerfragen, Bonn

Hohmann, M. (1989): Interkulturelle Erziehung – eine Chance für Europa? In: Hohmann, M./Reich, H.H. (Hg): Ein Europa für Mehrheiten und Minderheiten. Diskussionen um interkulturelle Erziehung. Münster: 1-32, Waxmann Verlag

Informationen zur politischen Bildung. Aussiedler. Heft 267/ 2000, Hrsg.: Bundeszentrale für politische Bildung, Bonn.

Ingenhorst, Heinz (1997): Die Russlanddeutschen. Aussiedler zwischen Tradition und Moderne. Frankfurt am Main; New York: Campus Verl.

Keck, Rudolf W.(2001): Die Funktion der Schule im Kontext ethnischer Vielfalt. In: Golz, Reinhard/Keck, Rudolf W./Mayrhofer, Wolfgang (Hg.): Humanisierung der Bildung. Jahrbuch 2001 der Internationalen Akademie zur Humanisierung der Bildung (IAHB), Frankfurt am Main: Peter Lang GmbH: 148-159

Klemm, K. (1987): Die Bildungsbe(nach)teiligung ausländischer Schüler in der Bundesrepublik. In: Pädagogische Beiträge, H.12: 19-21.

Krüger-Potratz, M.(1997): Ein Blick in die Geschichte ausländischer Schüler und Schülerinnen in deutschen Schulen. In: Kordon, Ch.(u.a.) (Hg.): Vergleichende Erziehungswissenschaft. Herausforderung – Vermittlung – Praxis. Band 2. Köln, 656-672.

Marshal, Barbara (2000): The New Germany and Migration in Europe. Manchester and New York: Manchester University Press.

Nieke, Wolfgang (2002): Interkulturelle Erziehung und Bildung. Wertorientierungen im Alltag. 2. überarb. u. erg. Aufl. Opladen: Leske+Budrich

Rapithwin, Sam (2001): Mein deutsches Kind,: Frankfurt a.m., Glaré Verlag

Schmalz-Jacobsen, Cornelia (1994): Zwischen Migration und Integration: Die Ausländerpolitik der Bundesrepublik von neuen Herausforderungen. In: Dippel, Horst (Hg.): Zuwanderung: Bedrohung oder Bereicherung? Münster; Hamburg: Lit Verlag: 1-11

Schmoll, Heike (2004): Der entscheidende Schritt. In: Frankfurter Allgemeine Zeitung: 08.07.2004, Nr.156, S.3

Strobl, Rainer/ Kühnel, Wolfgang (2000): Dazugehörig oder ausgegrenzt. Analysen zu Integrationschancen junger Aussiedler. Weinheim/München: Juventa – Verlag

Wenning, Norbert (1996): Migration in Deutschland: Ein Überblick. Münster / New York: Waxmann

Wenning, Norbert (2001): Minderheitenbildung in Deutschland zwischen Akzeptanz und Ignoranz. In: Golz, Reinhard/Keck, Rudolf W./Mayrhofer, Wolfgang (Hg.): Humanisierung der Bildung. Jahrbuch 2001 der Internationalen Akademie zur Humanisierung der Bildung (IAHB), Frankfurt am Main: Peter Lang GmbH: 160-178.

Zick, Andreas/Six, Bernd (1999): Akkulturation von Aussiedlern als sozialpsychologisches Phänomen: Modelle zur Vorhersage des Akkulturationsergebnisses. In: Silbereisen, R.K./ Lantermann, E.-D./ Schmitt-Rodermund, E.(Hrsg.): Aussiedler in Deutschland. Opladen: Leske+Budrich, S. 303-331

Zimprich, Stephan: Die verlorenen Schafe von Marzahn. In: Spiegel, 03.06. 2004
http://www.spiegel.de/politik/deutschland/0,1518,298564,00.html

Nicolae Rambu (University of Iasi, Romania)
Ana Pascaru (Academy of Science, Chisinau, Moldavia)

Cultural and linguistic conflicts between Romania and the Republic of Moldavia

Abstract
In this analysis we shall present the conflicts concerning the Moldavian language. In the cultural orthodox space there is a strong sensibility concerning the language because here the language is closely linked to the church. The language is essential for the cultural identity. This is the reason why the communist ideology tried to distort the truth about the native language spoken by most of the citizens of the Republic of Moldavia. In the Soviet period the Romanians from Basarabia were considered a Soviet people. After 1991 a specific Moldavian identity was adopted. The consequences of the Soviet russification of Basarabia after World War Two are still visible today, despite the rebirth of the Romanian national identity after 1989. A false Moldavian identity for the Romanian population is built in order to prevent an easy union between Basarabia and Romania.

1. The subject

In Eastern Europe, but not exclusively, the language has always represented a central part of the cultural and national identity. This is the reason why many political conflicts have had language as a starting point. In our opinion, a particular case is the Republic of Moldavia and the political conflicts between this country and Romania regarding expressions like "Moldavian language" (different from the Romanian language) or "Moldavian people". We have to mention that Basarabia, a part of the Romanian historical region Moldavia, was incorporated into the Soviet Union as a result of the Ribbentrop-Molotov pact. After 1989 this territory became the Republic of Moldavia. In the following analysis we shall present the conflicts concerning the Moldavian language. As a starting point we shall refer to the dramatic political fights in Chisinau caused by the use of the Romanian language and the Latin alphabet during the last period of the Soviet Union. This analysis will continue to the present day when, under the communist government from Chisinau the Romanian language became the Moldavian language.

In the cultural orthodox space there is a strong sensibility concerning the language because here the language is closely linked to the church. From a theological perspective it is essential to pray in your native language and to be able to understand all the religious ceremonies. For example, for a Catholic from Spain or Romania it is not a problem to go to a Catholic church in Germany. However, a Romanian orthodox who lives in Germany would definitely prefer a sermon in his native language and he will go to a Romanian church like the one in Munich even if, for example, there is another orthodox church where the sermon is held in German. This is the reason why the nationalism is stronger in orthodox countries. But what is the connection between these aspects and the Republic of Moldavia? If some people say that the Moldavian language is the dominant language in the Republic of Moldavia and other people say it is the Romanian language, then the linguistic schism will generate a religious schism too. In the Republic of Moldavia there are two orthodox institutions: The Bishopric of Chisinau and Moldavia, subordinated to the Moscow Patriarchy, and The Bishopric of Basarabia, subordinated to the Romanian Patriarchy from Bucharest.

2. Conflicts concerning the "Moldavian language"

For a Romanian-speaking citizen from the Republic of Moldavia the problem of identity is much more complex than for a French-speaking Belgian. The language is essential for the cultural identity. This is the reason why the communist ideology tried to distort the truth about the native language spoken by most of the citizens of the Republic of Moldavia. In multiethnic states most of the identity conflicts arise from the language.

After the Soviet occupation of Basarabia as a result of the Ribbentrop-Molotov pact, the Latin alphabet was replaced with the Cyrillic one in an attempt to prove the existence of a Moldavian language, different from the Romanian. These Stalinist actions were rejected by the national liberation movement before 1989.

The language is the study object for philological sciences. Only the scientists can decide if a certain language, spoken in a certain area, is Slavic, Romanic or another language. It is also a strictly scientific problem if the language spoken by a certain community is a dialect etc. Today in the Republic of Moldavia, 14 years after the democratic transformations in Eastern Europe, the communist ideologists, not the scientists, are debating the origin of the language spoken in this country, mostly resuming the old Stalinist ideas.

As for the "Moldavian language", regarded as different from the Romanian language, three concepts emerged:

a) The Moldavian language is a Slavic one and thus it must use the Cyrillic alphabet, the same way that it happened in the Soviet Moldavia and that is now happening in the pseudo-republic Transnistria.

b) The Romanian language and the Moldavian language are Latin languages, related but different, this leading to the publishing in 2003 of a bizarre Moldavian-Romanian dictionary.

c) Based on the self determining principle each society can decide the name of its language and the main ethnic population in the Republic of Moldavia has the right to say that they speak the "Moldavian language", even if from a scientific point of view, it is the same as the Romanian language.

The "Moldavian language" created a dispute between the communist government from Chisinau and the Romanian government. In the years 1995-1996 the movement called "Pro Moldova" asked the Republic of Moldavia government to call back the Moldavian students and the PhD students from Romania and to stop the "Romaniazation" of Basarabia.

Any linguist can see that the Moldavian language does not exist, that it is not even a dialect of the Romanian language.

3. Disputes around history

"Generally speaking, the historians from the Republic of Moldavia are divided in two main trends: pro Romania and pro Russia"[1]. In the period 1989-1993 the pro Soviet history is replaced by the pro Romanian one but then the Moldavian ideology resumes in general the concepts of the Soviet historiography.

Some of the historians from Moldavia, defining the difference between the Moldavians and the Romanians, put the accent on "the historical right of each people, including the Moldavian one, to self determination". This principle is essentially reasonable, but the term "people" is confusing in that the national claims can be applied in many regions of a country. From this point of view Romania and Moldavia are no exception. If, for example, the people from the Romanian territory occupied by the Soviets are called, in the name of the self determination principle the "Moldavian people", then Transnistria, part of the Republic of Moldavia, in the name of the same "historical principle" invoked its self determination as well and the people from that region is now called the "Transnistrean people". But this is happening in the Western Europe too: Corsica, the Basque region, Catalonia, Flanders are just a few examples. Many regions may pretend the right to self determination in the lack of a clear definition of the concept of "people". "Because it is about a general principle, it can be theoretically claimed by all the human groups that are invoking this quality"[2]. The first countries which took advantage of this principle after the World War One were those from the former Austro-Hungary and the Ottoman Empire (Czechoslovakia, Greece, Serbia). But the principle of self determination, formulated by President Wilson in 1918 could not be applied to the colonized peoples from Asia and Africa nor to the "peripheral nations" like the Catalans or the Scotts which were integrated into powerful

[1] Chifu 2004, p. 13.
[2] Dieckhoff 2003, p. 76.

104

states. However, gradually, "the subjugated peoples from Africa and Asia will master this emancipator grammar and will turn it back against the colonial powers in order to accomplish their fight for independence"[3].

In Western Europe the aspiration towards independence, also called "internal colonialism", partially materialized in Spain by a partial autonomy of Catalonia and the Basque region as well as in Belgium, by the federalization of the country.

Once the Soviet Union ended, the former Soviet Republics made their claims for self determination but their frontiers had already been arbitrarity marked by the Stalinist regime. In all the occupied territories the frontiers are arbitrary because they divide unitary human communities.

Returning to the way in which the history of the Republic of Moldavia is taught in the schools and to the conflict of opinions with the Romanian historians we have to mention that there are certain authors who support the return to the old historical province of Moldavia which was successively occupied by Romanians or Russians. Starting with the year 1995 in all the high schools and universities of the Republic of Moldavia "The History of the Romanians" course was replaced with "The History of Moldavia" course. The latter describes the history of the medieval state Moldavia ignoring the relations with the other Romanian participates. "In exchange, every Moldo-Russian relation is amplified and considered a supreme achievement in order to underline the peaceful co-habiting obtained with the constant help given by Russia to the Moldavians"[4]. All the events referring to the independence movement from the Republic of Moldavia were considered by the pseudo-historians from Chisinau as actions that did not respect the constitution of RSSM. The declaration of independence from August 27, 1991, is considered as an act imposed by Romania.

4. Basarabia, a falsified identity through "cultural revolution"
In the Soviet period the Romanians from Basarabia were considered a Soviet people. Sincer 1991 a specific Moldavian identity has been adopted.

During the Soviet occupation teaching in Basarabia was in Russian and the Latin alphabet was replaced by the Cyrillic in order to create a false cultural identity. The false idea that the Moldavian people are different from the Romanian people was spread in the whole educational system. Another false idea was that Basarabia was occupied by Romanian and German nazists and that it was then liberated by Stalin's army.

The Romanian cultural identity of Basarabia was falsified by the Soviets through the so-called "cultural revolution" which destroyed the educational system in the

[3] Dieckhoff 2003, p. 76.
[4] Chifu 2004, p. 17.

Romanian language, the literature, art, press, as well as the Romanian Orthodox Church. The goal of the "cultural revolution" was to propagate the communist ideology and to eliminate the representative elements of the Romanian culture.

On February 10, 1941, the Supreme Soviet of the RSSM carried "the law concerning the introduction of the Cyrillic alphabet in Basarabia". The use of the Latin alphabet was prohibited and the Russian language became the official language in the occupied Romanian territory. "The main works propagated by all means were the documents of the Communist Party, the USSR constitution, the works of Marx, Engels and Stalin, the History of the Communist Party and the USSR, the Soviet periodicals... All this demonstration of force was meant to melt the Romanian identity from the occupied territory into the great masses of fraternal peoples, without identity other than the communist one"[5].

The consequences of the Soviet russification of Basarabia after World War Two are still visible today despite the rebirth of the Romanian national identity after 1989. The Soviet occupation authorities created a cultural non-Romanian elite in the cities. At the same time people were arrested, deported or sent to death simply because they were Romanians. In order to sustain the russification policy the Soviets invented the theory of "Moldavianism" to create a certain identity of the occupied territory. The "cultural revolution" wanted to create an artificial identity, aberrantly called the "Moldavian people" or the "socialist Moldavian nation".

Between 1989 and 1991 the intellectuals from the Republic of Moldavia managed to start a vast social movement in order to replace the aberrations of the Russian pseudo-historians. The Cyrillic alphabet was enthusiastically replaced by the Latin one and the Romanian language. In schools the History of the Romanians was taught again and the Romanian state hymn as well as the flag was adopted.

The communists replied immediately. "Their positions being threatened and frightened by the proportions of the attitude which was trying to impose a real identity to the country resulted from the fragmentation of the Soviet colonial empire, the so-called communist political elite used the already prepared "Moldavianism" ideology, starting a strong offensive against the national rebirth movement"[6].

5. The diplomatic conflict between Romania and the Republic of Moldavia

After 2001, when the communists together with the President Voronin won the elections, the Soviet ideas about a Moldavia identity were reasserted. The gov-

---

[5] Chifu 2004, p. 92.
[6] Chifu 2004, pp. 122-123.

ernment from Chisinau took measures in order to strengthen the Russian domination in Basarabia: they declared the Romanians a minority emphasizing the difference between the Romanians and the Moldavians; they replaced "The History of the Romanians" with "The History of Moldavia"; the Russian language became the official language in the Republic of Moldavia.

From 1992 there are two religious orthodox institutions in the Republic of Moldavia: one subordinated to the Patriarchy of Moscow and another one, the Bishopric of Basarabia, subordinated to the Romanian Patriarchy. After the Soviet occupation of the territory between the rivers Prut and Nistru, the Bishopric had to cease its activity. The Romanian Patriarchy never accepted its suppression. After years of conflicts with the Moldavian authorities and the Patriarchy of Moscow, in September 2001, the Bishopric of Basarabia was recognized by the communist government from Chisinau in front of the European Court for the Human Rights. The representative of the Republic of Moldavia, the Ministry of Justice Ion Morei attacked Romania saying that the Bishopric of Basarabia is "an instrument of Romanian imperialism" and that Romania is an aggressive state trying to occupy the territory over river Prut[7]. Despite this pleading, the European Court for Human Rights forced the Republic of Moldavia to officially recognize the Bishopric of Basarabia, subordinated to the Romanian Patriarchy.

The diplomatic and cultural conflict between the communist authorities from Chisinau and Romania soon became absurd. The Romanian donations of books are systematically confiscated, the scholarships for pupils and students offered by the Romanian government are refused and qualified as "an interference into the internal problems of the Republic of Moldavia", the frontier with Romania is of Soviet type, and the Romanian artists are not allowed to organize shows in the Republic of Moldavia.

Before the admission of Romania into NATO, the communist government from Chisinau, probably following Moscow's instructions, tried to stop this process by starting a diplomatic conflict. Romania would have territorial claims from the Republic of Moldavia. The Romanian President Ion Iliescu said that the Republic of Moldavia is a second Romanian state because 65% of its citizens are of Romanian origin.

After the intervention of the Ministry of Justice from Chisinau at the European Court for Human Rights saying that Romania is an imperialist state which is interfering with the internal problems of the Republic of Moldavia, the Romanian government canceled the official visit of the Prim Minister Adrian Nastase in the Republic of Moldavia. The Romanian official statement reminded that the decla-

---

[7] cf. Chifu, p. 232.

rations of the Moldavian Minister are based upon the concepts of the Communist Party of the Soviet Moldavia.

As a reply to the russification actions from Basarabia the Romanian government decided to support some Moldavian publications in Romanian with important funds. It also supported the retransmission of the Romanian TV channels as well as the students coming to study in Romania. But for the authorities from Chisinau a scholarship for a Moldavian student means "imperialism" and "interference into the internal problems of the Republic of Moldavia".

On March 13, 2001, the Romanian military delegate from Chisinau was accused of spying, declared "persona non grata" and expelled from the Republic of Moldavia. The Romanian government replied in a similar way, expelling a councilor from the Moldavian Embassy in Bucharest.

In the Republic of Moldavia as well as in the Baltic countries the recovery of the collective identity is difficult because of the Russian minority which is part of what some authors (e. g. Dieckoff) call the "imperial minorities". The majority of the Russian population from the Republic of Moldavia, Estonia, Leetonia and Latvia, was brought in by the Soviet state after 1945 at the time when the USSR was a world super-power. The Russians became a minority in these small countries and suffered from a certain grandeur complex. Despite the new reality they continue to consider themselves the members of a great nation, the Russian one. The Russians from Moldavia or the Baltic countries should learn to be a minority, as Dieckoff says.

In Moldavia the problem of collective identity is even more complicated because, being strongly sustained by the communist pro-Russian government from Chisinau, the "imperial Russian minority" is continuously expanding. In the meantime a false Moldavian identity for the Romanian population is built in order to prevent an easy union between Basarabia and Romania.

References
Chifu, Iulian (2004): Basarabia sub ocupatie sovietica. Bucuresti: Politeia-SNSPA.

Dieckhoff, Alain (2003): Natiune si ratiune de stat. Identitatile nationale in schimbare. Bucuresti.

Anja Mihr (University of Magdeburg, Germany)

Human Rights Education in a Transformation Process

Abstract
The main argument of this article is that Human Rights Education (HRE) is a pivotal factor for any democratic transformation process. HRE contributes to creating a strong civil society, establishes a political culture of trust and fairness. Hence, it is a method for complying with universal human rights standards in a transformation process through consolidating democratic institutions and structures. In order to transform a society, HRE has to be clearly defined and made an integral part of the education system within a society. This, however, is fostered mainly by the informal education sectors, namely civil actors and Non-governmental organisations (NGOs).

Human Rights Education

Human Rights Education (HRE) is currently discussed as one of the primary means of establishing sustainable and long-term stable democratic societies. It plays a crucial role in transforming societies and maintaining consolidated democracies as well. In transition countries, including many Eastern-European countries, its most general purpose is to teach people about their human rights to claim certain freedoms as well as individual political participation in the changing society. In stable democracies, like Western European countries and North-America, HRE helps to emancipate and empower civil society to improve and manifest its current civil and political structures.

HRE, however, became a particular term in the academic and NGO community in the 1990s. HRE contributes to the dissemination of the Universal Declaration of Human Rights (UDHR) from 1948 and helps create a culture of human rights. There are dozens of international legal and political binding human rights frameworks, such as conventions and treaties of the United Nations (UNO), the Organization of American States (OAS), the African Union (AU), the Council of Europe (CoE) and the Organization for Security and Cooperation in Europe (OSCE). They are all founded on the thirty articles of the UDHR, which outline and promote human rights standards and norms, covering civil and political as well as social, economic and cultural rights. In 1993 the UNESCO promoted a World Plan on Education for Human Rights and Democracy in Montreal, Canada and in the same year during the UN-World Conference on Human Rights in Vienna, Austria, promoted the view that HRE "is essential for the promotion and achievement of stable and harmonious relations among communities and for fos-

tering mutual understanding, tolerance and peace".[1] This approach was empha-
sised by the UN-General Assembly by calling for the UN-Decade for Human
Rights Education (1995-2004) in 1994.

What is Human Rights Education? Human Rights Education is much more complex than mere awareness-raising. It consists of legal standards, knowledge,
awareness and skills and it aims to influence political and social behaviour. HRE
is constituted by seminars, teaching programmes and training material in the
formal, informal and non-formal educational sector for teachers, university professors, students, social workers, security forces, lawyers, company managers
and others. The overall goal of HRE is to educate people to respect each other.
This is the ground for any anti-bias, peace, tolerance and anti-discrimination education, and it sets the grounds for a culture of human rights as it is outlined in the
UDHR. Hence one of the core elements of HRE is to specifically refer to human
rights standards and their broader meaning. If people are not able to precisely
state their rights and those of others, they will not be able to claim nor will they
be able to fight for them.

To define the complexity of Human Rights Education we can divide it into three
levels:
(1) **The cognitive level:** This is the mere knowledge and information about hu-
    man rights standards. Teaching on a cognitive level includes also the devel-
    opment and the history, genesis and roots of human rights based on natural
    law, the Universal Declaration of Human Rights (UDHR), the seven treaty
    bodies and committees of the UN-System, the Council of Europe's treaty
    bodies and monitoring system, the International Criminal Court, the Organi-
    zation of American states (OAS), the African Union (AU) and other interna-
    tional human rights organizations and non-governmental organizations
    (NGOs) and their monitoring systems. The cognitive level is in most terms
    the simplest level, because it informs about human rights but does not lead
    necessarily to any actions.
(2) **The emotional and awareness level**: This means being conscious of and
    feeling a sense of responsibility towards human rights violations, for example
    the direct and indirect experience of injustice, madness or the experience of
    human rights abuses and atrocities. This experience usually causes sadness or
    anger about injustice and pain and motivates people to react and become ac-
    tive. It is this crucial moment of personal feelings, emotions and awareness

---

[1] UN-Vienna Declaration and Programme of Action UN-Doc. A/CONF.157/23 from 12 July 1993, paras.
78-82.

towards the importance that violations of one's human rights are unjust and lead to ongoing threat, anger and pain. This moment will change peoples' attitude and behaviour (Stellmacher/Sommer/Imbeck 2003, p.162). It is the most difficult level of all three because it can easily be manipulated through one-sided information or propaganda. Still people react differently to the same set of circumstances. Some people get upset about injustice others while do not care. But in any case, it can be stated today that without this emotional touch and these feelings of sadness, there will be no activities in favour of human rights. Surveys have shown that people have a natural understanding of injustice and become active participants if they (a) have a sense of self esteem and (b) have had experiences of great injustice either personally or through stories being told to them (cf. Müller 2002, p.17-18; Krajulec 1999, p.367-369).

(3) **The active level**: Finally become active! This is to empower people and promote their skills to detect human rights violations and injustice, for example knowing national and international legal and court systems; claiming rights via ombudsmen; becoming an active member of a NGO, demanding lawyers to use international law to claim someone's human rights. It is not only to stop human rights abuses through lobbying of decision-making bodies asking for the abolition of the death penalty or torture, or to overcome injustice and violations during a peace building process - it is also to promote human rights as part of preventive work to avoid human rights violations in daily life.

(Figure 1) To make HRE more visible, I present following picture:

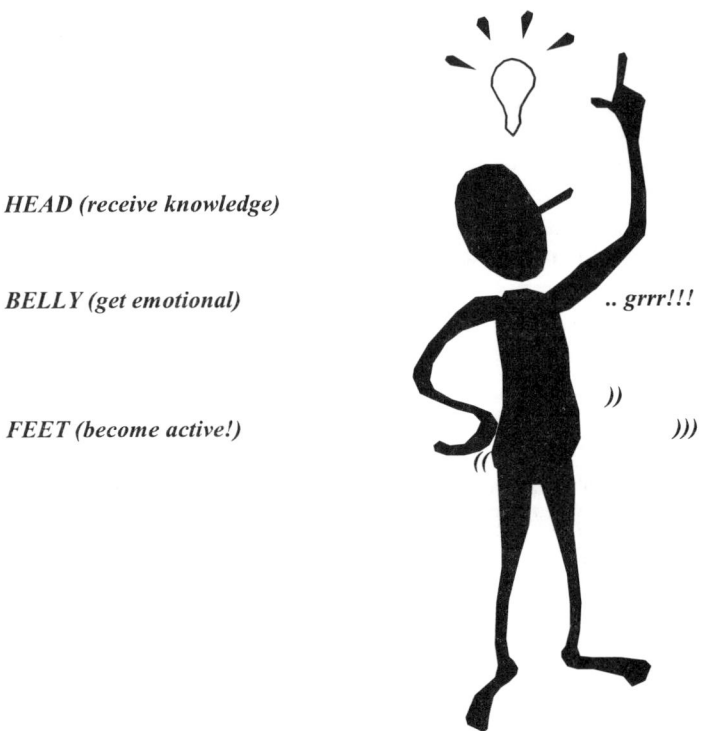

HEAD (receive knowledge)

BELLY (get emotional)   *.. grrr!!!*

FEET (become active!)

Hence the content of Human Rights Education is based on the universal concept of justice and injustice, which we know from the discourse about natural law. It contains information (head... get informed), emotions (belly... get angry and become aware) and skills (feet... get started, go and do something about it) which can be taught and understood face to face by everyone. Betty Reardon, who taught human rights for many years at Teachers College at Columbia University in New York, defines HRE as value education for peoples' dignity (Reardon 1995, pp. 3-4). The social scientist Weinbrenner defines Human Rights Education as a set of different aims and objectives which are (1) knowledge, through data and a concept of human rights; (2) attitudes and values, through self respect and fair treatment and (3) skills, both intellectual and action-based, informed by critical thinking and capacity building (Weinbrenner/Fritzsche 1993, p. 8). All attempts to define HRE are similar and focus on a concept of cognitive, emotional and active learning. This can also be found in the educational model of Paulo Freire's "educaca problematizadora", which focuses on individual consciousness and awareness-raising. An "education to problematise" should enable people to analyse problems independently through a reflection on one's own situation. This is crucial for any transformation process in society (Freire 1995).

Awareness can not be achieved by studying mechanisms, systems and human rights norms alone. Neither awareness nor societal change can be taught through the mere gathering of knowledge; rather, there needs to be an awareness-building process, including day-to-day examples, experience and reflection. It is a mixture of all three levels that makes HRE successful. Similar stages are described in Lawrence Kohlberg's analysis of different levels of moral development, in which he defines six steps towards moral learning. To reach high moral awareness and act according to it, each individual has to go through a stage of interpersonal learning orientated toward social standards in order to reach a post-conventional stage of thinking and acting in accordance with universal ethnical principles (Graz 1996, p. 55, 87).

Moral universal values are defined by global standards and best practices of moral norms all over the world. We find them in the so-called Golden Rule: "Do not do unto others that which is disagreeable to you" as the basis for ethical behaviour.[2] To define this more than 2,500 year-old Golden Rule, one can argue philosophically with Immanuel Kant that these norms and values have developed over centuries through critical self-reflecting awareness building, which has led to the basis for ethical behaviour as outlined in Kant's maxim of the categorical imperative: "If the maxim of your action is not such as to stand the test of the form of a universal law, then it is morally impossible" (Kant 1990, p. 421).

After the Cold War and due to a certain degree of human rights euphoria in the 1990s, academics, experts and NGOs consider more and more the impact of HRE. It is assumed that HRE is more sustainable than all preceding peace, tolerance and anti-bias teaching concepts and that we should learn from the misinterpretation and short term impacts of the re-education, civic-education and peace-education of the past. HRE is more than peace, re-education or civic education. It is inclusive, not exclusive. This means that it aims to teach all people, regardless

---

[2] The first written evidence of the Golden Rule can be found in the religious writings and moral value collection of Zoroastrianism 800 B.C (Dadistan-i-Dinik 94,5). It can also be found in Judaism, Christianity, Confucianism, Hinduism, Buddhism, Taoism, Humanism and the writings of the Bahá'i community.

of their citizenship, ethnic background, legal status or status as former enemies and combatants. Civic and citizenship education, for example, target only those people within a society or nation who are citizens of particular states. This excludes all non-state-citizens, foreigners, immigrants and members of minority groups. Peace-education is for people who have been former enemies, members of at least two parties in conflict or former combatants. Re-education is made only for those who have been suffering under dictatorship propaganda, promoted by a manipulative education system. Peace and re-education programmes can be used in post-crisis periods and as crisis-response mechanisms during peace-building and reconciliation processes. Exclusive education programmes – however important they may be for specific target groups – are made exclusively for specific "closed" target groups and not for all people within a community or nation. Such education programmes carry human rights elements in them but do not entail a holistic approach to human rights, including social and economic rights as well as individual and political rights. This holistic concept of human rights refers to the whole document of the UDHR and empowers people to behave and act according to the universal human rights norms and values stated already in the Golden Rule some 2,500 years ago. HRE can be part of the teaching curricula in the formal, non-formal and informal education sectors. It can cross-cut all subject areas and can be implemented in extra curricular activities, such as theatre plays, sports and fine arts.

Human rights can be taught to all target groups in a given society: police, politicians, NGOs leaders, security forces, social workers, physicians, children, students and scholars of all different social backgrounds and ages. A core concept of HRE can be taught to adults and children – there is no limit of age or required social status. Betty Reardon and Nancy Flowers define core concepts of HRE with regard to age and developmental stage: early childhood, later childhood, adolescence, youth and adulthood. For each of the developing stages, the content of HRE programmes can vary depending on social background, social and political circumstances and culture (Flowers 2000, p. 14; Reardon 1995, p. 14). Nonetheless, each programme's content must always incorporate the holistic concept of human rights, including social and individual human rights at the same time.

There are numerous effective methods of teaching human rights. They consist of lectures, role plays, paintings, observations, research of history and biographies, field research of current events, statistical analysis, panel and group discussions, essays, excursions, movies, interviews, talks, oral history or interactive exchange of experience. Each method depends on the degree of information a teacher wants to give to the students (Table 1). Even though it is important to take the different cultural backgrounds, social circumstances and developing phases in consideration, it is also vital to teach a holistic approach to human rights. HRE is meant to achieve a complete concept of human rights rather than a mere concept of anti-bias and peaceful behaviour. Hence, the UDHR should be the foundation for any methodological concept of teaching human rights.

History and the genesis of human rights, combined with knowledge about human rights standards and skills, are important methodological elements of HRE. To include these elements in HRE programmes for different target groups can bring groups to reflect upon their own social contexts, to raise awareness, to overcome prejudice and stop discrimination. People will become empowered to claim human rights for themselves and for others.

If we take the cognitive, emotional and active levels into account, the concept of HRE can lead to several outcomes depending on the age and stage of development of people as shown in Table 1. Depending on the time and resources available, HRE activities and courses can either be long or short term and sometimes lead to a specific goal. Thus HRE is methodologically successful if discussing human rights issues in in-school and adult-curricula becomes routine through shadow curricula. HRE has then reached a stage in which it goes beyond enthusiasm, emotions and short term activities. The overall goal is to enable and empower individuals to act according to their own abilities and responsibilities. Thus, HRE has successfully achieved its aims if human rights become an inclusive part of the overall behaviour of people.

Table 1: Concept of Human Rights Education during different stages in life.[3]

	Knowledge through information	Awareness through emotions	Activities through skills
Early Childhood	- convention on the rights of the child - family values - community values	- cases of racism and sexism - child labour	- practice fairness and respect - help children in other parts of the community of the world through letter writing / drawing activities
Childhood	- Universal Declaration for HR - History of HR - UNICEF - laws	- cases of discrimination, sexism, racism - prejudice - poverty and hunger	- activities in schools and community - NGO participation - letter writing campaign
Youth	- International law (UNO etc) - Moral values - World economy	- cases of injustice through political and social oppression - globalization - environmental issues - torture and death penalty	- research activities and oral history - community activities - research work / essays on HR cases - talks with politicians and lawyers - NGOs activities - visiting prisons - role playing
Adults	-history and genesis of HR - International HR-regime (UNO, CoE, OAS etc) - International laws, treaties and declarations and development of HR norms	- face to face talks to victims and perpetrators of HR violations - torture and death penalty - genocide -excursions to prisons, refugee camps	- activities in local or international NGOs - helping asylum seekers and refugees - demonstrations and letter writing campaign - newspaper articles - contact with politicians - becoming an ambassador of HR

---

[3] Table 1 shows examples of teaching contents and activities. It is not a complete list of all possible topics, methods or types of activities that can be part of a HRE programme. For sources and related concepts see Betty Readon (1995) and Nacy Flowers (2000).

Human rights and moral values change and go through different phases of interpretation and implementation during transformation processes. Hence, German
philosopher Jürgen Habermas argues for the need for a discourse on human
rights. Habermas aims to demonstrate that rationality potentialities are set within
the communicative everyday praxis: discourse or speech. Habermas' answer is
based in his theory of communication, which culminates in a conception of reason. This concept of reason claims the capability of joining universal foundations
and concrete contexts of every day life such as experience of injustice and a universal understanding of human rights (Habermas 1995). In other words, human
reason is able to combine the Golden Rule and moral values with every day life
experience. It is reflecting upon owning one's day-to-day environment and to
enabling oneself to start an ideal dialogue in favour for ethical behaviour and,
hence, a transformation of society.

Transformation and Civil Society
The democratic transformation of societies has one goal: to change attitudes and
behaviour in order to consolidate a strong civil society and democracy. Civil society and NGOs, play a crucial role in any such transformation processes. They
are vital for demanding change in institutions, for checking and monitoring the
implementation of laws, raising public awareness and asking for reforms, if
needed. In political system in transformation or in so called "new democracies,"
civil society and NGOs try to claim individual freedom for people and their work
focusing on the protection of individuals against state arbitrariness. Through their
self-reflective power they contribute to the balance of power, and at the same
time, they educate citizens and non-citizens to claim their human rights.

To transform a society from an authoritarian regime to a democracy, civil society
and individuals have to define their human rights; ask for the protection of individuals, accountability, participation and observation of the implementation
process of democratic laws and human rights standards. If this is done, the transition towards democracy can be considered successful. Thus, in stable democracies, basic democratic rules, the implementation of human rights in the constitu-
tions and the establishment of a constitutional state are already accomplished.
However, in consolidated democracies civil societies and well organised NGOs
play a major role in the conflict solving process. They monitor political decisions
and social developments and – in case needed – call for reforms. Respect, acceptance, trust in institutions, fairness and the rejection of the use of force to keep
peace in a given country are the key issues to be maintained in these societies
(Merkel/Lauth 1998, pp.6-9). In order to do so, civil society has to be aware of

and at the same time enjoy its human rights, for example, to participate in the decision-making process, and use its self-reflecting abilities to actively transform and change democratic societies wherever and whenever it is needed. To claim their rights people have to know and enjoy them regardless if they live in a country during a transition period or in a consolidated democracy. Hence, to implement HRE at all levels of society in children and adult education is an integral part of any transition process in order to accomplish a long term consolidation of democracies.

Non-Governmental Organizations (NGOs)

NGOs are considered the gatekeepers that try to fulfil the claims of the international organisations and they play a crucial role in transformation processes. The international human rights treaties are often their base for diffusion. NGOs have become more strategic in their work to spread the idea of human rights. One of their measures to spread it is through HRE. NGOs such as Amnesty International or the Peoples Decade for HRE (PDHRE) remind state governments to fulfil their duties and comply with human rights standards and the implementation of HRE. They use organizations of the international human rights regime, such as the UNO, to put pressure on governments, consult with human rights commissions and disseminate shadow-reports on human rights issues in particular countries to the UN-human rights committees and other decision making bodies. Since the 1980s, it can be noted that NGOs have become some of the most important actors in transformation processes for the establishment of civil society as well as in promoting and protecting democracies. Creating democracy no longer depends only on political actors and their parties (Schmitter/Brouwer 1999, pp. 6-7). If we talk about defining and building up democracies, NGOs are an overall integral part of this process.

NGOs legitimise their impact on both national and international levels through: (1) public support and civil society, for example: through letter writing campaigns, membership dues and public participations and (2) through their expert knowledge and contribution to different international governmental organizations, such as UN-bodies, the Council of Europe and others. Thus, the role of NGOs has been crucial in defining international human rights norms and developing institutional mechanisms to ensure adherence to international norms and monitoring of national and local human rights practices. They can start discussions, lobby and develop long term sustainable strategies, promoting them publicly as conflict solving procedures and models. In the past decades, a lot has been achieved in this respect and this change can undoubtedly be credited to the work of NGOs (cf. Keck/Sikkink, 1997; Risse/Ropp/Sikkink, 1999).

According to various studies, human rights NGOs have four major areas of activity: (1) standard setting; (2) monitoring compliance with international standards; (3) enforcement of human rights, and; (4) education. The latter is ranked and mentioned highest in the four areas by more than 60 % of human rights NGOs. Eighty percent of the same NGOs even claim to organise programmes in an effort to inform the general public about human rights (Smith/Panucco/Lopez 1998, pp. 379-412). However, if we take a closer look at these surveys, it is interesting to see that the general understanding of HRE is to raise public awareness about human rights abuses. Generally it is understood as the following: "to organise public actions, events and activities" and "to educate general public about human rights" (which means to raise public awareness via media reports and campaigns). To get the public and civil society involved in NGO activities constitutes the main source of legitimisation and credibility of NGOs when putting pressure on governments. In this context, HRE as awareness-building is useful only to respond to human rights violations and to react on a short-term basis.

However, awareness-building is one part of the more complex HRE concepts. NGOs partially provide some of the measures necessary in a non-strategic and non-systematic way. But so far, HRE is only a secondary element of their human rights work and, therefore, it neither reaches its goals nor is it sustainable. Even strong and well established NGOs, such as Human Rights Watch, have no resources or as in the case of Amnesty International (AI), the Human Rights Education Associates (HREA) or the People Decade for Human Rights Education (PDHRE) only very limited resources to implement and promote Human Rights Education. They depend completely on voluntary donors, private sponsors or fundraising.

NGOs are in a dilemma because they need to cooperate with governments but also want to be independent of them. This is particularly important in transition countries. Meanwhile the popularity, public presence and support of NGOs through public and governmental grants give the impression that governments leave the issue of human rights to NGOs. This type of "outsourcing" includes the trend that governments neglect their responsibility to implement human rights in daily life. This is particularly true for transition states in which NGOs take the biggest share in supporting human rights activities and offering HRE courses. Currently it can be stated that NGOs take up the highest share to promote HRE in the formal and non-formal sector worldwide. These organizations have realised within HRE a strategic approach by which to diffuse the idea of the UDHR. The promotion of HRE will increase their credibility and legitimacy in the area of human rights. Hence, NGOs currently face the following main obstacles in their work; (1) Responding to human rights violations by shaming governments does not necessarily mean that state actors and responsible groups understand and respect human rights; and (2) in many transition countries, human rights norms and institutions do not work because there is no common understanding of human rights, nor is there any attempt to implement human rights standards in politics, the legal system or daily life through HRE; (3) NGOs collaborate mostly on a horizontal level within states and on an international level. This includes ties to state representatives on international and national levels, to opposition leaders and representatives of other NGOs. But these ties do not necessarily reflect actual needs of people or human rights issues. Therefore NGOs have to concentrate on a vertical and internal level if they want to transform attitudes towards human rights and implementations of Human Rights Education. This is one goal of Human Rights Education which NGOs can focus upon.

To overcome the limits and obstacles NGOs face in their work, they have to increase their strategic efforts and focus on sustainable and long term implementation of HRE. If NGOs use international legal standards for HRE as a basis for diffusion to increase their impact and credibility, they need:

1. To cooperate with national governmental institutions in order to gain access to local decision-making bodies and local target groups; although this sometimes creates a dilemma for them.
2. To continue and strengthen their focus on long term strategies and public and mass HRE (publicly funded schools, universities, security forces and police academies, journalism academies etc).
3. To encourage opinion-makers, educators and political actors to ask for the implementation of mass HRE. NGOs have to lobby stronger decision-makers to implement these HRE methods in teaching curricula.
4. To collaborate with regional international governmental organizations and with the UNO in advocating and promoting good HRE practices and in monitoring human rights improvements.
5. To build HRE networks, such as the European Association for Education of Adults, the Asian Human Rights Commission, the HREA, and the PDHRE, on international and regional levels with focus on the promotion of HRE (Claude 1997, pp. 395-415; Mihr 2003; Schnabel/Horowitz 2002).

Conclusion

Human Rights Education is a key measure in the process of democratic transformation. It not only educates people about their human rights, but it also aims to teach them to understand the holistic concept of human rights and to claim it. To claim and enjoy human rights is crucial during a transformation of systems. Freedom and participation rights and the protection of individuals are important human rights issues that have to be maintained during transformation periods, especially in transition countries. However, the cooperation between civil actors, such as NGOs and political actors and governmental institutions, is vital in order to (1) claim and implement that HRE becomes an integral part of the formal and public education systems and (2) to establish and maintain a democratic culture of trust, respect and fairness and, hence, to consolidate democratic systems.

References

Andreopoulos, G.J./Claude, R. P. (Ed.) (1997): Human Rights Education for the Twenty-First Century. Philadelphia.

Claude, R.P (1997): Global Human Rights Education. The Challenges for Non-governmental Organizations. In: Adreopoulos, G.J./Claude, R.P. (Ed): Human Rights Education for the Twenty-First Century. University of Pennsylvania Press: pp. 395-415

Flowers, N.(2000): The Human Rights Education Handbook. Effective Practices for Learning. Action and Change. University of Minnesota: Human Rights Resource Center

Freire, P. (1995): Pedagogy of Hope. Reliving Pedagogy of the Oppressed. New York

Graz, D. (1996): Lawrence Kohlberg zur Einführung. Hamburg

Habermas, J. (1995): Theorie des kommunikativen Handelns. Frankfurt a.M.

Kant, I. (1900): Grundlegung zur Metaphysik der Sitten. (GMS) Akademie-Ausgabe (AA): Bd. IV.

Keck, M. E./Sikkink, K. (1997): Activist beyond borders. advocacy networks in international politics. Cornell University Press

Krajulec, P.(1999): Was geht mich das an? Sozialpsychologische Konzepte des Hilfeverhaltens. In: Sommer, G./Stellmacher, J./Wagner, U. (Ed): Menschenrechte und Frieden. Aktuelle Beiträge und Debatten. Philipps-Universität Marburg: Schriftenreihe des Arbeitskreises Marburger Wissenschaftler: AMW und IAFA: Vol. 22: pp. 364-374

Mahler, C./Mihr, A. (Ed.) (2004): Menschenrechtsbildung – Bilanz und Perspektiven. Frankfurt a.M.: pp.105-116

Merkel, W./Lauth, H.J. (1998): Systemwechsel und Zivilgesellschaft: Welche Zivilgesellschaft braucht die Demokratie? In: APUZ. B6-7: pp.3-12

Mihr, A. (2003): Menschenrechtsbildung und Menschenrechtsverständnis im Vergleich: Deutschland, USA, Großbritannien. In: Woyke, W. (Ed.): Neue deutsche Außenpolitik. Beiträge zur wissenschaftlichen Grundlegung und zur Unterrichtspraxis. Nr. 2

Müller, L. (2002): Menschenrechtserziehung an Schule und Hochschule. Arbeitsgemeinschaft Menschenrechte. Universität Trier: Occasional Paper Nr. 6

Reardon, B.A. (1995): Education for Human Dignity. Learning about rights and responsibilities. New York: K-12

Risse, T./Ropp, S.C./Sikkink, K. (Ed) (1999): The Power of Human Rights, International Norms and Domestic Change. Cambridge University Press.

Schmitter, P.C./Brouwer, I. (1999): Conceptualizing, Researching and Evaluating Democracy Promotion and Protection. European University Institute Working Paper SPS No 99/9

Schnabel, A./Horowitz, S. (2002): NGOs critical role in advancing human rights in transition societies. In: International Tolerance Network. Bertelsmann-Stiftung: Podium No. 2: pp. 1-2.

Smith, J./Panucco, R./Lopez, G. (1998): Globalizing Human Rights: The work of transnational Human Rights NGOs in the 1990s. In: Human Rights Quarterly 20: pp. 379-412.

Stellmacher, J./Sommer, G./Imbeck, J. (2003): Psychologische Ansätze zu einer positiven Menschenrechtserziehung-Determinanten der Einsatzbereitschaft für die Einhaltung von Menschenrechten. In: Witte, Erich H.(Ed.): Sozialpsychologische politische Prozesse. Lengerich: et al: pp. 143-166.

Weinbrenner, Peter/Fritzsche, Karl-Peter (1993): Teaching Human Rights, Suggestions for Teaching Guidelines. Bonn/Braunschweig: German Commission for UNESCO and Georg-Eckert-Institute

Emmy Jerono Kipsoi (Moi University, Kenya)

A Case for Peace Education in the Kenyan School Curriculum

Abstract
Africa has experienced a lot of conflict. Kenya as an African country has had to deal with the effects of these conflicts. There have been both internal and external conflicts. Internal conflict has been manifested in tribal and political wars. External conflict effects have been wars that her neighbours have been experiencing; Uganda and Rwanda on the west, Sudan and Ethiopia on the north, Somalia on the south had been constantly been at war. This has been that Kenya has had to serve as host to several refugees who seek to escape wars in their home countries. This situation has jeopardised meaningful and sustainable development in Kenya. It is behind this backdrop that this paper presents a strong case for the management of conflict through peace education in the Kenyan school curricula.
It is urged that since change of attitude and prejudices may not be effectively achieved through the family setting, the school can make a significant contribution in the empowering of the youth with conflict management and resolution strategies. It is hoped that this will enable peace-related issues to be internalised and hence become integrated into their daily lives. Peace education in the Kenyan education system will enlighten the country's youth on the dangers posed to human life by violence, war, poverty and oppression

Background
Kenya on the attainment of its political independence in 1963 from Britain had several concerns for its citizens. Top in the list of priority was the kind of education Kenya could give its citizens, thus the Ominde report of 1964-65, which was commissioned to review the Kenyan Education. The concern at the time of independence was to develop skilled middle and high-level manpower that could replace the colonialists that were leaving. Kenya has since over grown this need and several commissions have been formed with the view of reviewing the education system to meet the needs of the time. There has been Gachathi report of 1976, Mackay report of 1981, and the most recent is the Koech report 2001. Kenya currently has six national educational objectives.

1. *Education must serve the primary needs for national development.*
2. *Education must assist in fostering and promoting national unity.*
3. *Education must prepare the youth of the country so that they can play an effective role in the life of nation whilst ensuring that opportunities are provided for the full development of the individual's talents and personality.*

4. *Education must assist in the promotion of social equality and train in social obligation and responsibilities.*
5. *The education system must respect, foster and develop the rich and varied cultures of Kenya.*
6. *The education system should promote international consciousness.*
    (cf. Getao 1996, p. 55)

Paulo Freire says the true aim of education is the development of the whole human person as in so doing, man becomes critically aware of his reality in a manner that leads him to take critical and effective action upon it. Other philosophers such as Jacques Maritain and Russel agree that the refinement of the individual person is the true aim of education. Kenneth Kaunda of Zambia says the foundation lies in an educational system that recognizes the truth that it is a person and not just a brain that is being trained (cf. Bogonko 1992, p. 9).

The Kenyan educational objectives seem to seek to develop what these philosophers believed in. However there is a need to make a more conscious effort to prepare the students to deal with and manage the challenges they face in the 21st century, specifically, the ever presence of conflict and violence in the society. Kenya has and continues to witness all manner of conflict from within and outside the country's border.

External Conflict

Kenya borders to the North Sudan and Ethiopia, to the East Somalia, to South Tanzania, to the West Uganda and the far West Rwanda and Burundi. All of these countries have had their share of war. Sudan has had an internal war that has lasted more than 40 years the Muslim North region has been fighting with the Christian Southern region over the demand that the South are seek to break away from the predominately Muslims region so far over 1 million people have been killed. Ethiopia has been politically unstable. Somalia has been without a stable government and presently there is effort to seek to restore peace in that country. Uganda also has had decades of war when rebels were seeking to overthrow the dictator government of Amin, the memories of the 1994 genocide that took place in Rwanda are still fresh in the minds of many people world over. The results of these were the creation of six refugee campus (three in Dadaad and three in Kakuma) having a total population of almost 200,000 refugees. Not to mention many more who opted to live outside the refugee camps that cannot be accounted for in numbers.

The borders of Kenya/Sudan, Kenya/Ethiopia, Kenya/Uganda and Kenya/Somalia have to this day witnessed conflict from neighboring tribes who fight over cattle, grazing land and water points. The conflicts have been deadly leading to the loss of lives and destruction of property; these conflicts have been promoted by availability of Arms in these regions as a result of the wars in these countries. According to a small Arms survey report, the number of small Arms in sub Sahara Africa, including Kenya is much lower than previously expected. However Kenya reportedly has a considerable stockpile of weapons (500,000 – 1,000,000) and also some domestic capacity to produce small arms and ammunition. (cf. Armed conflict report Kenya 2003, p. 1)

Internal Conflict
Within the borders of Kenya a lot of violence exists. Notwithstanding the national Education objectives, there is no safe haven for the Kenyan child, violence surrounds him/her. Domestic and gender violence is on the rise in Kenya there have been documented cases of spouses fighting even killing themselves, in this the children also have not been spared. Cases of children being abused in the family set up have been reported.

School violence in Kenya has been of great concern. There have been reports of students burning down their schools in expressing their displeasure at something as minor as a change in the school diet. Teachers and students have been reported killed in the progress. Students have also vented their anger at the larger society by destroying property in the neighborhood. The most notorious of this school unrest are the state university students who have been known to stop at nothing when expressing their anger, in fact they made it a tradition to riot.

Violence in the larger society range from political violence, that is when political rivals fight each other along with their supporters, tribal clashes when one tribe rises against the other just in the name of tribe the most destructive occurred in 1992 and 1997 where an estimate of 3500 people were killed and 320,000 were made homeless (cf. Armed conflict report Kenya 2003, p. 2). What has come to be known as Mob Justice where a suspect of a crime is lynched has become the order of the day in Kenya's urban streets.

The above is a pointer to the presence of destructive conflict in the country, which has not been addressed. The question is who should address this pertinent issue? And how should it be addressed?

The Concept of Peace Education

The transmission or reproduction of culture has been characterized as one of the functions of education. The school has been changed with the responsibility of socializing the youth. Peace together with freedom, equality and justice is one of the most desirable values in almost every society. It has become a universal symbol. Thus it is not surprising that many societies decide to educate its young ones in the light of this new symbol. The education system realizes this mission for societies through the school system, which has the authority, the legitimacy, the means and the conditions to carry it out.

Peace education envisaged a society without indirect violence, such as political or economic oppression, discrimination and the destruction of the environment (cf. Bray 2003, p. 138).

Peace education needs to be an integral part of a child's overall education. We teach the 3R's we can also teach them the 4th R – Relationship. Education for the 21st century needs to address human relationship – how to live without the tremendous conflict and the suffering conditioned relationships produce worldwide. Children educated in understanding what prevents peace, that is what creates conflict will have a tremendous effect on the community at large. As adults they will be more capable of understanding the conditioned reaction that underlie domestic, social, national and international conflict.

The situation suggests that there is a vacuum in the school curriculum. The children are not prepared to deal with conflict in school and later when they leave school.

Peace education has been practiced in several countries in the world. Each country having its own specific objectives according to the needs; for example in Australia peace education focuses on challenging ethnocentrism, chauvinism and violence on the one hand and promoting cultural diversity, nuclear disarmament and conflict resolution. Japan's objectives on peace education mostly targets issues of nuclear disarmament, militarism and the nature of responsibility for violent acts performed in the past. The United States is concerned with prejudice, violence and environmental issues (cf. Solomon/Nevo 2003, p.1).

In Africa, South Africa is currently pre-occupied with structural violence, human rights and economic inequality. In Sierra Leone, peace education is aimed at understanding the past and re-building a secure society. Kenya has not focused on peace education in its curriculum. There has been only one pilot project for refugee's education in Kenya, which has incorporated peace education, and environmental education that was implemented in 1996 and is currently on its third phase. The project is funded by UNHCR's environmental trust fund. The peace education program was developed in response to perceived needs of the refugee camps.

Therefore there is a need to expand peace education to reach out the larger school population because as it has been pointed earlier violence exists, and the scale of conflict is high in Kenya. Kenyan children have to be exposed to a curriculum that will help them cope with the violence around them, as with every other society, the only institution that still has a chance to mould its young is the school. It is the place where the child spends the big part of his/her childhood. The average Kenyan child starts school at age 3 years and finish at the age of 23 years.

Content of Peace Education
Peace education in Kenya should aim on developing certain skills, which should be the focus of its content. Below is the proposed content for peace education.

Communication
Kenyan children have to learn the skills of communication. This include listening skills, be able to express their feelings (emotions), the ability to empathize with the other person understanding of bias and its limitations.

In a country with more than 73 ethnic communities, who have lived together fighting and in fear of each other, children have to be introduced to understanding the stereotypes that the communities hold on each tribe. The discrimination and prejudice that arise from the stereotyping of communities. The children should be able to see the falsehood of these stereotypes, in doing so Kenya may well be able to say that it has attained education for national unity.

Appropriate assertiveness
The students should be able to understand themselves as distinct individuals, as well as understanding others around them. The students in the course of their studies should be able to clearly see the similarities between for instance the ethnic communities in Kenya as well as appreciate the differences. Unless children learn to appreciate these similarities and differences between communities peace will be an elusive feature.

Development of values and attitudes
Students should know how to appropriately assert themselves, how to show aggression and when and who they should submit to. This is viewed in the context of school violence where the bullying of younger and new students exists and goes on unchallenged.

The curriculum should seek to develop values such as trust, tolerance, self-respect and respect for others. Open mindedness and social responsibility. The importance of co-operation should also be emphasized. The students should also be assisted to understand and practice positive conflict response like mediation and negotiation among others. Related to this are examples from the United Nations Peace Keeping strategies. These might help students to not only know how to separate and restrain destructive conflict but also to critically think of the best methods of maintaining peace.

Methodology for Teaching Peace Education
Peace education can be taught as a separate subject or spread across the curriculum or be a whole school approach. Each of these approaches has its benefits. This paper could wish to state for the Kenyan situation it is suggested that all the three main approaches to peace education be embraced.

In teaching, one specific subject the children/students will be exposed to specific skills, knowledge and experience related to conflict resolution.

For the benefit of reinforcing certain skills there will be need to integrate aspects of peace education into the entire curriculum and teachers will take time to emphasis on peace education. Subjects as Humanities could form a rich ground for peace education.

The whole school approach will require that the school administration to make a commitment to promote peace in its school. For example it could have policy on fighting in school and ways for reconciling the fighting students. The students should be taken through the process of forgiveness and reconciliation.

Foreseen Challenges to Peace Education in Kenya
Peace education is all about changing of attitude and this process takes a long time. The development and change of attitudes take place slowly and gradually. For the implementers of peace education it may be one long frustrating journey.

Subjects that are examination oriented may overshadow peace education because it is difficult to examine the subject.

Implementers of peace education should be aware of the political climate. Kenyan politicians have worked on tribal sentiments to gain in leadership. It is possible that efforts such as peace education may be received with some resistance from political leaders (tribal leaders) as peace education is about human rights. Students will be educated on human rights, justice, interdependence and gender among others. Those in political leadership may receive these issues with a lot of difficulty. Young democracies like Kenya are still struggling with the practice of justice and human rights. The sphere of justice has in most cases been for the use of the ruling class to punish its opposition in this case therefore human rights is abused.

This paper therefore proposes that curriculum developers in Kenya take the cue and design a specific curriculum for the entire school system for peace education in Kenya. For unless a culture of peace is cultivated the education system will be failing in meeting its educational objectives, that of education for national unity and promoting and preserving its diverse cultures.

References

Armed Conflicts report Kenya (2003): Conrad Studies: Institute of Peace and Conflict(Unpublished), Grebel College Canada.

Bray, M. (2003): Comparative Education. Continuing Traditions, New Challenges and New Paradigms. Dordecht: Kulwer Academic Publishers.

Bogonko, S. N. (1992): Reflections on Education's in East Africa. Nairobi: Oxford University Press.

Datta, A. (1992): Education and Society: A Sociology of African Education. Hong Kong: Macmillan Press.

Getao, F. N. (1996): International Education System Textbook in Comparative Education. Nairobi: Lectern Publications.

Salomon/Nevo (2003): Peace Education. The Elusive Nature of Peace Education (Unpublished).

Temesgen Fereja (Addis Ababa University, Ethiopia)

Multiculturalism and Education in Ethiopia: Historical Issues and Current Status

Abstract
This paper briefly discusses some historical issues, current developments and challenges about multiculturalism and education in Ethiopia. It is revealed that the 'Assimilation model' characterized Ethiopian education history. After the fall of the socialist oriented government in 1991, several significant developments are, however, achieved in this regard. The introduction of the mother tongue as a medium of instruction in the primary schools was one major development. It is pointed out that some challenges are still evident today. After an analysis of the situation, finally, it is argued that the emphasis on unity without due regard for diversity may threaten the existence of the country as a nation and, thus, genuine multiculturalism should be promoted in schools.

A Brief History of Multiculturalism and Education Issues in Ethopia

A glance at the history of Ethiopia shows that there existed a dominant-minority relationship in the Ethiopian society. The present day Ethiopia is a result of Amhara conquest and expansion from the northern part of Ethiopia southwards in the late 19th and early 20th centuries. This brought the vast ethnic, cultural and linguistic groups in Ethiopia under the rule of the Amhara led by Menelik II. It laid a historical foundation for Amhara rule in the history of Ethiopia for about a century and the dominance of the Amhara in every aspects of the lives of Ethiopians including the system of education until recently. Menelik utilized discriminatory policy systems favouring the northerners (mainly the Amhara) and imposed Amhara culture and the Amharic language on his subjects.

A successor of Menelik, Haile Selassie, who led Ethiopia from about 1930-1974, used the same means of rule by more and more institutionalizing Amhara domination. In this period, again, Amhara culture and values were given supremacy in every walks of the lives of Ethiopians, and although the language of a numerical minority, Amharic became the national language and the medium of instruction in the primary schools. Curricula also reflected Amhara culture and values and the few who have attended schools experienced denigrations of their culture and were made to accept their culture as inferior (Hamdesa, 1982). There were also educational disparities between the different regions, the sexes, between urban and rural areas (Asyeghn, 1978 cited in Hamdesa, 1982); an indication that educational opportunities were also given mainly for the Amhara as most of the towns were occupied by them and many of the schools were found in the towns (Hamdesa , 1982).

In general, no mention was made about the pluralistic nature of the Ethiopian society in either national or educational documents during the imperial regime. One very important comprehensive educational document in the history of Ethiopian education, Education Sector Review (1972), which was developed during the end of Haile Selassie's rule and which was hoped by many to solve the Ethiopian educational problems at that time failed to discuss the pluralistic nature of the Ethiopian society recommending Amharic language in all educational activities once again.

Neither the Derg (1974-1991), a military rule which brought an end to the feudal regime and which was hoped by many Ethiopians from diverse ethnic backgrounds to solve the existed social, political, economic as well as educational inequities, responded appropriately to multicultural issues. The Derg being put under pressure by the old status quo and by using socialist propoganda undermined ethnic questions and intensified the cultural and linguistic domination of one ethnic group. One among the four guiding principles of the Derg stated: "Above all, the unity of Ethiopia will be the sacred faith of all our people" (Government Declaration, 1974: 58). Unity of the country was overstated without giving room for diversity for fear that responding to diversity appropriately will divide the nation.

One important development during the Derg worth mentioning from the point of view of multiculturalism was that unlike the past regimes it recognized the plurality and equality of the societies in Ethiopia. "All Ethiopians of whatever religion, language, sex or local affinity shall live together in equality, fraternity, harmony and unity under the umbrella of their country in which justice, equality and freedom will prevail" (Government Declaration, 1974: 58). And the Derg for the first time in the history of Ethiopia proposed the use of the mother tongue in the primary schools. However, unfortunately, it was not implemented, and a universal basic education, which was proposed, did not materialize as well. There were simply many promises during the military regime, and no significant development was achieved.

A good lesson for education in multicultural societies today from this brief history of the issue of pluralism in Ethiopian education is that diversity has survived more than a century of repression and that 'the assimilation model ' did not work rather than aggravating ethnic tensions and becoming a hindrance to development.

Current Status of Multiculturalism and Education in Ethiopia

In many countries like the USA, Canada and many other countries in the world the idea of addressing the issue of diversity in education was brought particularly by civil right and gender movements. In Ethiopia it was a result of a continious struggle of the diverse cultural, linguistic and ethnic minorities. However, some ethnic liberation fronts particularly the Tigray Peoples Liberation Front (TPLF) and the Oromo Liberation Front (OLF) who were the main actors during the heated debate of how to reorganize Ethiopia soon after the fall of the Derg deserve the credit for forging the principles of reorganizing Ethiopia on the basis of multiculturalism.

The basis of multiculturalism in Ethiopia today is 'the Constitution' (The Constitution of the Federal Democratic Republic of Ethiopia, 1995). In the preamble of the Constitution it is stated: "...the full respect of individuals and peoples fundamental freedoms and rights to live together on the basis of equality and without any sexual, religious or cultural discrimination." And, all languages in Ethiopia are also given equal recognition in the Constitution (p.78).

In the New Education and Training Policy (NETP, 1994) it is further stated that education should play role in promoting respect for human rights and democratic values and in creating condition for equality, mutual understanding and cooperation among people. A bold step was also taken for introducing the mother tongue in the primary schools, which has been practiced in about 17 languages since then. Moerover, much emphasis is given for the education of females and the disabled children (NETP, pp. 9-12). It should not surprise us that as a result of the introduction of the mother tongue children enjoyed ones own culture and achievements increased, and parental involvement has also increased. Although disparities in educational achievement were reported, girls enrollment has also significantly increased (MOE, 1999).

This does not mean that the introduction of multicultural principles is equally liked by all Ethiopians and there is uniform and smooth development all over the country. From the first day of its proposal, the introduction of the mother tongue was highly opposed and criticized by those group who were enjoying cultural and linguistic dominance, for the same old reason that it will disintegrate the nation, and indeed for fear that they will lose their old status and privileges in the society. There is a tendency from this group to reverse current developments to the old status quo to this date.

On the other side, there exists a flourishing ethnonationalism which to some extent led to ethnocentrism in some of the regions which are exercising the right of using their languages and developing their cultures in schools. An authentic multicultural education which can lead to the development of general national feelings without compromising students cultural, linguistic or ethnic identities is , thus, very much desirable .

There are also no uniform developments all over the country. For example, in schools in the capital city, Addis Ababa, one can say that the issue of language, culture or ethnic identity is not much better than it was during the imperial regime or the Derg. The students encounter assimilation. They do not exercise their families language or experience the culture of their ethnic backgrounds, and there are no occassions at all where plurality of the society is discussed boldly or recognized in the schools. For students coming from the regions it is a must that they "take off" their language, culture or identity to be integrated into the schools. This puts the full commitment of the government under question.

Generally today we see that multiculturalism in education found its way into Ethiopian education landscape. However, not only the school community (teachers, students and school administrators) but also curriculum design or teacher preparation programs and personnel are less informed about the what, why and how of education in multicultural, multiethnic and multilingual settings. It is also discouraging that government education reform efforts currently undergoing under the name of TESO (Teacher Education Sytem Overhaul) does not stress the significance of multiculturalism in education in Ethiopia. The efforts to introduce multiculturalism, in general, seem to be fragmented as emphasis are shifting from one aspect of diversity at one time to the other aspect at another time.

Conclusion

'Assimilation model' characterized Ethiopian education history, and it now failed, although there are few who still favour this model. It should be underlined that the emphasis on unity without due regard for diversity is a blind move that may threaten the existence of the country as a nation further leading to ethnocentrist moves on the other hand among the diverse cultural, ethnic, linguistic and religious groups in the country. Full commitment and follow up on the part of the government in implementing the stated ideals in the policy is very much important. No question that multiculturalism in Ethiopian education is at its infancy stage. The experiences of other nations in developing and implementing multicultural policies is, thus, crucially important. As Ethiopia strives for multiculturalism in education, focus should be given to system wide change rather than fragmented efforts as it is seen now.

References

Baxter, P. T. W. (1978): Ethiopia's unacknowledged problem: The Oromo, African Affairs, 77, pp. 283-296

Hamdessa T. (1982): Minority Education in Ethiopia, Africa, Rivista Trimestriale di Studi e documentazione, vol. 37, No. 3

The Constitution of the Federal Democratic Republic of Ethiopia, Addis Ababa, 1995

Transitional Government of Ethiopia, Education and Training Policy, Addis Ababa, 1994

UNESCO, Experiments and Innovations in Education, Innovative reform in Ethiopia, IV. An International Bureau of Education Series No. 34. Paris, 1978.

Ian Andrews (Simon Fraser University, Vancouver, Canada)

Transformation in Education: The Intercultural Agenda of Internationalizing Teacher Education – A Canadian Perspective

> "Internationalization is a process that prepares the community for successful participation in an increasingly interdependent world. In Canada, our multicultural reality is the stage for internationalization. The process should infuse all facets of the education system, fostering global understanding and developing skills for effective living and working in a diverse world" (Francis 1993a, p. 5)

A.   Introduction
Transformation in society as a form of social change has been the major focus and professional commitment for my work as a teacher and a teacher educator ever since I was a student teacher at Simon Fraser University in 1969. Over the past 35 years (25 internationally) I have recognized as well as experienced how social forces within society enormously impact how we as educators attend to the development and implementation of the curriculum of our schools, colleges and universities. Consequently as the transformation of education is undoubtedly manifested in curriculum reform I feel privileged to be addressing this issue in this collection of papers edited by scholars at the Otto-von-Guericke-Universität Magdeburg (Germany).

Along with my colleagues Goodith White, Ken Hall from Leeds University and Erika Hasebe-Ludt from the University of Lethbridge we are addressing the theme of this book from the perspective of our work as teacher educators from Britain and from Canada. We are members of a consortium of European and Canadian institutions engaged in a student mobility program involved in the development of a teacher education program focusing upon intercultural/multicultural curriculum. This transatlantic consortium involves student teachers and beginning teachers as they work to enhance their professional intercultural knowledge and skills in socio-cultural contexts of multicultural classrooms in the different countries of this consortium.

The objectives of this mobility program include:

- The strengthening of the intercultural approaches to teaching and learning;
- The promotion of the internationalization of teacher education in Canada and Europe;
- The development of action research as part of professional inquiry of beginning teachers; and

- The expansion of the integration of technology into professional practice.

This chapter will examine the intercultural and multicultural agenda when internationalizing teacher education. I will do my best to define the context of this theme from a Canadian perspective and address the basic premises of intercultural competence and professional teacher pedagogy. I will close by identifying certain practices that I hope enhance transformation in teacher education regardless of the national or cultural context of the faculty and students social change agenda.

B.   Canadian-European Mobility Program

The Student Mobility Project that my colleagues and I are involved in is entitled "Internationalization, Cultural Difference, and Migration: Developing a Curriculum for Teacher Education". This three year mobility program will involve 48 Canadian and 48 European pre-service and first year graduate teachers in a 10 - 12 week international university/school placement as part of their teacher education program. The main objective is to strengthen intercultural approaches to teaching and learning, and the key activity will be the development and implementation of a culturally responsive curriculum for teacher education. The key outcome will be teacher education programs that are more responsive to the intercultural and global realities of multicultural classrooms. These programs aim to prepare teachers with increased competencies to work in culturally diverse settings.

The six institutions which are involved in this Project and their faculty participants are:

1. University of Leeds (England)– Goodith White, Ken Hall, Gary Pulleyn
2. University of Jaen (Spain)– Antonio Bueno-Gonzalez, Nieves Pascual-Soler, Salvador Valera-Hernandez
3. Otto-von-Guericke University of Magdeburg (Germany)– Reinhard Golz, Olaf Beuchling, Holger Kersten
4. University of Regina (Canada)– Sonya Corbin-Dwyer, Kathleen O'Reilly-Scanlon
5. University of Lethbridge (Canada)– Erika Hasebe-Ludt, Cynthia Chambers
6. Simon Fraser University (Vancouver, Canada)– Ian Andrews, Sharon Wahl and Don Northey

C.   Internationalization and Interconnecting Concepts

As you are aware internationalization of higher education has become an important initiative in many European and North American post secondary institutions. However, the extent to which internationalization has been firmly institutionalized widely differs from country to country, institution to institution. Fundamental to the establishment of internationalization at the post secondary level is the presence of significant intercultural programming in the various disciplines. One specific strategy that internationalization should hopefully address are the intercultural and international transformative issues that occur among the teaching and learning of students and faculty in the context of multicultural and intercultural contexts. One area that should address and incorporate these intercultural parameters within its academic mandate is the teacher education programs of our universities.

A brief overview of some key definitions that offer a foundation of this presentation from a Canadian point of view need to be introduced. These definitions describe four separate but interconnecting concepts that are critical to the work undertaken in teacher education at my university at Simon Fraser as well as to the interconnecting concepts that we are exploring in this Canadian-Europe Mobility Program. They are:

1.   **Intercultural Education:**
"Intercultural education fosters an understanding of the tightly integrated relationship between language, communication, and culture. Intercultural curricula focus on how individuals are shaped by the norms, values, beliefs, and the language of their culture" (Franco/Shimabukuro 1992, p. 4).

2.   **Multicultural Education:**
"...encompasses a variety of policies, programs, and practices that entail the management of diversity within the school setting. It includes processes associated with the formation of a healthy identity, cultural preservation, intercultural sensitivity, awareness of racism and cross-cultural communication" (Fleras/Elliot 1992, pp. 183-184).

3.   **International Education:**
"...includes the study of relations among nations particular regions of the world foreign languages and cultures, comparative and international approaches to particular disciplines, and the examination of issues affecting more than one country" (Pickert 1992, p. 20).

4.   **Global Education:**
...is a perspective which underlies and shapes the teaching and learning processes. Through it students develop knowledge about, and critical understanding of global issues as well as skills to enable them to address those issues. Through it, they acquire values that give priority to ecological sustainability, global interdependence, social justice for all the world's people, peace, human rights, and mutually beneficial processes of economic, social and cultural development. (CIDA 1994)

D. Canadian Program – International Teacher Education Program (ITEM)

In 1996 three members of our Faculty of Education at Simon Fraser University established a teaching module of 32 students to focus upon the theme of the internationalization of education. This initiative was supported by the Faculty and endorsed by the BC College of Teachers, the teacher certification agency in the province of British Columbia, Canada.

This module focuses on the theme of "internationalization" of education. Specifically, student teachers examine the issues and challenges for teachers and students in British Columbia schools where diversity, global education, English-as-an-additional language and intercultural communication have become critical and integral components of classroom life and the curriculum. In addition to the "internationalization" theme, the other major themes of ITEM emphasize the teacher as a self-directing professional, and the building of a creative community of social action. In 1999, the ITEM program evolved to comprise international practica components: ITEM Trinidad and Tobago, and ITEM Mexico. Half of the module studies and teaches in Port-of-Spain, Trinidad and Tobago for nine weeks while the other half studies and teaches in Oaxaca, Mexico. Both groups then complete an extended 3-month practica and a semester of course work in Vancouver.

It is our belief that through ITEM, students gain an increased and heightened awareness of the various factors that influence the education of students in culturally diverse and when possible international educational settings. We believe teachers must be able to respond to the many challenges this creates with respect to multicultural, multilingual and intercultural aspects of educational practices. Helping children and youth recognize and take on these challenges in their learning in a variety of settings becomes an educational responsibility for teachers. Along with the obligation of teachers to nurture and foster students' intellectual and emotional growth, teachers also need to be prepared to help students become more aware of diversity in their community and for them to learn to make informed and responsible decisions on how they interact with their classmates.

In essence, we emphasize to our student teachers that their pupils belong to many different communities, and the ways we become part of them and how we make meaning of them are important considerations for us as we come together as learners and teachers in these ethnically diverse classrooms; and in the larger societal and global environment. Hence, as teacher educators we recognize that all participants bring different and valuable resources to the study and practice of education. The transformation of these understandings by our student teachers becomes the core of our curriculum. As a former graduate Salima has stated:

"The make-up of our world now is such that the traditional majority is not always the majority. ITEM seemed to me to be a place where aspiring teachers of all backgrounds would come together, share ideas, share personal histories, and help to break the barriers of silence that traditional curricula have often created."

Consequently through the Professional Development Program experience at SFU student teachers come away with a sound developmental sense of their own beliefs, clear goals related to those beliefs, and instructional plans that will make it possible to implement these goals. This requires active involvement in the process as well as the ability to understand that in teaching there are no "right" answers, but only important questions. Part of working hard in PDP is learning to become a professional and taking the professional development process seriously. Part of being a professional suggests engaging in on-going growth and commitment to becoming exceptional in one's field of study. I believe that the Canadian European Mobility Program universities involved in this project are excellent international places to continue to develop this ethos so that it becomes a natural part of professional practice.

E.   International – Intercultural Learning Outcomes
A Report written by BCCIE, British Columbia Center for International Education (Stanley/Mason 1997) developed a set of international learning outcomes "for Preparing Graduates for the Future". The Report addressed the question "what competencies do students require to succeed as citizens and professionals in today's global society. A qualitative study to identify these learning outcomes was undertaken involving professionals in Canada from post-secondary institutions, government, non-profit organizations, business and finance, environmental firms, advanced technology and consulting firms. A framework for the effective internationalization of post-secondary curriculum and the preparation of graduates was developed from this research. This document greatly assisted the curriculum developers of ITEM to establish the learning outcomes for our students to address.

The results of the study identified international learning outcomes to be organized into 5 basic themes. These are:

- Adapting business English and business etiquette to the needs of international clients
- Acquiring basic skills in an additional language or languages
- Developing Canadian and global perspectives

- Developing intercultural competence
- Demonstrating coping and resiliency skills

A key finding of the report was that graduates of post-secondary institutions who combine international know-how with a firm foundation of skills and experience in one or more technical, business or professional areas are the ones most likely to find work in professional fields in international activities of Canadian businesses or with international firms including education agencies or institutions. Emphasizing the importance of language and communication skills, the study indicates that graduates seeking international opportunities should be able to carry on a conversation, read a newspaper and follow technical instruction in at least one language other than English. While it is acknowledged that English is the language of international business, speaking English in an international situation, graduates must be able to adapt their use of language and their behavior to the formality of the situation or culture and the listener's comfort level in English.

With it was recognized that increasing global interdependence is the need for all Canadians to act as global citizens. The study found that not only should graduates be able to speak confidently about the issues affecting Canada, but should also be able to relate these issues to past and present Canadian international relations as well as to global trends and concerns. To do so, they need a thorough understanding of Canadian and world history, geography, social, religious and political structures and current events.

The study confirmed that today's graduates need to develop intercultural competence which involves not only a knowledge of other cultures, but the ability to value individual and cultural differences. In working with other people, with other cultural backgrounds both inside Canada and internationally, graduates must exhibit a willingness to risk being a stranger, to learn about other cultures and to adapt to them.

Finally, recognizing that adapting to other cultures is stressful, the study indicated that graduates need skills in coping with stressful situations and in developing emotional resilience. These skills include developing a strong sense of personal identity so that one's integrity is not threatened by other's values and beliefs.

Through the process of defining international learning outcomes, the study helps provide faculty with a framework for developing internationally focused curricula and gives students a language and structure to reflect on their own international education, to evaluate how successfully they have acquired these skills, knowledge and attitudes. The definition of these outcomes and the methods by which they are acquired will better prepare educational institutions and students themselves to present their international abilities and accomplishments to prospective employers.

In addition to recommending that the international learning outcomes be incorporated into curriculum as the critical element, the Report emphasizes the need of institutions to adopt a variety of educational strategies to help students achieve the outcomes. Issues to be addressed in the design, planning, organization and articulation of education programs at various levels are also noted. Key strategies identified include the use of participatory techniques and exchange programs as it is recognized that direct experience is powerful and an effective method for developing international skills and understanding.

In examining intercultural competencies closely specific international learning outcomes were emphasized. The following are those intercultural competencies that are critical for all professions, including the teaching profession. They include:

- Demonstrate the qualities of tolerance, sensitivity to others and tact
- Demonstrate open-mindedness and curiosity with respect to other countries
- Recognize and respect individual and cultural differences
- Recognize issues that may be sensitive to other cultures and peoples and respect their beliefs
- Identify one's own biases and attitudes
- Subjugate the need to impose one's own structure and ideas on others
- Demonstrate willingness to adapt to others' standards of political, cultural, social, and religious behaviour
- Practice good listening skills (learn to speak less, listen more)
- Demonstrate an ability to problem-solve issues related to one's professional competence in different cultural contexts
- Understand the differences in respect for persons, adult-child relationships, gender relationships in other cultures
- Examine own assumptions about other cultures
- Take initiative to facilitate social interaction
- Demonstrated flexibility while retaining the stability of one's own identity and values

These learning outcomes are in some cases hard to quantify when evaluating student performance. However with qualitative strategies clearly identified for both teachers and students with the curriculum materials intercultural competencies may be demonstrated and documented.

F.   Internationalization of Teacher Education – Future Agenda

As my colleagues involved in this Canada-European Mobility Program work together to develop a curriculum framework for our students, and faculty instructors' various priorities for institutional consensus of curriculum outcomes are emerging; they include:

- More cultural responsive teacher education programs at the participant universities
- Strengthen intercultural and international curriculum for teacher education
- Development of curriculum materials and resources, modules and software
- Collaborative networks and research
- Dissemination of the results of the project
- Establish a research agenda that will investigate and document the fundamental objectives, activities and learning outcomes of the curriculum.

To ensure these curriculum priorities are realized an agenda for the internationalization of teacher education program is emerging. This agenda emphasizes that internationalization and multiculturalism must become critical elements of post secondary education, particular in teacher education programs. The agenda of curriculum in schools must have competent and knowledgeable teachers. Consequently internationalizing the curriculum that will incorporate multicultural and intercultural perspectives must be introduced and modeled in the teacher's pre-service and in-service training for all teachers.

Such courses will challenge pupils to think in more complex ways about identity, ethnocentrism and to avoid cultural stereotyping (Wachter 2003).

In addition international education and the opportunities to expand student mobility should become fundamental to intercultural experiences for our students. I believe that mobility program exchange programs should also involve students from countries with different economic contexts with those of the more affluent nations within our global community wherever possible. The ITEM program in Mexico and Trinidad has tried to address issue and it has proven to be most important to the context of the intercultural and socio-economic learning for our students.

Another priority to consider is that elements of a socially transformative agenda of teacher programs that wish to promote an international-intercultural agenda should model pedagogical principles that integrate the conceptual with the practical. International community service and experiential learning in local multicultural contexts will promote intercultural rich pedagogical practices.

Finally the manifestation of intercultural learning may be realized as intercultural competence as suggested by Stanley and Mason. Consequently a student whose intercultural knowledge, attitudes and skills are enhanced by effective interactions through mobility programs it is hoped that a strong focus on developing curriculum that promotes these understandings will be prevalent.

Establishing effective student mobility programs that will require a critical commitment by teacher education institutions to work collaboratively to frame these experiences for students' when studying in a different cultural context is the fundamental challenge of the Canada-Europe Mobility Program presently underway.

G. Summary

In summary it becomes essential that a core curriculum must internationalize our faculty colleagues' pedagogical and philosophical perspectives regardless of discipline, subject area and the age level focus of the students in the schools. As a result we must:

- Infuse content and materials from different countries, cultures and perspectives
- Include different methodologies and cultural approaches to the subjects being taught while recognizing the cultural diversity of the students
- Include material that encourages an awareness of global diversity
- Integrate international students' experiences and their cultural and national perspectives with local domestic students' cultural, national and international experiences in developing the curriculum.
- Include and value our international partners' academic knowledge and contributions in the teaching and learning experiences that we collaboratively develop.
- Establish an intensive research agenda among the faculty and students involved in the transformative international agenda.

This discussion will continue in this collection of papers when my colleague Goodith White examines the research agenda and the critical questions that could be pursued to illuminate the issues that the Canada-European Program will encounter and explore.

In the past, world views of Canadian students have been shaped largely by Western European and Northern American perspectives. I definitely believe that these perspectives must be broadened to include East European, Asian, Central and South American and African views. Hopefully this opportunity will be fostered more evidently in the future mobility programs financially sponsored by the Western – European funding agencies.

References

Fleras, A./Jean L. E. (1992) : Multiculturalism in Canada: The Challenge of Diversity. Scarborough: Nelson Canada.

Franco, R. W./Shimabukuro, J. N. (Eds.) (1992): Beyond the classroom: International Education and the Community College. Honolulu, HI: Hawaii University.

Pickert, S. M. (1992): Preparing for a Global Community. Achieving an International Perspective in Higher Education. Washington, DC: Washington, DC. School of Education and Human Development.

Stanley, D./Mason, J. (1997): Preparing Graduates for the Future: International Learning Outcomes. Vancouver, BC: BC Centre for International Education.

Wachter, B.: Intercultural Learning and Diversity in Higher Education. In: Thousand Oaks: Journal of Studies in International Education, 2003: Vol. 7

Ken Hall and Goodith White (University of Leeds, England)

Research in progress - Internationalization, Cultural Difference, and Migration: Developing a Curriculum for Teacher Education

Abstract
This project includes three Canadian universities from each of the western provinces: Simon Fraser University in Burnaby, British Columbia, the University of Lethbridge in Lethbridge, Alberta and the University of Regina in Regina, Saskatchewan; and three European universities: the University of Leeds in England, the University of Jaén in Spain, and the Otto-von-Guericke Universität in Magdeburg, Germany. Between 2004 – 2006, a total of 96 students will be involved in international school placements, 48 from Europe and 48 from Canada. The key activity is the development and implementation of a culturally responsive curriculum for teacher education and will produce teachers who are better prepared to teach in multicultural and international settings.

Project Rationale
As a result of internationalization, urban and rural settings on both sides of the Atlantic are becoming more diverse ethnically, racially, linguistically, religiously, and socio-economically. To address the issues, and potential tensions, which arise from this increasing diversity, this project has been developed to help increase understanding and promote a broader knowledge of the languages, cultures and educational institutions of the European Community and Canada. Between 2004 and 2006, a total of 96 students, 48 from Europe and 48 from Canada, will be involved in international school placements, with the key focus on the development and implementation of a culturally responsive curriculum for teacher education. In the case of the Canadian students and the European students from Spain and Germany, participants will be trainee teachers and the placement will form an integral part of their initial training, whereas the students from the UK will be Newly Qualified Teachers (NQTs) who have just successfully completed their year of initial teacher training and obtained the qualification of Secondary GCE with Qualified Teacher Status QTS.
The curriculum to be developed will be based on current theoretical and pedagogical approaches and concepts pertaining to cultural difference as well as on activities and assignments including action research projects and e-learning technologies. The curriculum will incorporate formative evaluation and be continually informed by the experiences and insights gained during school and community placements in Canada and Europe. Pre-service (beginning) teachers will experience at first-hand an unfamiliar cultural, linguistic, and educational setting,

which is likely to have a profound effect on their understanding of, and attitudes towards, the culturally diverse classrooms they will encounter throughout their professional life. Both the activities they will engage in and their reflections will inform the sustainable development of a strengthened intercultural and international curriculum for teacher education in all partner institutions and countries. This curriculum will be responsive to changing local and global classroom realities and provide a contextual framework for promoting harmonious social relationships and successful academic achievement. It will enable future teachers to become more competent in providing for teaching and learning in increasingly diverse cultural and linguistic school and community contexts.

Objectives

To achieve the objectives of strengthening intercultural approaches to teaching and learning, and promoting the internationalization of teacher education in Canada and Europe, the initial activities will include the development of a teacher education curriculum for use in the participating institutions and communities on both sides of the Atlantic. This curriculum will challenge trainee teachers' attitudes, and develop knowledge and skills in culturally responsive education and intercultural communication in local and global contexts through in-school placements and action research projects. In order to gather information and insights which will inform the development of the curriculum, the tools to be used by pre-service teachers during the placement will be identified.

The development of action research as part of professional inquiry will involve designing action research assignments (questioning, action and reflection) and seminars to be organized at host institutions at which visiting pre-service teachers will present.

Given the transnational character of the project, distance learning technologies will be developed in order to expand access and to facilitate communication between all stakeholders. The use of electronic communication between all sites will extend the period of learning before, during and after the international placements as well as enlarging the number of pre-service teachers who are able to exchange ideas, opinions and best practice with their peers from across the Atlantic. Moving beyond information exchange, the interaction on-line will be carefully structured so that groups of pre-service teachers across sites conduct scholarly investigations on specific topics and report their findings to the larger group. Specifically, e-mail and video conference links will be integral elements of the preparation for the teaching practicum and for monitoring the progress of the students whilst on their placement. ICT hardware and software will be used by students to plan, develop and deliver teaching materials. A project web site will be set up and maintained with the purpose of sharing information and knowledge and, as the project develops will be a prime resource for sharing outcomes.

An inter-cultural project such as this will enable participants to have access to colleagues facing similar challenges, and to share in ways of addressing these challenges. Schools will benefit from the presence of pre-service teachers from other countries, and local communities will have the chance to reaffirm the important role they play in education.

Results and Outcomes

Results and outcomes for the teacher education programmes of the participating institutions will include: a sustainable curriculum for culturally responsive education and intercultural communication, including teaching materials and resources, modules, and software; strengthened working partnerships and networks of communication and collaboration between Canadian and European institutions; improved quality and focus regarding inter-cultural approaches to teaching and learning; and joint publications.

Results and outcomes for the participating pre-service teachers from the 6 institutions will include increased cultural awareness and sensitivity, particularly an increased understanding and broader knowledge of the languages, cultures and educational institutions of the European Community and Canada; improved ability to assess and reflect on one's own professional practice in other socio-cultural contexts; development of language skills; increased employability in the global community; completion of academic programme requirements; and an increase in skilled use of distance learning technologies.

Benefits and Added Value of Transatlantic Multilateral Collaboration and Co-operation

Because of the influence of globalization and the reasons for population shifts, there are both similarities and striking differences between the historic and current experiences of multicultural education in Canada and Europe. In the past Canada has experienced waves of inbound migration, and migrant groups have for the most part been able to retain both their own ethnic identity while also becoming 'Canadians.' It has also had the experience of enforced resettlement (rather than migration per se) of large numbers of Aboriginal, first nation, peoples in Saskatchewan, Alberta, and British Columbia. Until fairly recently, Europe more typically experienced outbound migration to 'the New World', but now, like Canada, 'old Europe' has become a site for inward migration from other parts of Europe and former colonies, as well as from political and economic refugees, creating new challenges for intercultural education. Working collaboratively in these specific transatlantic settings will lead to increased knowledge and understanding of cultural difference for both pre-service and university teachers.

International Collaboration

While this project creates new partnerships, it also builds on existing links between some institutions. In particular, there is a collaborative working agreement between Simon Fraser University in Vancouver (Canada), and the University of Leeds (UK). This agreement was established in 1999 with shared activities commencing in 2000. The University of Leeds and the University of Jaen (Spain) also have an existing student and staff exchange for their respective Schools of Education under the European Socrates programme.

Informal links have existed between the University of Lethbridge (Canada) and Otto-von-Guericke University, Magdeburg (Germany) for the past four years, and they are currently in the process of negotiating and signing an institutional agreement.

Typically, links between western Canadian institutions and European institutions have not been as prolific as links between Canadian and Asian institutions. This programme is, therefore, an excellent opportunity to promote greater contact with European institutions.

In-school Placements and Practica

The pre-service teachers who participate in the project will gain experience in one or more educational contexts in the host country. Placements will be arranged by the host institutions in collaboration with local school boards and consortia partners in a variety of educational settings to complement the teacher training programmes of the students' home country. Participants will be asked to discover and document how each school and community setting deals with diverse populations of students, parents, and other community members, and to reflect on the personal challenge of being a foreigner and newcomer in each environment. This experience is likely to have a profound effect on their understanding of, and attitude towards, the mix of students whom they will meet in their future classes.

Prior to the exchange visit, students will follow and orientation programme which will include language training, where appropriate, and briefing sessions on the education system of the host country. Students will also design and undertake research (including the educational systems and culture of the cities/countries in which students will be studying), develop instructional technology activities and action research projects (to be conducted with their Canadian and European peers), communicate with other project participants, set goals, and plan instructional units and lessons.

Whilst on placement, participants will be required to become involved in
- an in-school practicum (including planning, teaching, and reflection);
- interactive instructional technology activities (to extend the project beyond those students directly involved);
- an action research project;
- formative on-going project evaluation (including self assessment, peer feedback, surveys, interviews, etc.);
- meetings at the host institutions (which may include presentations to other groups of students and teachers).

At the end of their placement in the host country, and on return to their home institution, students will participate in
- a summative evaluation of the project;
- the communication of the results of their action research projects;
- further design and development of instructional technology activities;
- the development of curriculum and related materials;
- dissemination of outcomes, including writing research papers.

During the placement students will be accommodated through home stays. This will provide them with a connection to the local community, facilitate personal adjustment, promote inter-cultural understanding and friendship, and reduce isolation. It is anticipated that students will also participate in welcome celebrations in the host institution to meet local pre-service teachers and faculty.

Evaluation of Outcomes
The project outcomes will be assessed both formatively and summatively by various methods, including:
- the results of the pre-service teachers' action research projects;
- the results of instructional technology activities;
- interviews (individual and group) of project participants (particularly the pre-service teachers and the supervising teachers in their practica);
- surveys of project participants;
- an independent evaluator at each institution.

While the surveys and interview questions will be determined during the initial curriculum development phase of the project, the criteria used for assessment of the project activities will include:
- the personal and professional development of pre-service teachers
- pre-service teachers' increased cultural awareness and sensitivity in approaches to teaching and learning

- pre-service teachers' foreign language training
- pre-service teachers' increased knowledge of education in the global community and how this knowledge impacts their role as teachers in European and Canadian classrooms
- integrating technology into professional practice
- sustainable curriculum for teacher education programmes
- teachers as role models and leaders who are responsive to global and local cultures
- strengthened working partnerships between Canadian and European institutions

Conclusion

The overall objectives of this project are to develop and implement a curriculum for teacher education that is more responsive to the global realities of multicultural classrooms and to strengthen intercultural approaches to teaching and learning. It offers students a unique opportunity to gain invaluable experience in teaching and learning in a multicultural context, and develop into rounded professionals who are consequently more qualified and more confident to teach effectively in multicultural and international settings.

Terry Carson (Alberta University, Edmonton, Canada)

Becoming Somebody Different: Teacher Identity and Implementing Socially Transformative Curriculum

Introduction

Speaking about democracy and education John Dewey famously stated that: "It is not the place of the school to educate citizens for a democracy, rather it is the role of the school to create the public for a democratic society". The distinction that Dewey is making is an important one. He is reminding us that the school's curriculum and teaching should not be viewed instrumentally, in the service of some pre-defined purpose, no matter how laudable this purpose might be. Rather, the point of an education is to exemplify, that is to literally become the change that is wanted.

Dewey's distinction between instrumentalism and immanence in achieving society's goals through public education are worth considering in our contemporary situation, in which the public school is being asked to deal with an array of often contradictory concerns that range from satisfying demands for rights of inclusion for children with special needs on one hand, to strengthening scores on international test scores in an effort to ensure competitiveness and prosperity in a global economy on the other. Clearly hopes and worries about the future are bound to coalesce around increasing demands and expectations on the public school. Certainly the political responses to these demands have put pressure on an already overburdened school system, along with a host of measures designed to control the curriculum and assessment practices in the interests of securing greater accountability.

Viewing teachers and curriculum instrumentally has intensified within the present landscape of increased expectations and accountability for public education. This is a global phenomenon (cf. Carson 2003). And concomitant with the intensification of efforts to bring about social change through the public school system there has also been a corresponding explosion of interest in understanding the mechanisms for effecting educational change.

The contemporary literature on educational change, as exemplified in the work of Michael Fullan and Andrew Hargreaves (1992), has moved away from interpreting change as a problem of curriculum implementation, to now regarding it as question of teacher development. Fullan's work in particular reflects insights gained from the implementation studies of a number of the ambitious national curriculum change projects during the 1960s. These change agent studies blamed failures of implementation on a failure to involve teachers as active participants in change. This accounts for a shift in focus, which appears to place teacher professional development at the centre of the change process. And while teacher development forms the focus of one stream of the current literature on educational change, there are other streams that examine educational leadership (cf. Fullan 2001) and organizational change.

While the new writing on educational change has become more nuanced and appears to centre on the participants as active agents of change, William Pinar reminds us that the change literature owes its lineage to research on these national curriculum projects whose very purpose was to remove the curriculum from the control of teachers and local developers. In his recent book entitled, *What is Curriculum Theory?* (2004), Pinar traces the impetus for turning over the development of these national curriculum projects to the academic disciplines to the response of the Kennedy administration to Soviet scientific ascendancy in Cold War. Educators were held responsible for allowing American standards to slide and were not to be trusted with solving the problem.

Change As a Question of Identity

As Dewey intimated in his claim that achieving democratic society is a matter of creating a democratic public, bringing about socially transformative change implies the formation of new identities. Conceptions of the public are no longer the same. Maxine Greene points out that Dewey and his contemporaries spared little thought for "gender difference or cultural diversity or even for class divisions as factors relevant to education and public life" (Greene 1996, p. 33). Creating the democratic public for a diverse society lies at the heart of multicultural and anti-racist education. In this country, at least, it is the challenge of creating a public that respects Canadian society as one that does not to assimilate difference, but in the words of Charles Taylor (1993), "recognizes and accepts a deep diversity".

Adoption of a multicultural and anti-racist education -- that is achieving the implementation of multicultural and anti-racist education that contributes to the creation of a democratic public for a diverse Canadian society, can hardly be considered to have been a resounding success. Although multicultural education is now often included as a topic in school subjects, like social studies, literature and the fine arts. And despite the fact that some schools in ethnically mixed neighbourhoods have worked hard both to accommodate and to honour cultural difference, many schools and most curriculum subject areas largely ignore the relevance cultural difference for teaching and learning. One recent national survey conducted by the Canadian Council for Multicultural and Intercultural Education, indicated that more than half of the teachers polled have had no workshops on multicultural education or anti-racist education (cf. Young/MacKay 1998). The authors of the report went on to point out teachers who had taken workshops had these as isolated events. These had limited influence on teachers' attitudes or on the priority placed on cultural difference and teaching.

Participants in teacher education programs have expressed similar concerns. Most graduating teachers feel that their teacher education has not prepared them well to cope with the cultural differences, yet they know full well the diversity that constitutes present classrooms in Canada will there throughout their teaching careers (cf. Carson/Johnston 2003 p. 27).

While legitimate concerns are raised about the lack of information about multicultural and anti-racist education for in-service and pre-service teachers, the fact that questions of identity are at stake may be seen in the resistances to knowledge, especially in the case of anti-racist education. Anti-racist educators become frustrated by the lack of willingness to learn about racism precisely from those of whom they consider to be most in need of anti-racist education. Often those who refuse to listen having had little personal experience of racism or sexism themselves, will deny the experiences of others who have, or feel the need to counter with their own stories of discrimination. Mistaking a passion for ignorance for naïve ignorance, anti-racist educators reach a pedagogical impasse, having raised awareness of the problem, but having little idea of what to do with the guilt and anger that now suffuses the classroom (cf. Carson/Johnston, 2001).

Identity and Resistances to Knowledge

Psychoanalytic theory can be deployed to provide some insights into the questions of identity that are revealed in this resistance to knowledge in anti-racist education. Psychoanalytically, we can say that knowledge will be resisted when it threatens familiar identities and unsettles the integrity of the self. Jacques Lacan explains the dynamics of resistance as originating in an essential split between twin sources of identity formation in the imaginary order and the symbolic order (cf. Felman 1987). We wish to present ourselves as having coherent single identities, but this is impossible because of the different sources of identity formation. In the imaginary order identity is formed in social relations with others, who reflect back to me who I am. The symbolic order forms identity through language. As we take on language, the traditions and authority that is handed down through language also discipline us.

Normally, we go through daily life as if we have coherent identities. Mere information seldom disrupts identities, nor will knowledge that does not activate the essentially split identity. Such is the case with multicultural education, which is easy to identify with in imaginary realm – I know myself to be a person who ac-

cepts others, and the symbolic realm – Canada has a policy of official multiculturalism. Anti-racist education disrupts this sense of the coherent self, suddenly
introducing dangerous knowledge of the existence of racism which one must re-
ject responsibility for in the interests of restoring integrity.

Identities are Negotiated

A psychoanalytical interpretation of resistance alerts us to the pedagogical complexity of creating a public for a deeply diverse democratic society. Because
transformational change implicates identity we need to understand that identities
are negotiated both inter-subjectively and intra-subjectively. Knowledge of racism is bound to be dangerous knowledge because people like me, a white male,
fifth generation Canadian of Anglo-Irish ancestry, who grew up speaking English
at home, will come to feel personally implicated in the dispensation that has produced racism. This comes to me as a new idea, and an unwelcome one at that.
My identity as a white male, hitherto unproblematic, has both enabled me to escape racism and to remain personally ignorant of the experience of those who
have. By being introduced to the experiences of these others my former sense of
myself – a self that believes that it has achieved what it has through personal effort, and not by virtue of being a white, English-speaking male – is disrupted. For
these reasons I am likely to resist this knowledge, and will only be able to change
when I have the necessity and the opportunity to re-identify with the other that
has experienced oppression. It is not simply a matter of learning something new,
but in truth, it is, for me, a matter of becoming someone who is different.
I have indicated that discourse of teacher development began in the problems of
curriculum implementation. Having repositioned the teacher more appropriately
as the acting subject, who in many respects "is" the change that is being sought,
the teacher development literature has exhibited a curious lack of interest in questions of identity. And yet it is the identity of the teacher that is being re-
negotiated in socially transformative educational reforms. Multicultural and anti-
racist education is being introduced within the contexts of already existing identities that have been constructed by social norms, school structures and curricula,
of times past. As Deborah Britzman states, "our identities, over determined by
history, place and sociality, are lived and imagined through the discourses or
knowledge we employ to make sense of who are, who we are not, and who we
can become" (1994, p. 58).
The history, place and sociality of public school educators who have been
enlisted to carry out the transformative projects of multicultural and anti-racist
education depends upon teachers whose identities have been formed in provin-
cially controlled Canadian school system that had been established originally to

protect English and French rights of language and culture. For much of Canada's history the school systems in the province of Quebec and those in the provinces of English Canada had developed quite separately, as "two solitudes" – as suggested in the title of Hugh McLennan's 1945 novel. In English Canada students were assimilated into an English Canadian/British identity, in Quebec into a French/Catholic identity. Newcomers were integrated into these already existing identities. In an egregious example of forced assimilation during a thirty-year period that ended in 1969, aboriginal children were removed from their families and communities and sent to church run residential schools to remove their native languages and cultures.

Finding the Right Language to Speak of Teacher Development
The teacher development literature has left us groping around in the darkness of educational change, recounting stories of what seems to have worked in past situations, deriving some conclusions about the change process and hoping that these will somehow hold lessons for future action. Contrary to the titles of the many editions of Michael Fullan's famous books on the "Meaning of Educational Change" and the "New Meaning of Educational Change", the meaning of educational change for teachers remains fundamentally opaque, because it lacks an adequate sense of the teacher as the subject who is changing. Therefore the strategies of teacher development are still basically limited to convincing teachers of the wisdom of reform and providing the necessary knowledge and skills that are thought necessary to enact the change. These strategies are inadequate to the challenges of the deeply socially transformative change facing democratic societies in the 21st Century, as indicated by the two examples described here; Curriculum 2005 in South Africa and multicultural and anti-racist education in Canada. Socially transformation necessarily involves negotiating new identities.
A language for attending to questions of identity is absent in these discourses of teacher development, because they lack an explicit theory of the subject. Lacking any alternative theory of the subject we are left with simplistic notions of unitary identity and transcendent human nature. Social change and the responses of public education require an explicit alternative theory of the subject.
Post-structuralism provides such an alternative theory. A post-structuralist theory of the subject allows productive insights into the dynamics of identity formation and institutional change. Foucault has summarized a post-structural theory as "tracing the constitution of the subject within a historical framework" (1980, p. 117).

References

Britzman, D. (1994): Is there a problem with knowing thyself ? In T. Shanahan (Ed.). Teachers thinking, Teachers knowing. Urbana, Ill.: National Conference on Research in English: pp. 53-75.

Carson, T./Johnston, I. (2003): Education for cultural difference: Reviewing some curriculum initiatives in a Canadian teacher education program. Humanization of Education, 1, 2003, pp. 25 – 32.

Carson, T./Johnston, I. (2001): Cultural difference and teacher identity formation: The need for a pedagogy of compassion. JPCS: Journal for the Psychoanalysis of Culture & Society, 6(2), Fall 2001, pp. 259 – 264.

Carson, T. (2003): Negotiating identities: subjectivities, curriculum change and teacher development. Paper presented at the First World Curriculum Studies Conference of the International Association for the Advancement of Curriculum Studies, East China Normal University, Shanghai.

Fullan, M. (2001): Leading in a culture of change. London: Jossey-Bass.

Greene, M. (1996): Plurality, diversity, and the public space. In: A. Oldenquist (Ed.): Can Democracy be Taught? Bloomington: Phi Delta Kappa Educational Foundation.

Hargreaves, A./Fullan, M.(Eds.) (1992): Understanding teacher development. New York: Teachers College Press& Cassell (U.K.).

Taylor, C. (1993): Reconciling the solitudes: Essays on Canadian federalism and nationalism. Montreal & Kingston: MeGill Queens Press.

Young, J./MacKay (1999): Multi-cultural in-service teacher education in a period of school reform. Multiculturalism/Interculturalisme: Journal of the Canadian Council for Multicultural and Intercultural Education 19(1), pp. 5 – 16.

Nadine Pantke (University of Magdeburg, Germany; Alberta University, Edmonton, Canada)

Cultural Diversity as an Educational Condition and Challenge: A Comparison Detailing the Cultural Differences within the German and Canadian School Systems – A Research Project -

Zusammenfassung

Der vorliegende Bericht über ein Forschungsprojekt thematisiert den Vergleich des Umgangs mit kultureller Vielfalt in deutschen und kanadischen Schulen. Im Mittelpunkt der empirischen Erhebung wird eine Befragung von LehrerInnen und SchülerInnen ausgewählter Schulen in den deutschen Bundesländern Sachsen-Anhalt und Brandenburg und den kanadischen Provinzen Alberta und British Columbia stehen. Die Untersuchung bedient sich somit vorrangig der qualitativen, aber in bestimmten Kontexten auch der quantitativen Erhebungsmethoden. Das deutsche und kanadische Bildungssystem wird verglichen unter Berücksichtigung der Bildungschancen, die sich für Kinder und Jugendliche aus Migrantenfamilien ergeben. Die Auswirkungen, die kulturbezogene Konflikte in der Schule auf das Handeln von LehrerInnen und SchülerInnen haben, werden von zentraler Bedeutung für den Vergleich sein. Indem die Bildungssysteme und Umgangsformen mit soziokultureller und sprachlicher Differenz in deutschen und kanadischen Schulen verglichen werden, wird ein Beitrag zur Diskussion der gegenwärtigen Reformprozesse geleistet. Letzteres gilt speziell für die migrationsunerfahrenen Regionen Brandenburg und Sachsen-Anhalt.

Introduction

This research project has been accepted by the University of Magdeburg and describes how cultural differences are dealt with within the German and Canadian school system. It is founded of past academic and personal experiences in public schools in Canada, especially in connection with experiences with ethnic minorities like the Native population. The idea of this project was born during a stay and active participation in an elementary school in Alberta / Canada and has been specified mostly during the last year.

Research Background

What makes Germany and Canada comparable? The new immigration country Germany and the classical immigration country Canada have experienced mobility processes that have had strong consequences to their educational systems. Either in the past or present, both countries had and have to deal with cultural diversity that represents a challenge in schools. Today's professionals, especially teachers, need to be intercultural competent in a world of internationalization and globalization and skills like cultural sensitivity are often seen as basic. According to Bender-Szymanski (cf. 2003, p. 156; 2000) intercultural competence is the infinite endeavour of the culture-bound person for using the potential of her cultural ability not to react on unfamiliarity with inclusion and exclusion, but to creatively use her new experiences across ethnic-national boundaries too in order to bring the points of view of all participants to a careful balance at the individual as well as at the institutional level. How Germany and Canada deal with cultural differences in their societies will affect their social and educational systems and will put it against new and unknown challenges. Cultural diversity is a condition for the Canadian society; it should be a challenge for Germany.

From 1989 to 1992, Germany became one of the most popular immigration countries in Europe, especially for immigrants from Eastern Europe and the former Soviet Union. These mobility processes have had strong consequences, most of all to the six new German states (East)Berlin, Brandenburg, Mecklenburg Western-Pomerania, Saxony, Saxony-Anhalt, Thuringia, and their educational systems. Professionals had almost no experiences dealing with cultural diversity and it is still an on-going process. Compared to other regions in Germany like Hamburg, Baden-Wuerttemberg, or Berlin, we are looking at a low number of immigrants where certain issues arise in Eastern German states and affect their educational systems – Brandenburg 2,5 %, Saxony-Anhalt 1,8 % (cf. Statistisches Bundesamt 2001). Recently published research projects about the national educational situation of German children and youth and the results of the PISA-Test show the importance of culturally founded problems in German schools. Especially children and youth with migration backgrounds are underprivileged and discriminated in our schools - the reason is often seen in the early separation of our educational system and social backgrounds (cf. Bos 2003).

Canada's good results of the PISA-Test support the multicultural educational system in general. The declared and bilingual immigration country is proud of its tradition of cultural and racial diversity – cultural minorities are able to keep their identity and fit in like a mosaic into the Canadian society (cf. Department of the Secretary of State of Canada 1987). The equality of all citizens, however, reaches its border by the time we look at relations with under representative ethnic groups like the Native population. The Canadian school system became specified because of cultural or language diversity and the distance learning of home schooling became more popular for the same reasons. This trend allows us to ponder the idea of multicultural education. Considering this development, we need to clarify an unproblematic multicultural education and if it seems to be possible in general. Highly discussed German problems have been noticed in Canada as well – if they have been solved under the idea of the multiculturalism, then what are the conclusions for the German society? This is one of the goals that have been set up for this dissertation project.

Objectives and Research Questions
Under these circumstances, the following objectives have been formulated:
- The detailed description of the German and Canadian school system considering the educational chances for children and youth with migration background.
- The description of teachers' individual everyday experiences (negative/positive) in dealing with cultural diversity and look behind the results of international empirical comparative research (PISA).
- The development of strategies in dealing with cultural diversity especially for teachers (and students, principals and parents) within inexperienced regions (of Germany) in order to make a contribution to presently discussed reform processes in the education system.

Under the conditions of the formulated objectives, the following academic research questions are pointed out:
- What differences and solidarities can be established considering the dealing with ethnic-cultural minorities in selected German and Canadian schools?
- How can the international success / failure of PISA be clarified and what are solidarities and challenges result for both education systems?
- Which problems determine the school day? Are problems culturally founded?
- How are cultural problems solved in German and Canadian schools? Where are the solidarities and where are the differences in the way of solution?
- How do teachers experience the dealing with children and youth from families that have migrated? Which individual problems determine the school day and how are they solved? Are teachers prepared? Do they get support? If yes, from who?
- How do students, with and without a migration background, experience the common education? Where do they see problems? Do ethnic-cultural problems exist for them in general and where do they see the reasons and solutions? Do they see their school education affected (negative / positive) because of their multicultural composition?

Research methods
The aforementioned objectives and research questions are part of a constantly changing process; they will be specified in the sequel of this dissertation project. The author plans to use qualitative research methods. The special term of indi-

vidual interest defend this decision. First, the research field in Germany and Canada need to be analysed – therefore naturalistic and participating observation seems to be the first methodical step. The problems in general will be discovered first and a relationship to the interview partner (teachers, students, principals, parents) will be established. Expert-structured interviews will follow non-structured or part-structure interviews – depending on the interview partner. It is planned that all interviews will be recorded, so that a detailed evaluation afterwards will be possible. This, of course, depends on the consent of the interview partner. It may be a good idea to use a structured questionnaire in combination with the interviews; so detailed questions like age, job experiences, and so forth will be captured after the interview talk and will not waste time. No more than 15 to 20 people will be interviewed; bigger groups would be desirable, but not possible because of the personal occupation of this research project. The author plans to record between 7 and 10 interviews in selected schools in Brandenburg and Saxony-Anhalt (Germany) and Alberta and British Columbia (Canada). Interview partners will be mostly teachers and students who are dealing with cultural diversity in school all day.

Concluding Statements

The state of research calls for the realization of this project. A qualitative educational comparison between Germany and Canada has never been realized, which increases the high rate of this research. Quite a large amount of books dealing with multicultural education have been published, especially in English-speaking countries. A higher interest in German-speaking areas has been noted especially after the results of the PISA-Test. International comparative educational research with a qualitative context, however, is not high rate published compared to quantitative Education or other research areas. Therefore, this project is very important for the integration process of ethnic-cultural minorities in educational institutions in different societies, especially in inexperienced regions of the German Republic.

References

Allemann-Ghionda, C. (2004): Einführung in die vergleichende Erziehungswissenschaft. Weinheim/Basel: Beltz.

Auernheimer, G. (Ed.) (2003): Schieflagen im Bildungssystem. Die Benachteiligung von Migrantenkinder. Interkulturelle Studien. Band 16. Opladen: Leske+Budrich.

Baumert, J./Artelt, C./Klieme, E. u.a. (2002): PISA 2000 – die Länder der Bundesrepublik im Vergleich. Zusammenfassung zentraler Befunde. Berlin: Max Plank-Institut für Bildungsforschung. In: Baumert, J/Artelt, C./Klieme, E. et al.: PISA 2000 – die Länder der Bundesrepublik im Vergleich. Opladen: Leske + Budrich.

Beauftragte der Bundesregierung für Ausländerfragen (2002): Bericht der Beauftragten der Bundesregierung für Ausländerfragen über die Lage der Ausländer in der Bundesrepublik Deutschland. Berlin/Bonn: Universitäts- Buchdruckerei.

Bender-Szymanski, D.: Learning through Cultural Conflict? A Longitudinal Analysis of German Teachers' Strategies for Coping with Cultural Diversity at School. In: European Journal of Teacher Education, (2000) 23, 3: pp. 229-250.

Bender-Szymanski, D.(2003): Interkulturelle Kompetenz bei Lehrerinnen und Lehrern aus Sicht der empirischen Bildungsforschung. In: Auernheimer, G. (Ed.): Schieflagen im Bildungssystem. Die Benachteiligung von Migrantenkindern. Interkulturelle Studien. Band 16. Opladen: Leske+Budrich, pp. 153-179.

Bos, W. u.a. (2003): Erste Ergebnisse aus IGLU. Schulleistungen am Ende der vierten Jahrgangsstufe im internationalen Vergleich. Münster/New York.

Carson, T./Johnston, I./Wiltse, L.: Negotiating Teacher Identity in Contexts of Cultural Diversity. In: Berulava, M.N./Golz, R./Keck, R. (Ed.): Humanisierung der Bildung. Internationale Zeitschrift für Pädagogik und Psychologie. Nr. 1/2001, Internationale Akademie zur Humanisierung der Bildung & Wissenschaftliches Bildungszentrum der Russischen Akademie der Bildung: Moskau – Sotschi, pp. 127-132.

Cohen, L./Manion, L./Morrison, K. (2000): Research Methods in Education. 5th Ed. London/New York: Routledge Falmer.

Department of the Secretary of State of Canada (1987): Multiculturalism... being Canadian. Minister of Supply and Services Canada.

Friebertshäuser, B. (1997): Feldforschung und teilnehmende Beobachtung. In: Friebertshäuser, B./Prengel, A. (Ed.): Handbuch Qualitative Forschungsmethoden in der Erziehungswissenschaft. Weinheim /München: Juventa: pp. 503-534.

Golz, R. (2001): A Comparison of Intercultural Education in Germany, Canada and Russia. In: Gumanizacija Obrazovanija. Moscow/Sochi: Nr. 1/2001, pp. 77-90.

Mayring, P. (2002): Einführung in die qualitative Sozialforschung. 5. Auflg. Weinheim/Basel: Beltz.

Nieke, W. (2000): Interkulturelle Erziehung und Bildung. Werteorientierungen im Alltag. 2. Auflg. Reihe Schule und Gesellschaft Bd. 4. Opladen: Leske + Budrich.

Ratzki, A. (2003): Skandinavische Bildungssysteme – Schule in Deutschland. Ein provokanter Vergleich. In: Auernheimer, G. (2003): Schieflagen im Bildungssystem. Die Benachteiligung von Migrantenkinder. Interkulturelle Studien. Band 16., Opladen: Leske+Budrich: pp. 23-31.

Schriewer, J. (Ed.) (2003): Discourse Formation in Comparative Education. Second Revised Edition. Frankfurt am Main: Peter Lang Verlag.

Erika Hasebe-Ludt (University of Lethbridge, Alberta, Canada)

Migration[1]

One cannot not speak of the scandals of an epoch. One cannot not espouse a cause. One cannot not be summoned by an obligation of fidelity.

—Hélène Cixous

In Linda Ohama's 1985 silkscreen print *Watari Dori/Bird of Passage*, the Sansei (third generation) Japanese Canadian artist from southern Alberta uses 23 individual layers of screens to overlay and blend together memories through subtle textures and colours. She uses blurred images—portraits and photographs—of her own family to represent the suffering of the different generations—Issei, Nisei, and Sansei. Uprooted from their West Coast homes in 1942, evacuated and interned during World War Two, thousands of Japanese Canadians endured the political and social stigmas that came with being labeled "enemy alien." The muted hues of the piece reflect, in the artist's words, "the softened voice of Japanese Canadians. We often feel very deeply but rarely shout out in a loud voice" (Artist Statement, 1985). *Watari Dori*, with its mixed images of a sacred crane in flight, newspaper text recounting the events of evacuation, and childhood photographs, brings together past and present generations towards a mixed-generation future. It portrays the artist's dual East/West sensibilities and points to signs of struggle larger than this individual's family history:

---

[1] A different version of this essay was presented under the title "Watari Dori" as part of a performance session on "The Credible and the Incredible in Autobiographical Research: A Canadian Curriculum Métissage" with Cynthia Chambers, Wanda Hurren, Carl Leggo, and Antoinette Ober, at the American Educational Research Association (AERA) Annual Conference in San Diego, California, in April 2004.

> Begin with a "picture bride" in a new found wilderness filled
> with salmon-haunted rivers of the pacific littoral. add a ravaged
> dream of a gold mountain. two world wars & unspoken night-
> mares of bereftments. begin. again. let the years swiftly pass.let
> them pass into the shape of a grown woman who carries an im-
> ageof her grandmother embedded in her...the two of them speak
> a single tongue, one that would tear away. all the abysmal years
> of silences. (Kiyooka, n.d.)

For Linda Ohama, *watari dori* constitutes a way of expressing the courage and inspiration as well as the pain of her grandparents' and parents' generations. A mother of three fourth-generation or yonsei daughters, her work speaks of the mindfulness of the currents of change in each generation, the bonds and differences created by memories both silenced and articulated.

For myself, mother of one fourth-generation daughter of mixed Japanese Canadian German heritage, *watari dori* signifies the mixed emotions of hope and fear that are part of my own and my Japanese Canadian German family's migration and immigration. The crane in flight conjures up images of the patterns of leaving and returning that have been part of my own life for so long, both forced and voluntary, that are not ever a comfortable flight. "...[T]he great fear is that departure is the state of being abandoned, even though it is you who leave," Edward Said (1999/2000, p. 414) reminds me while I try to keep alive the memory of my relations and the stories of the places they grew from in the face of a new generation's reshaping of the past. I think of my daughter whose heritage spans two races and three continents, and I wonder how she will braid the métissage of stories out of old and new geographies and genealogies. As she begins her own journey into teaching, the career she has chosen, her *currere* is already shaped by the mixed stories of her lineage. Born and raised in Vancouver, the curriculum she creates in her classroom will be seemingly simply Canadian—and yet connected to other origins of race and place, measuring the distance between Hiroshima and Berlin, alive with the memory of difficult uneasy imperfect stories, reinterpreting them with grace, courage, determination and fidelity. The passage of *Watari Dori* is impermanent and hopeful at the same time. Returning year after year, generation after generation, to a place of birth and beginning, we long to link with these migratory creatures in flight, returning home because of something deep inside, only to leave again...

References

Cixous, H. Cixous, H. (1991). *"Coming to writing" and other essays*. Cambridge, MA: Harvard University Press.

Kiyooka, R. (n.d.). *Celebration of Ohama, the artist*. Retrieved February 28, 2004 from http://www.whitepinepictures.com/seeds/i/8/biography.html

Said, E. W. (1999/2000). On writing a memoir. In M. Bayoumi & A. Rubin (Eds.), *The Edward Said reader* (pp. 399-415). New York: Vintage Books.

Aristi Born (Universität Magdeburg, Deutschland)

Zur Rolle der personalen Identität in aktuellen Transformationen

Abstract
Our world, with its variable social and cultural conditions, is rich in transformation and requests us to regulate our personal identity. This is a lifelong process, which is enforced when people have to cope with critical life events that break the routines of everyday life, e.g. incisive experiences due to the German reunification. Based on a coping-model, which combines the transactional stress theory of Richard S. Lazarus with the Ego identity status approach of James E. Marcia, this article presents two empirical studies. The first study concentrates on inhabitants of three East and three West-German „twin villages", which are situated very closely to each other, but which were separated by the wall. It reveals East-West-differences with regard to their identity diffusion, a status characterized by low exploration and lose commitments. In the second study, the adaptivity of a diffuse identity status is examined more specifically relating to coping and subjective well-being. For this study a questionnaire, which operationalizes four different subgroups of diffusion was constructed and distributed to 372 students in Magdeburg. The article concludes that it is worth to go on studying personal identity as a resource for coping with transformational change.

Einleitung

Der Künstler, Psychoanalytiker und Harvard Professor of Human Development Erik H. Erikson bezeichnete 1959 die Entwicklung einer personalen Identität als psychosoziale Entwicklung und betonte somit bereits die Wechselwirkung zwischen Individuum und Gesellschaft. Er definierte Identität als „unmittelbare Wahrnehmung der eigenen Gleichheit und Kontinuität in der Zeit [...] und die damit verbundene Wahrnehmung, dass auch andere diese Gleichheit und Kontinuität erkennen." (1959/1998, S. 18). Identität zeitübergreifend und in unterschiedlichen Kontexten zu wahren und zu regulieren ist eine zentrale Aufgabe für jedes Individuum, besonders in aktuellen Transformationskontexten, die über die Zeit und verschiedene Situationen hinweg eine Mannigfaltigkeit an Identitätsprojekten ermöglichen und dennoch vom Individuum verlangen, aus der Vielfalt eine Einheit zu schaffen.

Dieser Beitrag fokussiert das Zusammenwirken von personaler Identität und der Bewältigung aktueller Transformationsanforderungen. Aus einer Verbindung der transaktionalen Stresstheorie nach Richard S. Lazarus mit der Identitätsforschung in der Tradition von James E. Marcia wird ein Modell zur Transformationsbewältigung konzipiert. Basierend auf dem Bewältigungsmodell werden im empirischen Teil dieses Beitrags zwei Studien vorgestellt, die das Zusammenwirken von Identität, Transformationsbewältigung und Wohlbefinden näher untersuchen. Für die erste Studie wurden in je drei ost- und westdeutschen „Zwillingsdörfern", die in unmittelbarer Nähe zur ehemaligen innerdeutschen Grenze liegen, 59 Frauen und Männer zwischen 16 und 72 Jahren befragt. Es zeigen sich höhere Diffusionswerte der Ostdeutschen, die bezüglich ihrer Adaptivität im Bewältigungsprozess diskutiert werden, von dem die Ostdeutschen nachweislich stärker betroffen sind als ihre westdeutschen Nachbarn. Die Adaptivität der Identitätsdiffusion wird in einer zweiten Studie genauer untersucht. Im Zuge einer Befragung von 372 Studierenden in Magdeburg wurde ein Fragebogen zur Erfassung von vier Diffusionsformen konzipiert und untersucht, inwieweit die vier Unterformen mit Wohlbefindensvariablen zusammenhängen. Abschließend wird diskutiert, inwieweit personale Identität als eine Ressource bei der Bewältigung aktueller Transformationsprozesse angesehen werden kann.

Identität als Ressource
Gesellschaftliche Transformationsprozesse, bleiben nicht ohne Einfluss auf die Identität. Veränderte Lebensumstände und -umwelten, aus den Fugen geratene Alltagsroutinen sowie neue Perspektiven stellen das eigene Selbstverständnis infrage. Gravierende Einschnitte in den Lebenslauf, die mit den unmittelbar verfügbaren Handlungsressourcen und -routinen nicht bewältigt werden können, bezeichnet Filipp (1995) als *kritische Lebensereignisse*. Angesichts der deutschen Vereinigung erlebten viele Menschen vor allem jene kritischen Lebensereignisse, die im Lebenslauf der Person nicht normativ vorhersehbar waren, wie z.B. Handlungs- und Entwicklungsmöglichkeiten in der aktuellen Lebenssituation als unvereinbar mit den von ihnen verfolgten Lebenszielen und Identitätsprojekten. Dieses Diskrepanzerleben musste bewältigt und in eine neue Balance gebracht werden.

Gerade in der Auseinandersetzung mit Umwelt und Selbst liegen aber auch die Chancen für eine regulierte, *dynamische Identität*, mit der man sich wohl fühlen kann. Whitbourne (1982) befasst sich in ihrem Modell mit der Identitätsregulation durch emotionale, soziale und intellektuelle Erfahrungen. Bei der Identitätsassimilation werden neue Erfahrungen so wahrgenommen, dass sie in das Raster der vorhandenen Identitätsstruktur passen. Bei der Identitätsakkomodation hingegen wird die vorhandene Identitätsstruktur den neuen Erfahrungen angepasst; die Identität durchwirkt jedoch nicht die Erfahrungen, so dass diese nicht persönlich interpretiert werden können.

Whitbourne (1996) hält die *Ausgewogenheit der akkomodativen und assimilativen Prozesse* für bedeutsam, wenn es um eine gesunde Identitätsregulation geht.

Gelingt es Personen, ein Gleichgewicht zwischen den beiden Mechanismen der Differenzierung aufrechtzuerhalten, können sie sowohl neue Erfahrungen induktiv in ihre Selbst-Theorie integrieren, als auch deduktiv ihre Identitätskonzeption zur Erfahrungsstrukturierung nutzen. Identität wird somit zu einer Ressource, die mitentscheidet, ob kritische Lebensereignisse als bedrohlich oder herausfordernd eingeschätzt werden, welche Bewältigungsstrategie verfolgt wird und wie wohl man sich in der veränderten Situation fühlt.

Das Identitätsstatuskonzept

Basierend auf Eriksons Ansatz der psychosozialen Entwicklung konzipiert Marcia (1993a, 1993b) die Identitätsentwicklung als einen Wechsel von *empirisch zugänglichen Identitätszuständen*. Mit seinem bereits 1966 entwickelten Ego I-dentity Status Approach ebnete er damit den Weg für eine empirische Überprüfung der Ressourcenfunktion der personalen Identität. In seiner Operationalisierung unterscheidet Marcia je nach Bestehen bzw. Nicht-Bestehen einer inneren Verpflichtung und dem Vorhandensein bzw. Ausbleiben kritischer Exploration vier Identitätszustände.

Tab. 1: Die vier Identitätszustände nach Marcia

	kritische Exploration	keine kritische Exploration
innere Verpflichtung	erarbeitete Identität	übernommene Identität
keine innere Verpflichtung	Moratorium	Diffusion

Im Zustand der übernommenen Identität orientiert man sich an Standpunkten, die man von den Eltern oder dem familiären Umfeld übernommen und nicht in kritischer Auseinandersetzung erworben hat. Man fühlt sich diesen Standpunkten gegenüber verpflichtet, und sie strukturieren, z.B. in politischer oder religiöser Hinsicht, die Erfahrungswelt. Im diffusen Zustand fehlt die innere Verpflichtung gegenüber bestimmten Orientierungen. Statt sich kritisch mit verschiedenen Standpunkten auseinanderzusetzen, lässt sich das Individuum im „Meer der Möglichkeiten" treiben. Anders im Moratorium: Hier hadert man mit verschiedenen Sichtweisen und versucht, sich aktiv im „Alternativendickicht" zu orientieren. Diese explorative Auseinandersetzung wird oft als Krise erlebt, man fühlt sich hin und her gerissen und kann sich nicht entscheiden. Im Zustand der erarbeiteten Identität ist man in aktiver Auseinandersetzung mit unterschiedlichen

172

Standpunkten zu eigenen Überzeugungen gelangt, die einem helfen, die Erfahrungswelt zu strukturieren. Man kann sich bezüglich verschiedener Lebensbereiche in unterschiedlichen Identitätszuständen befinden, und der Weg von jedem Identitätszustand in einen anderen steht ein Leben lang offen. Auch Marcia betont somit den selbstkonstruierten, dynamischen Aspekt der Identität.

Die Identitätsdiffusion

1989 stellt Marcia fest, dass der Anteil junger Menschen mit diffuser Identität seit 1984 von zuvor 20% auf 40% angestiegen ist. Er plädiert dafür, den Identitätsstatus der Diffusion differenzierter zu betrachten. In zahlreichen Interviews findet er eine Untergruppe, die er "kulturell adaptive Diffusion" nennt, womit er auf die Passung zwischen dem indifferenten Subjekt und den Unverbindlichkeit fordernden gesellschaftlichen Bedingungen eingeht. Ferner unterscheidet er die "sorglos Diffusen" von den "gestört Diffusen". Der Gleichgültigkeit der "sorglos Diffusen" steht die soziale Isolation und der Ressourcenmangel der "gestört Diffusen" gegenüber, die Marcia (1989) als pathologisch bezeichnet. Für eine vierte Untergruppe stellt die Diffusion ein "Durchgangsstadium" auf dem Weg zur "erfolgreichen" Identitätsfindung dar. Kraus und Mitzscherlich (1995) haben in einem Projekt 150 Jugendliche in Bayern und Sachsen einem teilstrukturierten Interview zu Erwerbsverläufen, sozialen Netzwerken und ihrer Identitätsentwicklung unterzogen. In der Auswertung der Antworten konnten sie die vier von Marcia (1989) benannten Unterformen wiederfinden. Beide Arbeiten dienten als Grundlage für die *Entwicklung eines Fragebogens zur Erfassung der vier Diffusionsformen*, die sich wie folgt näher beschreiben lassen:

⇒ *Sorglos Diffuse oder Surfer im Meer der Möglichkeiten:*

gleiten dahin mit ständiger Positionskorrektur, ästhetische und hedonistische Motive ("gefällt mir eben!", "macht einfach Spaß!"), hohe soziale Fähigkeiten, viele Kontakte, sozial anerkannt/attraktiv, oberflächlich, innerlich leer, ideal für kurzfristige Beziehungen und -Denken.

⇒ *Gestört Diffuse oder Verlorene im Meer der Möglichkeiten:*

ohne Richtung und commitment, geben sich rat- und hilflos, Ressourcenmangel, konfliktbelastete Einzelgänger, suchen Trost in Engagement in Hobbys was sie ausmacht, steht nicht integriert nebeneinander; Diffusion à la Erikson.

⇒ *Kulturell adaptiv Diffuse oder Fischer im Meer der Möglichkeiten:*

nehmen etwas auf, ohne sich innerlich festzulegen; heute hier, morgen da, wenn es die gesellschaftlichen Verhältnisse verlangen, könnten auch anders; Exploration ja, aber ohne Krisenerleben; flexibel, anpassungsfähig, "jump at the first opportunity", ressourcenreich

⇒ *Durchgangsdiffuse oder Transitreisende im Meer der Möglichkeiten:*
haben diverse Überzeugungen, aber noch unentschieden; undeutliche Standpunkte, fehlende Verbindlichkeit, im Unterschied zum Moratorium kein Krisenempfinden, unkritisches Hadern ohne Leidensdruck, zunehmende Reflexion über eigene Überzeugungen, alterstypisch für junge Menschen am Übergang zum Erwachsenenalter.

Nach Erikson (1959/1998), bezeichnet die Identitätsdiffusion den negativen Gegenpol der Identitätsbildung. Gelingt es dem Individuum demnach nicht, Gegensätze innerhalb des erlebten und sozial vermittelten Selbst sowie über die Zeit hinweg zu integrieren, diffundieren die unvereinbaren Elemente. Aus heutiger Sicht wirkt diese Aufteilung normativ und einseitig. Der Gefahr der Identitätsdiffusion auf der einen Seite steht die *Gefahr einer erstarrten Identität* auf der anderen Seite gegenüber (vgl. Krappmann 1997). Im Spannungsfeld zwischen den dynamischen Polen Identitätsbildung und Identitätsdiffusion muss während des ganzen Lebens immer wieder neu eine individuelle Lösung entwickelt werden, die beide Pole integriert. Während Erikson für eine gefestigte Identitätsstruktur plädiert, betont Krappmann (2000) das Gestaltungspotential, das Diskrepanzen und Diskontinuitäten bieten. Seiner Meinung nach braucht der Mensch Divergenz und Wandel, um sich als eigenständiges Individuum zu etablieren. Er hält das Individuum für belastbarer, "wenn seine Identifikationen weniger fest sind, so dass ihm Spielraum und Distanz bleibt und damit ein Potential verfügbar wird, Konflikte aufzuarbeiten oder sich mit ihnen zu arrangieren." (Krappmann 2000, S. 92).

In der Diffusion fehlt sowohl das kritische Explorieren identitätsrelevanter Überzeugungen und das Hadern mit alternativen Standpunkten als auch die innere Verpflichtung gegenüber bestimmten Orientierungen. Statt sich kritisch mit verschiedenen Alternativen auseinanderzusetzen, lässt sich das Individuum im "Meer der Möglichkeiten" treiben. Marcia (1993a) beschreibt die Diffusion als einen relativ stabilen Zustand mit geringem Entwicklungspotential. Die Stabilität und Zunahme des diffusen Identitätszustands könnte man damit erklären, dass die Struktur- und Orientierungslosigkeit in transformationsreichen Zeiten durchaus *adaptiv* sein kann (vgl. Keupp 1997; Kraus/Mitzscherlich 1995).

174

Das Transformationsbewältigungsmodell

Für alle vier Identitätszustände wird postuliert, dass sie einen Einfluss auf die Bewältigung gesellschaftlicher Transformationserfahrungen haben (vgl. Born 2002). Transformationserfahrungen werden hier als kritische Lebensereignisse dargestellt, wie sie z.b. infolge der Wiedervereinigung in Deutschland erlebt wurden. Dieses Modell ließe sich auch auf andere Transformationskontexte sowie Migrationserfahrungen anwenden.

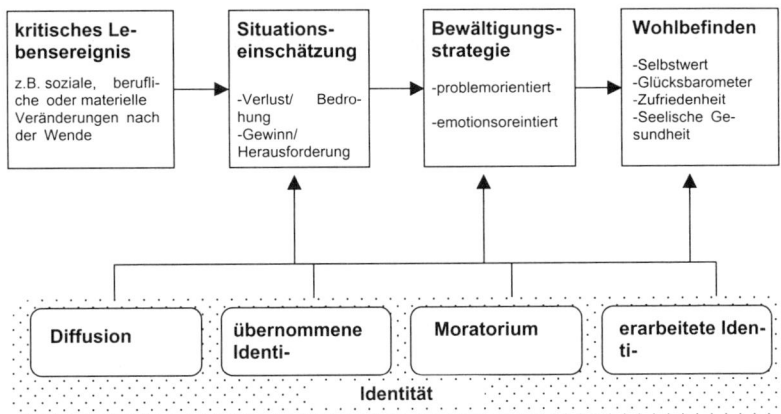

Abb. 2: Identitätseinflüsse auf die Transformationsbewältigung (Born, 2002)

Das Modell basiert auf der *transaktionalen Stresstheorie nach Lazarus* (vgl. Lazarus/Folkman, 1984; 1987). Demnach haben kritische Veränderungen im Zuge der Wiedervereinigung nicht unmittelbar Einfluss auf das Wohlbefinden. Vielmehr ist es entscheidend, ob man seine momentane Situation als verlustbringende Bedrohung oder aber als gewinnbringende Herausforderung einschätzt und ob man eher emotions- oder problemorientierte Strategien wählt, um sich mit der Situation auseinanderzusetzen (vgl. Jerusalem 1990). Objektive Veränderungen, beispielsweise ein Arbeitsplatzverlust oder Wohnortwechsel nach der Wende, liegen den kognitiven Einschätzungen zwar zugrunde, doch werden diese von einer Reihe weiterer Variablen beeinflusst. In der Stressforschung wird hier neben sozialen und ökonomischen Rahmenbedingungen wie der finanziellen Situation oder dem sozialen Netzwerk besonders die Ressourcenlage einer Person (erwartete soziale Unterstützung, Selbstwirksamkeitserwartung) fokussiert (vgl. Lazarus/Folkman 1987; Schwarzer 1996). In diesem Beitrag werden die Einflüsse der Identität auf den Bewältigungsprozess und das Wohlbefinden einbezogen. Identität wird über das Identitätsstatuskonzept nach Marcia (Marcia 1993a) operationalisiert. Das Modell dient als Grundlage für die nun folgenden zwei Studien.

Studie 1: Identität und Transformationsbewältigung in ost- und westdeutschen „Zwillingsdörfern"

Studie 1 untersucht Zusammenhänge zwischen den Identitätszuständen nach Marcia, der Bewältigung und dem Wohlbefinden in je drei *ost- und westdeutschen Zwillingsdörfern*. Die Dörfer liegen in unmittelbarer Nachbarschaft in Sachsen-Anhalt bzw. Niedersachsen und gehörten, von 1961 bis 1989 durch die innerdeutsche Grenze getrennt, unterschiedlichen gesellschaftspolitischen Systemen an. Es handelt sich hier um eine sehr spezifische Stichprobe, die gewählt wurde, weil die Transformationsprozesse im Zuge der Wiedervereinigung in den grenznahen ost-westdeutschen Dorfpaaren Hanum-Zasenbeck, Böckwitz-Zicherie und Döhren-Mackendorf sicherlich unmittelbar erlebt werden konnten. In dieser Studie soll überprüft werden, ob das Transformationsgeschehen seit der Wende in den ostdeutschen Dörfern starker in das Leben der Menschen eingegriffen hat als in den westdeutschen Nachbardörfern, und ob sich dies in einer unterschiedlichen Identitätsstatuszugehörigkeit widerspiegelt. Diesbezüglich lassen sich folgende Hypothesen formulieren:

Hypothesen

• Ostdeutsche waren und sind stärker von den gesellschaftlichen Umbrüchen in Deutschland betroffen als Westdeutsche.

• Ost- und Westdeutsche setzen sich unterschiedlich kritisch und verbindlich mit Standpunkten in identitätsrelevanten Bereichen auseinander.

• Die Identitätszustände haben Einfluss auf die Transformationsbewältigung und das Wohlbefinden.

Stichprobe und Untersuchungsdurchführung

In die Analysen gehen die 1997 gewonnenen Daten von 59 Einwohnern zwischen 16 und 72 Jahren aus je drei ost- (N = 20) und westdeutschen (N = 39) Zwillingsdörfern ein. Die Ost-West-Verteilung 1/3 zu 2/3 entspricht dem Größenverhältnis der Dörfer zueinander und spiegelt keine geringere Rücklaufrate in den ostdeutschen Dörfern wider. Die drei ostdeutschen Dörfer hatten nach Auskunft der zuständigen Einwohnermeldeämter im Untersuchungsjahr 1997 239 (Döhren), 199 (Hanum) und 97 (Böckwitz) Einwohner, die westdeutschen Nach-

bardörfer hatten 382 (Zasenbeck), 333 (Mackendorf) und 300 (Zicherie) Einwohner. Die Probanden lebten vor und nach der Wende in einem der Dörfer. Ost-West- oder West-Ost-Wechsler wurden nicht mit in die Analysen einbezogen. Das Geschlechterverhältnis war in der Ost- (45% Männer, 55% Frauen) und Weststichprobe (54% Männer, 46% Frauen) annähernd ausgeglichen. Der Altersmittelwert lag in beiden Teilstichproben bei 43,3 Jahren. Die Standardabweichung betrug in der Oststichprobe 16,3 Jahre, in der Weststichprobe 15,0 Jahre. In der Weststichprobe hatten sieben Personen (18% der Teilstichprobe) das Abitur sowie 32 Personen (82%) einen Haupt- oder Realschulabschluss. Einen entsprechenden Abschluss bzw. einen Abschluss der Polytechnischen Oberschule hatten in der ostdeutschen Teilstichprobe 13 Personen (65%), das Abitur machten drei Personen (15%), und vier Personen (20%) verfügten über keinen der genannten Schulabschlüsse. In beiden Teilstichproben verfügten annähernd 50% der Teilnehmer über bis zu 3500 DM monatliches Haushaltsnettoeinkommen, die übrigen Teilnehmer erhielten ein höheres Einkommen. In den ostdeutschen Dörfern lebten durchschnittlich 3,1 Personen in einem Haushalt, in den westdeutschen Dörfern 3,2 Personen. Von den 20 ostdeutschen Teilnehmern waren 14 verheiratet (70%), drei ledig (15%), zwei geschieden (10%) und eine Person (5%) verwitwet. Bei den 39 westdeutschen Teilnehmern zeigte sich folgende Verteilung bzgl. des Familienstandes: 26 waren verheiratet (67%), neun ledig (23%), zwei geschieden (5%), und zwei Personen waren verwitwet (5%).
Zunächst wurden alle Einwohner ab 16 Jahren per Brief über das Untersuchungsvorhaben informiert. Die angekündigte *Stichprobenrekrutierung* erfolgte persönlich vor Ort. Die interessierten Personen erhielten einen Fragebogen, den sie zu Hause ausfüllen und im frankierten Rückumschlag einsenden konnten. Nicht angetroffenen Personen wurde ein Fragebogen mit Rückumschlag im Briefkasten hinterlegt.

Beschreibung der Messinstrumente
Die Veränderungen seit der Wende wurden in Anlehnung an H.D. Mummendeys „Liste der Lebensereignisse" von 1995 operationalisiert. Erfragt wurden 14 *kritische Lebensereignisse* (z.B. Arbeitsplatzverlust seit der Wende) und biografische Änderungsmerkmale (z.B. andere Freunde als vor der Wende), deren Auftreten bzw. Nichtauftreten festgestellt wurde.
In Anlehnung an Jerusalem (Jerusalem, 1990) wurden die Pbn zusätzlich gebeten, ihre *momentane Lebenssituation* hinsichtlich der Aspekte Herausforderung („Ich finde meine jetzige Lebenssituation aufregend, weil ständig neue Anforderungen auf mich zukommen."), Gewinn („Ich profitiere von neuen Erfahrungen."), Bedrohung („Ich fürchte, mit Neuem nicht zurechtzukommen.") und Ver-

lust („Ich habe den Mut verloren, da alles nur schlimmer geworden ist.") einzuschätzen. Die Aspekte Herausforderung (drei Items) und Gewinn (zwei Items)
wurden mit der eindimensionalen Skala „positive Situationseinschätzung", die
Aspekte Bedrohung (vier Items) und Verlust (vier Items) mit der ebenfalls eindimensionalen Skala „negative Situationseinschätzung" erfasst.

Bei der *Stressbewältigung* (vgl. Jerusalem 1990) wurde mit je vier Items unterschieden zwischen problemorientierter Bewältigung („Ich setze mich mit meinen
Problemen auseinander, bis sie gelöst sind.") und emotionaler Bewältigung („Ich
lenke mich irgendwie ab."). Das subjektive *Wohlbefinden* wurde mittels vier
Verfahren operationalisiert, die sich in einer repräsentativen Ost-West-Studie von
Schmitt, Maes und Schmal (1995;1997) bewährt haben. Das Selbstwertgefühl
wurde über die deutsche Übersetzung der Rosenberg Self-Esteem Scale von Janich und Boll (1982) gemessen. Die Beantwortung der zehn Items (Bsp.: „Ich
glaube, dass ich eine Menge Stärken habe.") erfolgte auf einer sechsstufigen Likert-Skala. Das Konstrukt seelische Gesundheit wurde über die gleichnamige
Skala des Trierer Persönlichkeitsfragebogens von Becker (1989) erhoben. 18
Aussagen (Bsp.: „Ich fühle mich voller Energie und Tatkraft.") mussten hinsichtlich vier Häufigkeitsangaben (nie, manchmal, oft, immer) unter der Eingangsfra-
ge „Wie erleben Sie sich?" beurteilt werden. Als kognitiv-evaluatives Maß des
Wohlbefindens wurde die Lebenszufriedenheitsskala nach Fahrenberg verwendet
(vgl. Fahrenberg/Myrtek/Wilk/Kreutel 1986). Für die vorliegende Untersuchung
wurden die durch jeweils fünf Items repräsentierten Bereiche Arbeit und Beruf,
finanzielle Lage, mitmenschliche Situation und gesundheitliche Situation ausgewählt. Auf einer sechsstufigen Likert-Skala sollten die Probanden beispielsweise
angeben, wie zufrieden sie mit ihren Freundschaften sind.

Das *Identitätsstatus-Konzept* nach Marcia für die Bereiche Religion, Politik,
Weltanschauung, Freizeit und Freundschaft wurde über den ADAMS-
Identitätsstatus-Fragebogen (vgl. Kapfhammer 1995), einer deutschen Übersetzung des EOMEIS (Extended Objective Measure of Ego Identity Status) (vgl.
Bennion/Adams 1986), erfasst. Jeder der vier Identitätszustände wurde in den
fünf genannten Inhaltsbereichen mittels zweier Items gemessen, so dass das a-
daptierte Messinstrument aus 40 Items bestand, die auf einer fünfstufigen Likert-
Skala beantwortet wurden. Für den Bereich Politik soll für jeden Identitätsstatus
ein Beispiel genannt werden: „In politischen Dingen denke ich ziemlich dasselbe
wie mein familiäres Umfeld. Ich wähle dieselbe Partei usw.." = übernommene
Identität; „Im Grunde habe ich mich nie um Politik gekümmert. Politik ödet mich
nur an." = Diffusion; „Ich bin mir über meine politische Haltung nicht im Klaren;
aber ich versuche herauszufinden, wo ich stehe und was ich politisch denke." =
Moratorium sowie „Ich habe mir meine politischen Ansichten gründlich überlegt;

und ich lehne manches, wenn auch nicht alles, von dem ab, was mein familiäres Umfeld politisch denkt." = erarbeitete Identität.

Ergebnisse

Die signifikanten *Ost-West-Unterschiede* im Erleben kritischer Lebensereignisse, die mittels χ^2-Tests mit Kontinuitäts-Korrektur nach Yates festgestellt wurden, verdeutlicht Tabelle 2. Die absoluten Zahlen zeigen, ergänzt durch die prozentualen Häufigkeitsangaben in Klammern, wie viele Personen die Frage nach den entsprechenden *Veränderungen seit der Wiedervereinigung* positiv beantwortet haben. Die Ergebnisse in Tabelle 2 machen deutlich, dass der gesellschaftliche Umbruch für die Ostdeutschen mit mehr Veränderungen im beruflichen und finanziellen Bereich einhergegangen ist. Aber auch Lebensgewohnheiten, Tagesablauf und Wohnsituation haben sich besonders in den ostdeutschen Dörfern verändert:

Tab. 2: Veränderungen seit der Wende in den Zwillingsdörfern

	Ost	West	
	(N = 20)	(N = 39)	
Sind Sie seit der Wende in eine andere Wohnung oder in ein anderes Haus gezogen?	11 (55%)	9 (23%)	*
Hat sich Ihr gewöhnlicher Tagesablauf seit der Wende verändert?	14 (70%)	7 (18%)	**
Haben sich bei Ihnen seit der Wende irgendwelche Lebensgewohnheiten (z.B. Essensgewohnheiten oder Hobbys) geändert?	11 (55%)	4 (10%)	**
Hat bei Ihnen seit November 1989 ein Stellen-, Berufswechsel oder Berufs(wieder-)eintritt stattgefunden, oder haben Sie an einer Umschulung teilgenommen?	12 (60%)	10 (26%)	**
Hat sich Ihre finanzielle Situation seit der Wende verändert?	18 (90%)	14 (36%)	**
Haben Sie im Zeitraum ab November 1989 Ihren Arbeitsplatz verloren oder keine passende Stelle gefunden?	9 (45%)	4 (10%)	**

Anmerkung: $* p < .05$; $** p < .01$.

Obwohl Ostdeutsche häufiger kritische Lebensereignisse erlebt haben als ihre westdeutschen Nachbarn, belegen t-Tests für unabhängige Gruppen mit Blick auf die drei *Wohlbefinden*smessinstrumente lediglich einen Ost-West-Unterschied bezüglich der Gesamtskala Zufriedenheit: Ostdeutsche sind mit einem Mittelwert von 3.31 (SD = .62) auf dem 1%-Niveau signifikant unzufriedener als ihre westdeutschen Nachbarn, die einen Mittelwert von 3.84 (SD = .56) aufweisen. Ein signifikanter Zusammenhang meint im Folgenden, dass die Irrtumswahrscheinlichkeit für dieses Ergebnis unter 5% (p < .05) bzw. sogar unter 1% (p < .01) liegt.

Betrachtet man die einzelnen Unterskalen der Zufriedenheitsskala, sind Ostdeutsche signifikant unzufriedener mit ihrer finanziellen Situation als Westdeutsche. Bezogen auf die Fragen zur seelischen Gesundheit, zum Selbstwert, zur Situationseinschätzung und zu den Bewältigungsstrategien zeigen sich keine signifikanten Ost-West-Unterschiede.

Es zeigen sich jedoch signifikante Ost-West-Unterschiede bezogen auf die Identität: Die Varianz der Messwerte zur *Identitätsstatuszugehörigkeit* für die Bereiche Religion, Politik und allgemeiner Lebensstil lässt sich in einer multivariaten Varianzanalyse zu 20% durch Ost-West-Unterschiede erklären ($F_{(1/48)}$ = 2.76; p < .05; η^2 = 20%). Deutliche signifikante univariate Effekte sind bezogen auf den Zustand der Diffusion festzustellen. Ostdeutsche haben hier, verglichen mit ihren westdeutschen Nachbarn, die höheren Werte ($F_{(1/48)}$ = 8.63; p < .01; η^2 = 15%). Auch für das Alter ergibt sich ein signifikanter multivariater Haupteffekt ($F_{(1/48)}$ = 3.82; p < .01; η^2 = 25%). Die univariaten Analysen zeigen, dass Probanden bis einschließlich 40 Jahre (Mediansplit) geringere Werte bezüglich übernommener Identität ($F_{(1/48)}$ = 4.65; p < .05; η^2 = 9%) und höhere Diffusionswerte als die über 40-Jährigen ($F_{(1/48)}$ = 8.41; p < .01; η^2 = 15%) haben. Ein signifikanter multivariater Interaktionseffekt zwischen den beiden Variablen Alter und Ost-West-Zugehörigkeit ist ebenfalls zu finden ($F_{(1/48)}$ = 3.41; p < .05; η^2 = 23%). Bei den Ostdeutschen haben die bis 40-Jährigen in den univariaten Analysen niedrigere Werte als die über 40-Jährigen bezüglich erarbeiteter Identität ($F_{(1/48)}$ = 5.09; p < .05; η^2 = 10%), bei den Westdeutschen ist das Altersverhältnis umgekehrt. Die Diffusion hingegen ist bei den bis 40-jährigen Ostdeutschen deutlich höher als bei den über 40-jährigen Ostdeutschen ($F_{(1/48)}$ = 4.90; p < .05; η^2 = 9%), bei den Westdeutschen geht der Alterseffekt in die gleiche Richtung, ist aber signifikant geringer. Betrachtet man die *Identitätsbereiche Freundschaft und Freizeit*, sind keine multi- oder univariaten Ost-West-Unterschiede zu entdecken.

Um die *Zusammenhänge zwischen den Identitätszuständen, den Bewältigungs-und Wohlbefindensskalen* zu untersuchen, wurden Korrelationskoeffizienten nach Pearson (r) berechnet. Genannt werden nur die signifikanten Ergebnisse (* p < *.05; ** p < .0*). Der Korrelationskoeffizient (*r*) kann zwischen -1.0 und $+1.0$ variieren. 0 bedeutet keinerlei Zusammenhang. Bei *r*=±.10 spricht man von einem schwachen, bei *r*=±.30 von einem mittleren und ab *r*=±.50 von einem starken Zusammenhang (vgl. Cohen 1988).

Je höher die Diffusionswerte umso geringer die Zufriedenheit (r = -.32*) und das aktive Bewältigen (r = -.31*) und umso intensiver wird die eigene Situation als verlustbringende Bedrohung eingeschätzt (r = .32*).

Die erarbeitete Identität korreliert tendenziell positiv mit den Bewältigungs- und Wohlbefindensvariablen sowie mit einer Einschätzung der aktuellen Situation als herausfordernde Chance. Die Koeffizienten sind jedoch nicht signifikant.

Je höher die Moratoriumswerte umso geringer die seelische Gesundheit (Selbstwert: r = -.43**, seelische Gesundheit: r = -.53**, Zufriedenheit r = -.32*) und umso intensiver wird die eigene Situation als verlustbringende Bedrohung eingeschätzt (r = .51**). Personen mit hohen Moratoriumswerten bewältigen Anforderungen stärker emotional (r = .41**) und weniger aktiv (r = -.36**).

Die übernommene Identität korreliert durchweg gering mit Bewältigung und Wohlbefinden.

Diskussion

Die Ergebnisse verdeutlichen, dass der gesellschaftliche Umbruch nach der Wende erwartungsgemäß für die Ostdeutschen mit mehr Veränderungen im beruflichen und finanziellen Bereich einhergegangen ist. Aber auch Lebensgewohnheiten, Tagesablauf und Wohnsituation haben sich besonders in den ostdeutschen Dörfern verändert. Dabei handelt es sich um wichtige Bestimmungskomponenten der persönlichen Identität, so dass *Transformationsbewältigung und Identitätsarbeit für Ostdeutsche eine besondere Relevanz* besitzen.

Obwohl die Menschen in Ostdeutschland von der Transformation stärker betroffen sind und sich für sie die Aufgabe einer kritischen Auseinandersetzung mit sich selbst und ihrer sich wandelnden Umwelt dringlicher stellt als für Westdeutsche, schätzen Erstere ihr *Wohlbefinden nur bezüglich der Zufriedenheit geringer* ein als Letztere. Die geringere Zufriedenheit bezüglich der finanziellen Situation wird auch in anderen Studien berichtet (vgl. Brähler/Richter 1999; Schmitt/Maes/Schmal 1997). Die Zufriedenheit als evaluativ-kognitive Komponente des Wohlbefindens (vgl. Abele/Becker 1991) begründet sich hier auf einer objektiven finanziellen Benachteiligung der Ost- gegenüber den Westdeutschen. So verzeichnet das Statistische Jahrbuch (Statistisches Bundesamt Wiesbaden 1998) für Sachsen-Anhalt ein niedrigeres Haushaltsnettoeinkommen, einen geringeren Bruttostundenverdienst und geringere Spareinlagen als für Niedersachsen. Die Ost-West-Unterschiede auf den Skalen Selbstwert und Seelische Gesundheit werden jedoch nicht signifikant. Dass sich hier keine Ost-West-Differenzen niederschlagen, spricht dafür, dass die Ostdeutschen über Ressourcen verfügen, mit denen sie die intensiveren Transformationsanforderungen bewältigen können.

Betrachtet man nun, wie in dieser Studie, die *Identität als Ressource*, zeigen sich nur bezüglich der Identitätsdiffusion Ost-West-Unterschiede. Ostdeutsche haben höhere Diffusionswerte als ihre westdeutschen Nachbarn. Sie setzen sich, besonders in den Bereichen Politik, Religion und allgemeiner Lebensstil, weniger kritisch mit verschiedenen Standpunkten und Alternativen auseinander. Dieser Identitätsstatus der Struktur- und Orientierungslosigkeit könnte unter aktuellen gesellschaftlichen Bedingungen durchaus adaptiv sein kann (vgl. Marcia 1989; Keupp 1997; Kraus/Mitzscherlich 1995). Da man sich keiner Struktur verpflichtet fühlt, muss man sich auch nicht kritisch mit ihr auseinandersetzen. Wer sich nicht festlegt, riskiert auch nicht, bei der nächsten gesellschaftlichen Veränderung entwurzelt und aus der Bahn geworfen zu werden. Man kann flexibel auf sich ändernde Umweltbedingungen reagieren, ohne erst lange Standpunkte überdenken zu müssen.

Dass die bis 40-Jährigen höhere *Diffusion*swerte haben als die über 40-Jährigen, ist hypothesenkonform und spricht einerseits dafür, Diffusion als Durchgangsstadium auf dem Weg zu einer reifen erarbeiteten Identität zu begreifen (vgl. Goossens 1995), andererseits kann das Ergebnis aber auch unter adaptiven Gesichtspunkten betrachtet werden. Die bis 40-Jährigen sehen sich einer Vielzahl von Alternativen und möglichen Lebenswegen gegenüber. In dieser Altersgruppe ist es daher angemessener, sich (noch) nicht festzulegen, als bei den über 40-Jährigen, die viele Entscheidungen schon gefällt haben. Dies trifft besonders für die jüngeren Ostdeutschen zu, die die deutlich höchsten Diffusionswerte aufweisen. Sie wollen sich möglicherweise angesichts des Wendewandels alle Optionen offen halten (vgl. Kraus/ Mitzscherlich 1995). Der signifikante Interaktionseffekt zwischen Alter und Ost-West-Zugehörigkeit lässt sich diesbezüglich wie folgt erklären: Sowohl in West als auch in Ost haben die bis 40-Jährigen hypothesenkonform höhere Diffusionswerte als die über 40-Jährigen. Während sich das Diffusionsniveau bei den Älteren angleicht, klafft es bei den Jüngeren aufgrund des sehr hohen Diffusionswerts der bis 40-jährigen Ostdeutschen signifikant auseinander.

Die Zusammenhänge zwischen hoher Diffusion, geringer Zufriedenheit und geringer aktiver Bewältigung sowie einer ungünstigen Einschätzung der eigenen Situation sprechen aber nicht für die *Adaptivitätsannahme*, dass die Sorglosen und Gleichgültigen sich mit ihrer unverbindlichen und indifferenten Haltung wohl fühlen. Die Ergebnisse sprechen eher für die Theorie von Whitbourne (1982, vgl. Abb.1): Überwiegt im Zustand der übernommenen Identität die Identitätsassimilation, dominiert die Akkomodation. Die Identität wird ständig neuen Erfahrungen angepasst. Das für das Wohlbefinden förderliche, wenn nicht gar erforderliche Gleichgewicht zwischen assimilativen und akkomodativen Prozessen ist also in der Diffusion nicht zu finden.

Die Annahme von der *Identität als Ressource* zeigt sich nicht für alle Zustände, sondern tendenziell nur für die erarbeitete Identität. Die nicht signifikanten Zusammenhänge zwischen übernommener Identität und Wohlbefinden lassen an der Adaptivität dieses Identitätszustands in einer Zeit des sozialen Wandels zweifeln. Übernommene Sicherheiten und Klarheiten haben in einer Zeit der gesellschaftlichen Transformation ihre Passform verloren. So betont auch Keupp (1997), dass heutige Identitätsarbeit infolge gesellschaftlicher Wandlungsprozesse losgelöst von gegebenen Schnittmustern stattfinden muss und Lebensentwürfe in eigener Regie kreiert werden müssen. Das Moratorium erweist sich als Identitätsstatus mit viel Exploration und hohem aktuellen Krisenerleben, der aktuell negative Zusammenhänge zu Transformationsbewältigung und Wohlbefinden aufweist und wahrscheinlich eher langfristig positive Effekte hat, wenn die kritische Auseinandersetzung zu einem höheren Gleichgewicht führt. Dies wäre in Längsschnittuntersuchungen von individuellen Statusübergängen zu prüfen.

Für die *Diffusion* soll die besonders für junge Erwachsene plausible Adaptivitätshypothese nicht verworfen werden, zumal Marcia (1989) einen dramatischen Anstieg der Diffusion bei Studenten beobachtet hat und aufgrund seiner Arbeiten dafür plädiert, die Diffusion differenzierter zu betrachten. Eine differenzierte Operationalisierung und Betrachtung der Diffusion im jungen Erwachsenenalter soll daher in Studie 2 realisiert werden.

Studie 2: Identitätsdiffusion beim Übergang ins Erwachsenenalter

In Studie 2 soll nun der Versuch beschrieben werden, einen Fragebogen zur *Erfassung der vier Diffusionsformen* zu konzipieren. Daran anschließend soll untersucht werden, inwieweit die vier Unterformen mit dem Glauben an die eigene Kompetenz, der Selbstwirksamkeitserwartung, zusammenhängen und ob es unterschiedliche Zusammenhänge zwischen den Diffusionsformen und Wohlbefindensvariablen wie dem Selbstwert und der seelischen Gesundheit gibt. Die Ergebnisse fließen ein in eine abschließende und ausblickende Diskussion der Adaptivität der Diffusion.

Die Einflüsse der gesellschaftlichen Transformation werden in dieser Studie nicht an einem historischen Ereignis, wie der deutsch-deutschen Vereinigung, sondern in ihrer generellen Wirksamkeit betrachtet. Angesichts veränderter gesellschaftlicher Bedingungen in den Industrieländern, wie einer verlängerten Bildungsphase und einer verzögerten Gründung einer Familie, plädiert der US-amerikanische Psychologe Jeffrey J. Arnett (2000) dafür, den *Übergang ins Erwachsenenalter* nicht als kurzweilige Zäsur, sondern als eigenständige Lebensperiode zu betrachten. Auch in Deutschland sind diese veränderten Bedingungen zu verzeichnen. Nach Angaben des Statistischen Bundesamtes (2003; 2004) studieren im Wintersemester 2003/2004 so viele junge Menschen wie nie zuvor. Verglichen mit dem Vorjahr stieg die Zahl der Studierenden um 87.000 auf knapp über zwei Millionen. 35,6% der 20-29-Jährigen haben einen höherwertigen Schulabschluss (Fachhochschul- oder Hochschulzugangsberechtigung), damit sind sie führend vor allen anderen Altersgruppen. Das gemittelte Erstheiratsalter hingegen betrug im Jahr 1990 bei Männern 27,9 und bei Frauen 25,5 Jahre. 2001 heirateten Männer im Durchschnitt erst mit 31,6 und Frauen mit 28,8 Jahren das erste Mal. Das durchschnittliche Alter der Mütter bei der Geburt betrug 2001 29,7 Jahre.

Besonders in Industrieländern heiraten junge Menschen immer später und widmen sich zunächst Ausbildung und/oder Studium, bevor sie eine Familie gründen. Die verlängerte Bildungsphase ermöglicht und verlangt es, unabhängig von sozialen Rollenerwartungen und normativen Erwartungen identitätsrelevante Standpunkte bezüglich Liebe, Freundschaft, Beruf und Weltsicht zu explorieren. "Übergangs-Erwachsene" probieren unterschiedliche Formen des Zusammenlebens und der Liebe aus, sind mobil in Bezug auf ihren Wohnort und oftmals auch bezüglich ihres Studienfaches. Sie befinden sich in einer Lebensphase, in der noch viele Wege gehbar sind. Sowohl Arnett (2000) als auch Kroger (2000) halten die *Bereiche Studium/Beruf und Freundschaft* für zentrale identitätsrelevante Bereiche, in denen junge Menschen sich selbst in Auseinandersetzung mit den gesellschaftlichen Bedingungen behaupten müssen. Ein diffuser Identitätsstatus erscheint unter aktuellen gesellschaftlichen Bedingungen beim Übergang ins Erwachsenenalter besonders adaptiv (vgl. Kraus/Mitzscherlich 1995). Diesbezüglich werden folgende Hypothesen aufgestellt:

Hypothesen

- In der *sorglosen Diffusion* lässt man sich überwiegend treiben. Aufgrund der fehlenden Bereitschaft zur Exploration können daher keine eigenen Kompetenzerfahrungen entwickelt werden. Marcia (1993a, 1993b) schreibt der Diffusion eine externale Kontrollüberzeugung zu, die sich in dieser Unterform besonders zeigen müsste. Die sorglos Diffusen werden von situativen Erfahrungen am stärksten beeinflusst, da sie keine verantwortungsvollen Verbindlichkeiten eingehen und Geschehnisse nicht persönlich interpretieren wollen. Da das "Sich nicht festlegen wollen" unter den gegebenen gesellschaftlichen Bedingungen und vor allem für junge Menschen, denen noch alle Wege offen stehen, als adaptiv eingeschätzt wird, werden positive Zusammenhänge zum Wohlbefinden erwartet.

- In der *gestörten Diffusion* wird aufgrund des fehlenden Explorationsverhaltens ebenfalls ein negativer Zusammenhang zur Einschätzung der Selbstwirksamkeit erwartet. In diesem Zustand leiden die Personen aber nicht nur an ihrem Ressourcenmangel, sondern auch an der fehlenden Selbststruktur, die als organisierender Rahmen zur Erfahrungsinterpretation dienen könnte. Es werden negative Korrelationen mit den Wohlbefindensvariablen erwartet.

- Den *kulturell adaptiv Diffusen* werden Ressourcen zugeschrieben, die es ihnen erlauben, sich selbstbestimmt so zu verhalten, wie es unter den aktuell gegebenen Bedingungen adaptiv ist. Sie profitieren von den ihnen offen stehenden Möglichkeiten und fühlen sich wohl.

- Die *Diffusion als Durchgangsstadium* ist eng verbunden mit dem Übergang zum Erwachsenenalter. Man ist auf dem Weg zu einer kritisch erarbeiteten Identität und gewinnt im Zuge der zunehmenden Exploration verstärkt Zutrauen in die eigene Wirksamkeit. Im Gegensatz zum Moratorium à la Marcia hat man in der Durchgangsdiffusion kein Krisenempfinden und fühlt sich verhältnismäßig wohl.

Stichprobe und Untersuchungsdurchführung

Die *Stichprobe* besteht aus 148 Männern (40%) und 224 Frauen (60%), die den Fragebogen vor Beginn einer Vorlesung ausfüllten. Die Untersuchung fand im Sommersemester 2002 an der Otto-von-Guericke-Universität Magdeburg statt. Es nahmen überwiegend Studierende der Wirtschaftswissenschaften an der Befragung teil (N=275), die übrigen 97 waren Studierende der Sozialwissenschaften. Das Alter betrug im Durchschnitt bei den Frauen 21,9 Jahre und bei den Männern 23,0 Jahre. 95,4% waren ledig, aber 28,9% lebten in einer festen Partnerschaft. 96% hatten noch keine Kinder.

Beschreibung der Messinstrumente
Um einen *Fragebogen* zu den vier Diffusionsformen zu *entwickeln*, haben 18 PsychologiestudentInnen nach theoretischer Einarbeitung in vier Kleingruppen für jede Unterform zwölf Items formuliert, die sich zur Hälfte auf den Inhaltsbereich Studium/Beruf und zur anderen Hälfte auf den Bereich Freundschaft bezogen. Aus dem Itempool wurden die Items ausgewählt, die von den jeweils anderen Kleingruppen korrekt den vier Diffusionsformen zugeordnet werden konnten. In die endgültige Version gingen die 24 Items (je sechs pro Inhaltsbereich und Untergruppe) ein, die den größten Zuspruch erhielten. Förderlich für die Itemformulierung war, dass die Studierenden der selben Altersgruppe und Bildungsschicht angehörten wie die Probanden, für die der Fragebogen konzipiert war.

Skala	Bereich	Item- Beispiel	Reliabilität
sorglose Diffuison (9 Items)	Freundschaft	Ich habe viele kurzfristige Beziehungen.	$\alpha = .57$
	Beruf	Berufliche Verpflichtungen sind mir ein Graus.	
gestörte Diffusion (10 Items)	Freundschaft	Den größten Teil meiner Zeit verbringe ich allein.	$\alpha = .79$
	Beruf	Was ich im Studium auch tu, keiner nimmt mich richtig wahr.	
kulturell adaptive Diffusion (7 Items)	Freundschaft	Da wo ich mich gerade befinde, suche ich mir meine Freunde.	$\alpha = .64$
	Beruf	Für einen guten Job breche ich ohne weiteres meine Zelte ab.	
Durchgangs- diffusion (12 Items)	Freundschaft	Wer meine wahren Freunde sind, wird sich noch herausstellen.	$\alpha = .78$
	Beruf	Es wird sich zeigen, welcher Beruf zu mir passt.	
Selbstwirksamkeit (10 Items nach Schwarzer)		Wenn ein Problem auftaucht, kann ich es aus eigener Kraft meistern.	$\alpha = .85$
Selbstwert (10 Items nach Rosenberg)		Ich wünschte, ich könnte mehr Achtung vor mir selber haben.	$\alpha = .82$
Seelische Gesundheit (19 Items nach Becker)		Ich habe ein Gefühl der Teilnahmslosigkeit und Leere.	$\alpha = .90$

Tabelle 3 zeigt die verwendeten Skalen mit je einem Beispielitem und der Angabe von Cronbach´s Alpha (α) als Maß der internen Konsistenz.

Reliabilitätsanalysen ergaben für den selbstentwickelten Diffusionsfragebogen keine durchweg zufriedenstellenden Ergebnisse. Die Items, die eine Diffusionsform psychometrisch erfassen sollen, sind demnach nicht konsistent. Items mit einer Trennschärfe unter .30 wurden eliminiert, da sie wenig dazu beitragen, den Skalenwert einer Diffusionsform zu messen. Reduziert man die "unscharfen" Items, erhöht sich die innere Konsistenz, die Reliabilität, einer Skala. Cronbach´s Alpha (α) ist ein von der Anzahl der Items abhängiges Maß für die innere Konsistenz (je mehr Items umso höher Cronbach´s Alpha) und sollte gegen 1 gehen. In einer *konfirmatorischen Faktorenanalyse* bestätigte sich die Zuordnung der Items zu den vier Unterformen nicht durchgängig, was auch daran liegen kann, dass die vier Unterformen auch theoretisch nicht unabhängig voneinander sind.

Als personale Ressource wurde das Konstrukt *Selbstwirksamkeit* über eine 10-Item-Skala von Schwarzer (2000) erhoben. Es bezieht sich auf die optimistische Einschätzung der eigenen Kompetenz, bestimmte Handlungen ausführen zu können, die notwendig sind, um ein spezielles Ziel zu erreichen. *Selbstwertgefühl* und *seelische Gesundheit* wurden wie in Studie 1 erfasst. Zusätzlich erhob der Fragebogen Geschlecht, Alter, Beschäftigung vor dem Studium, Familienstand, Kinderanzahl, Job sowie wöchentliche Arbeitsstunden.

Ergebnisse

Signifikante *Geschlechtseffekte* zeigen sich in Varianzanalysen bezüglich sorgloser Diffusion und bezüglich kulturell adaptiver Diffusion. In beiden Fällen haben die Männer signifikant höhere Skalenmittelwerte.

Es werden nun Zusammenhangsanalysen (Korrelationen) berichtet, deren Korrelationskoeffizient (r) zwischen -1.0 und $+1.0$ variieren kann. 0 bedeutet keinerlei Zusammenhang. Bei $r=\pm.10$ spricht man von einem schwachen, bei $r=\pm.30$ von einem mittleren und ab $r=\pm.50$ von einem starken Zusammenhang (Cohen 1988). Ein signifikanter Zusammenhang meint im Folgenden, dass die Irrtumswahrscheinlichkeit für dieses Ergebnis unter 5% liegt. Es ergaben sich signifikante negative Zusammenhänge (je älter umso weniger diffus) zwischen *Alter* und sorgloser Diffusion (-.16) sowie zwischen Alter und Durchgangsdiffusion (-.20). Die übrigen Diffusionsformen korrelieren nicht signifikant mit dem Alter.

Die *sorglose Diffusion* korreliert nur in Bezug auf den Bereich Freundschaft positiv (je diffuser umso selbstwirksamer) mit Selbstwirksamkeitserwartung (.32). Bezogen auf Studium/Beruf beläuft sich die nicht signifikante Korrelation auf .02. Entsprechend sieht das Korrelationsmuster bezogen auf den Selbstwert aus

(Freundschaft = .24, signifikant; Studium/Beruf = -.05, nicht signifikant). Bezüglich seelischer Gesundheit ist die Korrelation zwischen sorgloser Diffusion im Bereich Studium/ Beruf sogar negativ (-.12), während die freundschaftsbezogene sorglose Diffusion positiv mit seelischer Gesundheit korreliert (.27). Getrennt nach Geschlecht ergeben die Analysen nur bei den Männern signifikante Zusammenhänge zu Selbstwirksamkeit und Selbstwert.

Die Zusammenhänge der gestörten Diffusion mit der personalen Ressource Selbstwirksamkeit sind für die Bereiche Freundschaft (-.39) und Studium/Beruf (-.40) negativ signifikant. Ferner hängt die *gestörte Diffusion* signifikant negativ mit dem Selbstwert (Freundschaft = -.50; Studium/Beruf = -.50) und der seelischen Gesundheit (Freundschaft = -.58; Studium/Beruf = -.57) zusammen. Diese Zusammenhänge zeigen sich bei Männern und Frauen.

Die *kulturell adaptive Diffusion* hingegen korreliert positiv mit Selbstwirksamkeitserwartung, sowohl im Bereich Freundschaft (.26) als auch im Bereich Studium/Beruf (.44). Die Zusammenhänge mit den Wohlbefindensvariablen Selbstwert (Freundschaft = .15; Studium/Beruf = .26) und seelische Gesundheit (Freundschaft = .24; Studium/Beruf = .33) sind ebenfalls positiv. Untersucht man die Zusammenhänge geschlechtsspezifisch, ist der Zusammenhang zwischen kulturell adaptiver Diffusion und Selbstwert nur bei den Männern positiv (.34), bei den Frauen jedoch nicht signifikant (.01). Die Zusammenhänge zu Selbstwirksamkeit und seelischer Gesundheit unterscheiden sich nicht in Abhängigkeit vom Geschlecht.

Die *Durchgangsdiffusion* hängt signifikant negativ mit Selbstwirksamkeitserwartung in den Bereichen Freundschaft (-.29) und Studium/Beruf (-.17) zusammen. Die Zusammenhänge mit den Wohlbefindensvariablen Selbstwert (Freundschaft = -.39; Studium/Beruf = -.19) und seelische Gesundheit (Freundschaft = -.45; Studium/Beruf = -.29) hängen ferner signifikant negativ mit der Diffusion als Durchgangsstadium zusammen. Die Zusammenhänge gestalten sich für beide Geschlechter ähnlich.

Diskussion

Zunächst muss kritisch darauf verwiesen werden, dass der Fragebogen die vier Untergruppen nicht durchgängig trennscharf und als vier unabhängige Faktoren erfasst. Abgesehen von der psychometrischen Kritik muss allerdings auch hinterfragt werden, ob die Diffusion über ein quantitatives strukturiertes Instrument zugänglich ist und nicht eher eine narrative Konstruktion darstellt, die sich einem geschlossenen Verfahren entzieht. Nunner-Winkler (1988) hält eine offene Befragung gar für unumgänglich, um ein Konstrukt wie Identität angemessen zu erfassen und um neben der "objektiven Welt" der beobachtbaren Sachverhalte und der "sozialen Welt" der geteilten Bedeutungen auch die "subjektive Welt" der inneren Erfahrungen und kognitiven Repräsentationen, die ein Subjekt über sich selbst hat, zu erheben. Sie kritisiert, dass eine "Zwei-Welten-Methodologie", wie sie in standardisierten Forschungsverfahren ihren Ausdruck findet, die "subjektive Welt" übergeht und einem "Drei-" oder gar "Mehr-Welten-Konstrukt" wie Identität nicht gerecht wird. Nunner-Winkler favorisiert hermeneutisch-rekonstruktivistische Verfahren, bei denen Befragte und Forschende in einer offenen Gesprächssituation Bedeutungsübereinstimmungen aushandeln. Identität zeigt sich hier in der Rekonstruktion von Denkstrukturen und an wohlüberlegten Überzeugungen, an denen der oder die Befragte trotz Gegeneinwänden begründet festhält. So drückt sich z.B. Kontinuität darin aus, wenn es mir gelingt, meine biografischen Wandlungsprozesse anderen plausibel zu machen. Ferner ist das Individuum auch als Korrelat zunehmender gesellschaftlicher Differenzierung zu betrachten, so dass weiterhin sozialhistorische und -statistische Analysen in den Methodenkanon aufgenommen werden sollten, um dem vielschichtigen Konstrukt Identität möglichst gerecht zu werden.

Sicher bedarf die Erfassung des komplexen Phänomens Identität vielfältiger methodischer Ansätze, doch sollte hier exemplarisch ein Einblick in einen empirischen Ansatz vermittelt und offen gelegt werden. Auch auf die Spezifität der Stichprobe muss verwiesen werden. Die Ergebnisse beruhen auf einer studentischen Stichprobe, die überwiegend Wirtschaftswissenschaften studiert, und können nicht auf andere Altersbereiche und Bildungswege generalisiert werden. Dennoch sollen die gewonnenen Ergebnisse nun vor diesem Hintergrund diskutiert werden.

Die *sorglose Diffusion* ist im frühen Erwachsenenalter besonders ausgeprägt. Dies scheint theoretisch plausibel, da man als junger Mensch zu Beginn seines Studiums noch vielem offen gegenüber steht und man sich aktuell keine Sorgen um die eigene Zukunft macht. Männer erzielen bezüglich dieser Unterform höhere Werte als Frauen. Dies könnte dahingehend diskutiert werden, dass junge Frauen selbstkritischer sind als Männer. Kroger (2000) berichtet, dass jugendliche Mädchen Bindungen ans Elternhaus als bedeutsamer für ihre Identitätsentwicklung erachten als Jungen, Diffusion jedoch mit geringer Bindung und geringer Autonomie einhergeht (vgl. Willemsen/Waterman 1991). Diesbezüglich ist interessant, dass auch nur bei den jungen Männern die erwarteten positiven Korrelationen zwischen Selbstwert, Selbstwirksamkeit und sorgloser Diffusion zu finden sind. Möglicherweise haben junge Frauen und Männer hier andere Erwartungen, die sich besonders im Freundschaftsbereich niederschlagen. Wenn dieser bindungsrelevante Bereich von jungen Frauen kritischer exploriert wird, kann die sorglose Diffusion hier nur für junge Männer adaptiv sein. Interessant ist auch, dass bei beiden Geschlechtern das sorglose Dahingleiten im Bereich Studium/Beruf negativ mit Wohlbefinden einhergeht. Hier wird das Auseinandersetzen mit Studiumsbelangen sicher als adäquater betrachtet und erlebt als das passive Dahingleiten. Die Adaptivität der sorglosen Diffusion gilt demnach nur eingeschränkt. Junge Männer scheinen im Freundschaftsbereich von ihr zu profitieren und sich beim sorglosen Treibenlassen wohl zu fühlen.

Die *gestörte Diffusion* steht erwartungsgemäß in deutlichen negativen Zusammenhängen zu Selbstwirksamkeitserwartung und Wohlbefinden. Im Sinne Eriksons leiden die jungen Menschen hier unter der Strukturlosigkeit und mangelnden Verbindlichkeit. Ihnen fehlt die sichere Basis zur selbstkritischen Exploration, sie bleiben konturlos und können sich nicht als kontinuierliches Wesen im Wandel entwerfen. Dies gilt sowohl für gestört diffuse Männer als auch für gestört diffuse Frauen, und sowohl im Freundschafts- als auch im studiumsbezogenen Bereich.

Die *kulturell adaptive Diffusion* trägt den Adaptivitätsanspruch schon im Namen. Männer haben hier im Durchschnitt höhere Werte als Frauen. Es sind auch nur die Männer, bei denen eine ausgeprägte kulturell adaptive Identität den Selbstwert erhöht. Die kulturell adaptive Diffusion begünstigt bei beiden Geschlechtern die seelische Gesundheit und geht bei Männern und Frauen positiv mit Selbstwirksamkeitserwartung einher. Bezogen auf Haußers Drei-Komponenten-Ansatz der Identität (1995), der sich auf eine sich selbst wahrnehmenden Komponente, eine Selbstwert- und eine personale Kontrollkomponente bezieht, scheint die kulturell adaptive Identität bei Männern und Frauen das Wohlbefinden im gesellschaftlichen Wandel zu begünstigen und die personale Handlungskomponente zu stärken. Die Unterschiede liegen in der Bewertung ihrer Selbstwahrnehmungen, die, über Zeit und Situationen generalisiert, den Selbstwert ausmacht. Womöglich bewerten Frauen ihre Selbstwahrnehmungen anders, haben andere Ideale oder setzen andere Akzente. Bei Items wie "Für einen guten Job breche ich ohne weiteres meine Zelte ab." kann für Männer der Flexibilitätsaspekt im Vordergrund stehen und positiv bewertet werden, für Frauen hingegen das Aufgeben ihrer alten Bindungen eine höhere, schmerzlich empfundene Priorität haben. Für die *Durchgangsdiffusion* als Durchgangsstadium im Übergang zum Erwachsenenalter spricht der Rückgang der Werte mit zunehmendem Alter. Was die negativen Korrelationen zum Wohlbefinden betrifft, ähnelt die Durchgangsdiffusion erwartungskonträr dem Krisenstatus Moratorium. Man hadert im Meer der Möglichkeiten und einem wird bewusst, dass das ehemals sorglose Dahingleiten kein Zutrauen in die eigene Wirksamkeit beschert hat. Nun steht man, übrigens Mann und Frau in gleicher Weise, vor der Aufgabe, eigene Standpunkte zu explorieren und zu einem unverwechselbaren Wesen im Wandel zu werden.

Die *unterschiedlich gerichteten Zusammenhänge* zeigen, dass es sinnvoll ist, die Diffusion auch weiterhin differenziert zu betrachten. Die positiven Zusammenhänge zwischen der kulturell adaptiven Diffusion und den Wohlbefindensvariablen könnten durchaus ein Hinweis auf die Funktionalität dieses Identitätszustands sein. Dennoch kann die Diffusion nicht als grundlegend adäquater Identitätszustand in aktuellen Transformationszusammenhängen bezeichnet werden, zumindest wenn die negativen Korrelationen der gestörten oder der Durchgangsdiffusion mit den Wohlbefindensvariablen als Beleg herangezogen werden.

Sind letztlich doch kritische *Exploration und Verbindlichkeit nötig*, um sich eine integrierte, differenzierte Identität zu erarbeiten, mit der man die gesellschaftlichen und postmodernen Transformationsanforderungen bewältigen kann? Côté (1997) betrachtet eine ausgewogene integrierte und differenzierte Identität als Kapital mit Ressourcencharakter in der Postmoderne. Kurtines (nach Schwartz 2001) favorisiert eine kritisch ko-konstruierte Identitätsarbeit und forciert in seinen Interventionen die Kreativität, um möglichst viele Alternativen zur Exploration zu finden. Er fördert die sachlogische Erörterung und Abwägung der Alternativen sowie deren kritische Evaluation und Diskussion mit SozialpartnerInnen. Die Interventionen führten abhängig vom Identitätszustand der TeilnehmerInnen zu einer subjektiven Erhöhung der Lebensqualität. Da die trainierten Problemlösetechniken eine Distanzierung von bestehenden Überzeugungen verlangen, profitierten TeilnehmerInnen mit hohen Diffusions- und im Moratoriumswerten stärker von der Intervention als Personen mit erarbeiteter und übernommener Identität. Möglich ist aber auch, dass die Personen mit festen inneren Überzeugungen von vornherein schon zufriedener waren.

Verfolgt man diese Ansätze, kommt der *Identität eine besondere Relevanz* zu: Sie wird zur Ressource, die darüber mitentscheidet, ob ich mich in den Freiräumen des gesellschaftlichen Wandels verliere oder die Gestaltungsfreiheit als Herausforderung erlebe und mich in aktuellen Transformationskontexten als integere Person erleben und präsentieren kann.

Literatur

Abele, A. /Becker, P. (1991): Wohlbefinden: Theorie, Empirie, Diagnostik. Weinheim: Juventa Verlag.

Arnett, J.J.: Emerging Adulthood: A Theory of Development From the Late Teens Through the Twenties. In: American Psychologist, (2002): 55 (5), S. 469-480.

Becker, P. (1989): Trierer Persönlichkeitsfragebogen. Göttingen: Hogrefe.

Bennion, L.D. /Adams, G.R.: A revision of the extended version of the objective measure of Ego Identity Status: An identity instrument for use with late adolescents. In: Journal of Adolescent Research, (1986): 1, S. 183-198.

Born, A. (2002): Regulation persönlicher Identität im Rahmen gesellschaftlicher Transformationsbewältigung. Münster: Waxmann.

Brähler, E./Richter, H.-E. (1999): Ost- und Westdeutsche – 10 Jahre nach der Wende. In:H. Berth /E. Brähler (Hrsg.): Deutsch-deutsche Vergleiche. Psychologische Untersuchungen 10 Jahre nach dem Mauerfall. Berlin: VWF.

Côté, J.E.: An empirical test of the identity capital model. In: Journal of Adolescence, (1997): 20, S. 421-437.

Erikson, E.H. (1998): Identität und Lebenszyklus. Frankfurt am Main: Suhrkamp. (Org.: Identity and the life cycle, 1959).

Fahrenberg, J./Myrtek, M./Wilk, D./Kreutel, K.: Multimodale Erfassung der Lebenszufriedenheit: Eine Untersuchung an Koronarkranken. In: Psychotherapie und Medizinische Psychologie,(1986) 36,S. 347-354.

Filipp, S.-H. (1995): Kritische Lebensereignisse. Weinheim: PVU.

Goossens, L. (1995): Identity status development and students perception of the university environment: A cohort-sequential study. In: A. Oosterwegel /R. Wicklund (Eds.), The self in European and North American culture: Development and process. Dordrecht: Kluwer.

Haußer, K. (1995): Identitätspsychologie. Berlin: Springer.

Janich, H./Boll, T. (1982): Übersetzung des Self-Esteem-Fragebogens von Rosenberg (1965). Trier: Universität Trier, Fachbereich I - Psychologie (unveröffentlichtes Manuskript).

Jerusalem, M. (1990): Persönliche Ressourcen, Vulnerabilität und Streßerleben. Göttingen: Hogrefe.

Kapfhammer, H.-P. (1995): Psychosoziale Entwicklung im jungen Erwachsenenalter. Berlin: Springer.

Keupp, H. (1997): Diskursarena Identität: Lernprozesse in der Identitätsforschung. In: H. Keupp/R. Höfer (Hrsg.): Identitätsarbeit heute. Frankfurt am Main: Suhrkamp.

Krappmann, L. (1997): Die Identitätsproblematik nach Erikson aus einer interaktionistischen Sicht. In: H. Keupp/R. Höfer (Hrsg.): Identitätsarbeit heute. Frankfurt am Main: Suhrkamp.

Krappmann, L. (2000): Soziologische Dimensionen der Identität. Stuttgart: Klett-Cotta. (Org. 1969).

Kraus, W./Mitzscherlich, B.: Identitätsdiffusion als kulturelle Anpassungsleistung. Erste empirische Ergebnisse zu Veränderungen der Identitätsentwicklung. In: Psychologie in Erziehung und Unterricht, (1995): 42, S. 65-72.

Kroger, J. (2000): Identity development: Adolescence through adulthood. London: Sage.

Lazarus, R.S./Folkman, S. (1984): Stress, appraisal and coping. New York: Springer.

Lazarus, R.S./Folkman, S.: Transactional theory and research on emotions and coping. In: European Journal of Personality, (1987): 1, S. 141-170.

Marcia, J.E. (1989): Identity diffusion differentiated. In: M.A. Luszcz/T. Nettelbeck (Eds.): Psychological development: Perspectives across the life-span. North-Holland: Elsevier.

Marcia, J.E. (1993a): The ego identity status approach to ego identity. In: J.E. Marcia, /A.S. Waterman/D.R. Matteson/S.L. Archer/J.L. Orlofsky (Eds.): Ego identity: A handbook for psychosocial research. New York: Springer.

Marcia, J.E. (1993b): The status of the statuses: Research review. In: J.E. Marcia/A.S. Waterman/D.R. Matteson, S.L. Archer /J.L. Orlofsky (Eds.): Ego identity: A handbook for psychosocial research. New York: Springer.

Mummendey, H.D. (1995): Selbstkonzeptänderungen nach kritischen Lebensereignissen. In: S.-H. Filipp (Hrsg.): Kritische Lebensereignisse. Weinheim: PVU.

Nunner-Winkler, G.: Selbstkonzeptforschung und Identitätskonstrukt – Ein Vergleich zweier Ansätze aus der psychologischen und der soziologischen Sozialpsychologie. In: Zeitschrift für Sozialpsychologie, (1988): 19, S. 243-254.Schmitt, M./Maes, J./Schmal, A. (1995): Gerechtigkeit als innerdeutsches Problem: Auswahl von Indikatoren seelischer Gesundheit. Trier: Universität Trier (Forschungsbericht).

Schmitt, M., Maes, J., /Schmal, A. (1997): Gerechtigkeit als innerdeutsches Problem: Analyse der Meßeigenschaften von Indikatoren der seelischen Gesundheit. Trier: Universität Trier (Forschungsbericht).

Schmitt, M., Maes, J. /Schmal, A. (1999): Ungerechtigkeitserleben im Vereinigungsprozess: Folgen für das emotionale Befinden und die seelische Gesundheit. In: M. Schmitt /L. Montada (Hrsg.): Gerechtigkeitserleben im wiedervereinigten Deutschland. Opladen: Leske + Budrich.

Schwartz, S.J.: The evolution of Eriksonian and neo-Eriksonian identity theory and research: A review and integration. Identity: In: An International Journal of Theory and Research, (2001): 1, S. 7-58.

Schwarzer, R. (1996): Psychologie des Gesundheitsverhaltens. Göttingen: Hogrefe.

Schwarzer, R. (2000): Stress, Angst und Handlungsregulation. Stuttgart: Kohlhammer.

Statistisches Bundesamt Wiesbaden (1998): Statistisches Jahrbuch für die BRD. Stuttgart: Metzler + Poeschel.

Statistisches Bundesamt Wiesbaden (2003): Statistisches Jahrbuch für die BRD. Wiesbaden: Statistisches Bundesamt.

Statistisches Bundesamt Wiesbaden (2004): Fakten und Trends: Deutschland aktuell.

http://www.destatis.de/download/d/veroe/f+t_d.pdf [10.05.2004].

Whitbourne, S.K. (1982): Identitätsentwicklung im Erwachsenenalter. In: S.K. Whitbourne/C.S. Weinstock (Hrsg.): Die mittlere Lebensspanne. Entwicklungspsychologie des Erwachsenenalters. München: Urban & Schwarzenberg.

Whitbourne, S.K. (1996): Psychosocial perspectives on emotions: The role of identity in the aging process. In: C. Magai/S.H. McFadden (Eds.): Handbook of emotion, adult development, and aging. San Diego: Academic Press.

Willemsen, E.W./Waterman, A.S: Ego identity status and family environment: A correlational study. In: Psychological Reports, (1991): 69, S. 1203-1212.

Reinhard Golz (University of Magdeburg, Germany)

Integration Problems of Russian Jewish Migrants in Russia and Germany

Abstract
The Jewish immigrants living in Germany mostly come from Russia, where they are often confronted with economic and social problems, uncertainties as well as anti-semitic attitudes from the Russian public. Germany is one of the most selected countries of the Russian Jewish migration. The living conditions of the Jewish immigrants in the German receiving society are also difficult due to increasing crisis developments, particularly in the social and economic domain. It is important to recognize and use the Jewish immigrant's intellectual capabilities and their eagerness to contribute to the German society.

Regarding the geographical structure, the multinational state of Russia looks for the same. Approximately 150 million people live on 17,075,400 km^2 in a federation of 20 republics (e.g.: Altaj, Dagestan, Chechnya, Chuwashia) and other large administrative regions and autonomous areas. There is hardly another country with such an ethnical heterogeneity. Russia was and is a country with a multi-layered process of immigration and emigration. Particularly since the 18th century under the rule of the Tsar, Zarin Katharina II, Germans immigrated in large numbers to Russia (see Brandes 1992; Bruk Smirnova 1994). An insignificant number of them later moved further, for example, to North America (see. Jansen 1997). To be mentioned in this context as well, are the late re-settlers who, until now and in the future, returned to Germany from Russia. Between 1989 and 1993 approximately 4,3 million people from other areas of the former Soviet Union immigrated to Russia. In this period approximately 2,8 million emigrated. There is further data, according to the time period from 1993 to 1999, that more than 3 million people from republics of the former Soviet Union moved to Russia, among them 40% from the South of the country (see Gukalenko 2000, S. 3). In the process of this inland migration within the former soviet state and in connection with the increasing socio-economic problems, the differences in culture, religious and educational traditions, which were before rather suppressed, became particularly clearly visible. This refers, e.g., to the Tatars coming from the entire former Sovjet Union (currently approximately 5.52 million Tatars live in the Russian Federation). This also affects different ethnical groups such as Kurds, Gypsies, Eskimos and others, who are without their own nationality, but with a multiforum Diaspora within the Russian Federation (see Matveev 1999).

The *non*-Russian population makes up approximately 20%, and there are about 120 (!) *ethnical groups* (e.g.: Armenians, Belorussians, Germans, Eskimos,

Finns, Greeks, Grusinians, Jewish, Kurds, Polish, Tatars, Chuwashians, Turks, Ukrainians, Gypsies). Some statisticians and ethnologists sometimes even count two to three times more ethnical groups (see Matveev 1999). Of special interest in this context are those groups living with citizenship in Russia and/or nationality outside of the Russian Federation, for example Germans, Greeks, Polish, Jewish and others in particular after the end of the USSR – Ukrainans, Belorussians, Moldavians, Grusins or Armenians.

Take here, for example, the Germans. While Germans live in many countries in the world, such as, in the USA (5 million), in Canada (1,2 million) or in Brazil (0.8), there are in all Eastern Central Europe and in Eastern Europe approximately 3.5 million. However, in the former Soviet Union in 1989 altogether approximately 2 million were spread throughout the Russian Federation (e.g. in the area around the city of Omsk approximately 134,200, in the Altaj Region approximately 127 700) and in other countries of the former Soviet Union (e.g. in Kazakhstan 957 500 or in Kirghizia 101, 300).

Currently, 0.54 million Jews live in Russia, of which 75 800 are in Moscow and 106500 in St. Petersburg as well as about 8 000 in the "Autonomous Jewish Area", belonging to Russia (refer to: Peoples of Russia, 1994). Concerning the problems with the determination of their minority status (What dominates: the nationality or the confession to the Jewish religion?) this cannot be taken further here (refer to this problem: Kugelmann 1995).

As in other places in the world, Jewish people in Russia often appeared and still appear to be confronted with characteristics bordering on Anti-Semitism. In the months of June/July 1999 more synagogs in Russia were bombed, arson attacks were committed and praying Jewish people were stabbed. According to the observations of the author, as well as other observers of the situation, Jews in Russia are often accused unfoundedly to be responsible for the bad economic situation and blamed for stealing billions of dollars from the International Development Funds. The increasing Anti-Semitism led to a rise of emigration, especially to Israel and Germany.

After the collapse of the Soviet Union, it was apparent that in the process of the social transformation that one was only insufficiently prepared for the handling of culture-conditioned conflicts between the peoples, which can be referred also to social handling and the conditions of socialization. The process of the inland migration already specified, strengthened the general problems of the transformation of Russia and affected also the attitudes of the Russian population opposite Jewish fellow citizens. Particularly in the educational and political discussions the thought of the national upswing, the national rebirth and the ethnical self-instruction (ethnopedagogy) always plays an even larger role. The aim of Russian pedagogy reflects the Russian patriot, the son of the people with highly developed feelings of national pride and human dignity. However, through observation there is a remarkable orientation towards Slavic and particularly Russian educational thoughts and actions as a component of the present Russian "Zeitgeist" (spirit of the time) (refer e.g. to: Volkov 1999; Nikandrov 1999). For the prominent Russian education scientist N.D. Nikandrov, for example, the "goal of the socialization and the education - now and perspectively - is the Russian patriot, who orientated himself on the priority of the national Russian values – by respecting the values of other cultures." (Nikandrov 2000, S. 266). Nikandrov is convinced that the return to a steady national idea will be the basis of the mental self preservation of Russia. It concerns (orthodox) religion, patriotism and solidarity of the people (refer ibid., p. 263). However, apart from such a nationally stressed educational direction, however, rather relative (moderate) directions are to be stated, which can only imagine the appropriation of the values of the home culture and the world culture in correlation (refer Golz 2001, p. 100).

The tendency towards a Russian Nationalism is both understandable and problematic in the view of the crisis of the Russian civil society: it is understandable from the lost (or allegedly lost) of national and human dignity. Yet, it is problematic from the view of the possible dangers that a national (patriotic) development can become a nationalistic one. There is also the danger, that the desired intercultural tolerance within Russia between the different cultures could become the undesirable dominance of the majority culture and thus lead to conflicts which may to some extend already exist (cf. Gersunskij 2002, p. 472).

These tendencies had and still have their specific negative consequences also for the integration of Jewish people into Russian society and have a strengthened affect on appropriate emigration decisions within this subpopulation. Jewish migration was and still is both inland migration and immigration just as emigration. There is hardly any other nation whose members had and continue to deal in a similar way with problems and come to terms with migration. While approximately 13 million Jews live in the whole world, there are for example in the USA 6 million, in Israel 4 million, in France 0.65 million. In 1933 approximately half a million Jews lived in Germany, and in 1945 - after the genocide - there were only 25. 000.

According to various data, at the present time approximately 150 000 Jewish citizens live in the Federal Republic of Germany. Of these citizens more than one third came from the former Soviet Union, which began in the 1990s. Regarding the "jewish contingent refugees" the problems and tasks exist particularly in economical, social and – if desired - religious integration. Concerning community formation is the development of a modern Jewish identity, over and above is the development of the "Jews in the former Soviet Union" into "Jews in Germany". In other words: the regional social structures and cultures of the respective Länder (provinces) of the Federal Republic are about the integration of the Jewish fellow citizens into the society of the Federal Republic of Germany.

Jewish contingent refugees are foreigners, in the context of humanitarian relief work in the Federal Republic of Germany, who were allowed to stay due to the distribution of residence permits or due to an explanation assumption after § 33 Abs. 1 of the "Ausländergesetz". (cf. Runge 2001). They can also be taken up according to an agreement of the Prime Ministers of the countries since February 15th, 1991 from the states of the Former Soviet Union in the BRD. Thus, they are to a large extent German citizens, in particular on equal footing with the social and unemployment relief and education assistance. German knowledge is obtained for integration in school, occupation and society. The refugees are distributed to match up to the total population numbers of all countries in the Federal Republic. As long as the immigrants are dependent on national assistance, they must maintain their assigned residence (cf. ibid).

According to the present valid rights, all persons are to be granted access, who can prove with documentation, to be of Jewish citizenship or at least be descended from one Jewish parent. However, according to Jewish religion teachings (Halacha), only such persons who either descended from a Jewish mother or who crossed over to Judaism through an orthodox or liberal rabbinical court (Rabbinatsgericht) with records can be recognized as Jewish and accepted to German municipalities.

Many people are by law allowed to come, however, are not recognized as members of Jewish municipalities. A further problem exists in the distribution of the new immigrants to the individual counties of the Federal Republic, which each deal differently with these immigrants. They are distributed either in cities with a Jewish municipality with the appropriate infrastructure or into assigned rural areas, in which there neither has been nor is a Jewish municipality, so that problems of support result (cf. ibid).

Jewish immigrants would theoretically have all the opportunities that German citizens also have. By law they can get an interpreter (usually Russian German); labour offices offer language courses for refugees contingent with the job market. While the language barrier is the largest challenge in all integration measures, it certainly represents the largest hurdle for the older Jewish immigrants. Many of them (university professors, poets, artists etc.) lived and worked in and with the language. In particular, they can no longer take part in the social life of German majority culture in their familiar language. They must argue with new terms, which mostly have a degrading meaning for them: "foreigner authority, social welfare assistance, living authorization, labour office". Those who are not in the job market due to age reasons, receive no German instruction. It is difficult for immigrants in Germany to be established socially and economically; nevertheless in the meantime the number of unemployed in Germany has risen to 5.2 million. The specifics of the Russian speaking Jewish population however, contrasts the other migrating groups- there are many professionally experienced scientists of all disciplines in the age group over 55: writers, film makers, teachers, physicians, engineers, musicians and economists. There are fastidious people with a high education, whose intellectual potential now lies bare. This is not a social psychological problem for these people, who can be underestimated. The feeling that their abilities and experiences are not as noteworthy and usable in the German receiving society, represents a large psychological part of it. On the one hand, at first glance it seems to be "only" a problem for these people, if they cannot integrate themselves even insufficiently in the German society. On the other hand, it is high time to offer these people more effective self-help assistance in order to realize that, what they want most is their specific abilities and talents to be used for the society and social circle.

An example of promising and already successful attempt of integration is the cooperation of the science combination in the synagog municipality to Magdeburg with the University of Magdeburg. The principle purpose on October 31, 1999 created a science combination to include all its members, education, sociological, scientific, technological, artistic-cultural and other life spheres, in the area of Magdeburg in Saxony-Anhalt and beyond to other projects in all areas of Germany. Members of this combination are professors emeritus, doctors and science candidates, inventors, diplomats from different ranges of science, technology, economics, art and culture. It would be highly advised that the German receiving society, which lies bare in various ways – for example in honorary and advisory functions – make their own contributions, not only for personal reasons, but also in the interest of the German society, in which they want to live permanently.

Literature:

Brandes, D. (1992): Die Deutschen in Russland und der Sowjetunion. In: Bade, K.J. (Hrsg.): Deutsche im Ausland – Fremde in Deutschland. München, S. 85-134

Bruk, S.I./Smirnova, T.B. (1994): The Germans. In: The People of Russia. Moscow, pp. 246-249 (russ.)

Geršunskij, B.S. (2002): Philosophy for the 21. Century. Moskau (russ.)

Golz, R. (2001): Terminologische Erkundungen zum Verhältnis von Ethnizität und Pädagogik im gegenwärtigen Russland. In: Humanisierung der Bildung. Jahrbuch 2001. Frankfurt a.M. (u.a.), S. 86-105

Gukalenko, O.V. (2000): Theoretisch–methodologische Grundlagen des [...] Schutzes von Migrantenschülern im polykulturellen Bildungsraum. Tiraspol (russ.)
http://www.nai-israel.com/israel/artikel/default.asp?CatID=3&ArticleID=140

Janssen, S. (1997): Vom Zarenreich in den amerikanischen Westen: Deutsche in Russland und Russlanddeutsche in den USA 1871-1928. Münster

Kugelmann, C. (1995): Die jüdische Minderheit. In: Schmalz-Jabobsen, C./Hansen, G. (Hg.): Ethnische Minderheiten [...]. München, S. 256-268

Matveev, K.P. (u.a.) (1999): Ethnic Groups. In: Davydov, V.V. (Red.): Russian Pedagogical Encyclopedia. Vol. 2. Moscow, pp. 635 et seqq. (russ.)

Nikandrov, N.D. (1999): The Russian National Idea (...) In: Humanisierung der Bildung. Jahrbuch 1999. Frankfurt a.M. (u.a.), pp. 64-77 (russ.)

Nikandrov, N.D. (2000): Russia: Socialization and Education (...). Moscow (russ.)

Runge, I. (2004): Zur Situation älterer Zuwanderer [...] (http://www.berlin-judentum.de [...]; www.fh-potsdam.de/~Sozwes/werkstatt/adf/ [...] [04.01.04])

Tiškov, V.A. (Red.) (1994): Peoples of Russia. Moscow (russ.)

Volkov, G.N. (1999): Ethnopedagogy. Moscow

Haci-Halil Uslucan (Universität Magdeburg, Deutschland)

**Ankommen in der neuen Heimat:
Akkulturationsbelastungen von Migranten[1]**

Abstract
The following study gives a short overview on some theoretical conceptions about the integration of migrants and focuses afterwards on the specific acculturative strains of Turkish migrants, who are, due to the relative great cultural distance of their country of origin to Germany, particularly exposed strong psychological stress situations. Subsequently, recurring to previous research on this area, the author presents some relevant social and psychological aspects like the voluntary of migration and the language competencies, which moderate the impact of the experienced acculturative strain. Then, in the following own empirical investigation with 357 Turkish migrants in Berlin, aged from 13 to 66 years (Mean: 34.3 years), the results of the experienced social threats and uncertainties on the one hand, and the experienced social support, as typical risks and resources of the integration process, are presented. The results exhibit a high level of experienced social threat, especially in the group of Turkish women, who came to Germany by the way of transnational marriages with Turks in Germany. But besides the high level of uncertainties and threats, Turkish migrants also seem to obtain a high degree of social, presumably familial support, which may soften the experienced stress. A remarcable aspect is that the stay of duration is irrelevant for the experienced stress: a longer duration seems not to soften the experienced stress, but rather lead tendentially to its rising.

1. Einleitung
Gegenwärtig gibt es in Westeuropa kaum ein Land, das nicht von Arbeitsmigration oder Flüchtlingsbewegung betroffen ist. Im Zuge der rapiden Globalisierungsbewegungen und der Vereinigung der europäischen Märkte treten Migrationsprozesse noch deutlicher als bislang in den Vordergrund und bilden eine große Herausforderung für moderne Nationalstaaten (vgl. Hoffmann-Nowotny, 1989). Diese Prozesse führen zu Veränderungen im Sozialgefüge sowohl der Entsende- als auch der Aufnahmestaaten.

Von Migration bzw. Migranten wird dann gesprochen, wenn es um die Bezeichnung von Individuen oder Gruppen geht, die einen sozialen und geographisch umgrenzten Raum verlassen und in einen anderen, im Prinzip auf eine längere

---

[1] Bei der Erhebung der empirischen Daten haben folgende Personen wertvolle Unterstützung geleistet, denen ich hiermit ganz herzlich danken möchte: Selvet Uslucan, Ertugrul Kirec, Dr. Ismail Kalayci, Dr. Adem Karabulut und Dr. Kerim Sultani.

Zeit angelegten, Raum ziehen, also bewußt keine Touristen oder Urlauber sind. Vielfach werden auch die Nachkommen über verschiedene Generation dieser ursprünglichen Einwanderer als Migranten bzw. Migrantenkinder bezeichnet. Die sprachliche wie sozialpolitische Sensibilität gebietet, eher von Migranten zu sprechen als von Ausländern, um diese Menschen nicht als "fremd", die die Bezeichnung des "Ausländers" nahe legt, zu stigmatisieren und sie dadurch einem begrifflich-ideologischem Ballast zu unterwerfen. Denn gegenwärtig sind sie vielfach keine Ausländer mehr, sind bspw. hier geboren und in ihrer subjektiven Selbstdefinition häufig der deutschen Kultur näher als der Ursprungskultur ihrer Eltern.

Zu Beginn der Migrationsbewegung in Deutschland kam in der politischen und wissenschaftlichen Diskussion dem Begriff des *„Kulturkonflikts"* eine Schlüsselposition zu. Dabei war in den Anfangszeiten der Migration kaum die Rede von einer „Integration" der Migranten. Ab etwa den 70er Jahren wurde kritisch auf die Notwendigkeit einer sinnvollen Integrationsstrategie hingewiesen. Insbesondere die Rückkehrorientierung und die starke Bindung an die Heimat der ersten Generation von Migranten in Deutschland, die von Anfang an ihre materiellen wie psychischen Investitionen in die Heimatkultur tätigte, erwies sich für die nachkommende zweite wie auch noch dritte Generation als ein Integrationserschwernis. Sie, die nachkommenden Generationen, verfügten weder über die kulturell gefestigten Basisorientierungen, noch waren sie unmittelbar in der Lage, kulturelle Orientierungen der Aufnahmegesellschaft nahtlos zu adaptieren.

Der Ansatz der „bi-kulturellen Sozialisation" (Schrader, Nikles & Griese, 1979) hob kritisch hervor, dass Migranten, besonders aber die Kinder, gezwungen sind, ihr kulturelles Bezugssystem zu wechseln und dass sie in diesem Kulturwechsel einen Prozess der Entwicklung und Veränderung ihrer Identität durchmachen, der mit einem kulturellen Konflikt einher geht, bei der entgegengesetzte Einflüsse der Familie auf der einen und die des Migrationslandes auf der anderen Seite auf das Kind wirken. Diese Diskrepanz der beiden „Kulturen" auf die Entwicklung von Kindern wurde in seinen Auswirkungen als eher negativ und identitätsbedrohend gedeutet. So wurde etwa angenommen, dass bei Jugendlichen, die in einem bi-kulturellen Kontext leben und die sie als ablehnend, feindlich und diskriminierend erleben, die Gefahr besteht, ein gebrochenes Selbstbild, bzw. allgemeine Symptome einer Identitätskrise, zu entwickeln. Im Gegensatz zu ihren Altersgenossen der Mehrheitsgesellschaft haben Migrantenkinder in der Adoleszens neben der allgemeinen Entwicklungsaufgabe, eine angemessene Identität, ein kohärentes Selbst zu entwickeln, sich auch noch mit der Frage der Zugehörigkeit zu einer Minderheit auseinander zu setzen und eine "ethnische Identität" auszubilden. In der Sozialisation von Migrantenkindern erweist sich ethnische Kategorisierung als ein relevantes Merkmal; denn dadurch wird über Zeiten und Generationen hinweg die Stabilität der Eigengruppe garantiert. Jedoch, so ist kritisch festzustellen, hemmt die nach wie vor mangelnde Repräsentanz der kulturell-ethnischen Minderheiten im deutschen Bildungskanon und der deutschen Öffentlichkeit den Aufbau eines positiven symbolischen Bezuges zur Herkunft.

Gleichwohl der Ansatz der bi-kulturellen Sozialisation auf zentrale Aspekte der Migrationssituation verweist, birgt er einige gewichtige theoretische Probleme: Die Ursachenzuschreibung bei Fehlentwicklungen in der Sozialisation von Migrantenkindern wird häufig einseitig auf den Kulturwechsel und der damit zusammenhängenden Konflikte zurückgeführt. Zwar ist festzuhalten, dass vermehrte interkulturelle Situationen in der Alltagswelt von Migrantenkindern und somit ihr unvermeidbarer Bezug zu zwei unterschiedlichen Kulturen wichtige Aspekte bilden, jedoch werden Kulturkonflikt-Konzepte reduktionistisch, wenn sie „Kulturwechsel" lediglich als eine Entwicklungseinschränkung des Individuums betrachten und nicht die Freisetzung von Entwicklungspotenzialen durch eine Migration sehen. Ferner führt eine ausschließliche Fixierung auf die Veränderungen der Heimatkultur - im Zuge einer Assimilation - dazu, dass die familiären und extrafamiliären sowie die gesellschaftlichen Bedingungen des Migrationslandes nicht im Kulturkonflikt-Konzept mit reflektiert werden.

Festzuhalten bleibt, dass im Prozess der Akkulturation, der allmählichen Aneignung von Schlüsselkompetenzen und Kulturstandards der Aufnahmekultur, Migranten und ihre Familien stets in einem doppelten sozialen Bezugsnetz involviert sind, sie also einerseits das Verhältnis zur eigenen Ethnie, andererseits zur Aufnahmegesellschaft, eigenaktiv gestalten müssen. Dabei lassen sich, folgt man Bourhis, Moise, Perreault, & Senécal (1997) in idealisierter Form vier Optionen unterscheiden: Integration, Assimilation, Separation und Marginalisierung. Während bei Integration und Assimilation Handlungsoptionen stärker auf die aufnehmende Gesellschaft bezogen sind, wobei Integration zugleich Bezüge zur Herkunftskultur bzw. zur eigenen Ethnie stärker berücksichtigt, ist Separation durch eine stärkere Abgrenzung zur aufnehmenden Gesellschaft bei gleichzeitiger Hinwendung zur eigenen Ethnie und schließlich Marginalisierung durch eine Abgrenzung sowohl von intra- als auch interethnischen Beziehungen gekennzeichnet. Diese Optionen können dabei bereichsspezifisch variieren und bringen nicht nur Unterschiede in personenbezogenen Präferenzen zum Ausdruck, sondern hängen wesentlich auch von den Erfahrungen mit Handlungsopportunitäten und -barrieren in der Aufnahmegesellschaft zusammen. So sprechen bspw. empirische Befunde dafür, dass Marginalisation und Separation mit höheren Belastungen verbunden sind als Integration und Assimilation (vgl. Berry & Kim, 1988; Morgenroth & Merkens, 1997).

Die unterschiedlichen Akkulturationsorientierungen von Migranten und Einheimischen lassen sich tabellarisch in dem theoretischen Konzept von Bourhis et al. (1997) veranschaulichen. Im Zentrum dieses Modells stehen die Interaktionsbeziehungen zwischen der Migrantenkultur und der aufnehmenden Mehrheitskultur. Dieses Modell berücksichtigt, gegenüber dem etwas starren Kulturkonflikt Ansatz, dynamisch sowohl die Aufnahmebereitschaft der Mehrheitskultur als auch gleichzeitig die Anpassungsbereitschaft der Einwanderergruppe.

Tabelle 1: Das Interaktive Akkulturationsmodell (IAM).

Aufnehmende Gesellschaft	Migrantengruppe			
	Integration	Assimilation	Separation	Marginalisation
Integration	*Konsens*	Problematisch	Konflikt	Problematisch
Assimilation	Problematisch	*Konsens*	Konflikt	Problematisch
Segregation	Konflikt	Konflikt	Konflikt	Konflikt
Exklusion	Konflikt	Konflikt	Konflikt	Konflikt

Modellhaft wird hier verdeutlicht, mit welchen Alternativen die aus psychologischer Sicht wünschenswerte Akkulturationsorientierung "Integration" theoretisch zu konkurrieren hat: So zeigt die Tabelle, dass lediglich das Aufeinandertreffen von integrations- oder assimilationsorientierten Haltungen der jeweiligen Mitglieder relativ wenig Probleme im alltäglichen Zusammenleben mit sich bringt; alle anderen Konstellationen dagegen latent problembehaftet sind, so z.B. wenn Migranten eine eher integrationsorientierte Haltung favorisieren, d.h. Schlüsselelemente der eigenen Kultur beibehalten wollen und gleichzeitig die Bereitschaft zeigen, Schlüsselelemente der Aufnahmekultur zu erwerben, die Aufnahmegesellschaft jedoch von ihnen eher eine Assimilation erwartet, d.h. eine Aufgabe der kulturellen Wurzeln und eine Adaptation der Normen und Werte der Aufnahmekultur wünscht.

2) Akkulturationsbelastungen von Migranten

Die Belastungen und Probleme von Migranten in ihrem Alltag erfahren - im Verhältnis zu ihrer psychologischen Dringlichkeit - kaum die angemessene Thematisierung im sozialwissenschaftlichen Diskurs. Dabei stellen Migranten mit weit über sieben Millionen Menschen etwa fast ein Zehntel der Gesamtbevölkerung der Bundesrepublik dar, sind somit keine zu vernachlässigende Population mehr. Prognostisch betrachtet wird diese Zahl eher zu- als abnehmen und die Frage um eine gelingende Integration dieser Population ihre Virulenz auch in nächster Zukunft nicht einbüßen. Die Schwierigkeiten der alltäglichen Lebensgestaltung sind dabei nicht nur ein Problem der Migranten selbst, fallen nicht nur auf sie zurück, sondern stellen auch die involvierten deutschen Berufsgruppen wie etwa Lehrer, Erzieher, Ärzte, Psychotherapeuten und Krankenschwestern vor eine besondere Herausforderung.

In der folgenden Studie wird das Augenmerk nur auf türkische Migranten gelegt. Die Begrenzung auf diese Gruppe folgt dabei zunächst einer relativ pragmatischen Überlegung: Mit fast zweieinhalb Millionen Menschen stellen türkischstämmige Migranten die größte ethnische Minderheit in Deutschland dar. Ferner ist die kulturelle Distanz zwischen Deutschen und Türken, im Vergleich zu anderen ethnischen Minderheiten wie etwa Italienern, Spaniern, Polen oder Griechen, wesentlich größer, so dass deutlich stärkere Unterschiede in der Lebensgestaltung und Orientierung zu erwarten ist. Deshalb ist in dem Diskurs über Migration und Migrantengruppen stets vor einer Nivellierung zu warnen; weder weisen alle ethnischen Gruppen dieselben Schwierigkeiten im selben Ausmaß auf, noch sind die Problemlagen innerhalb einer Ethnie gleich verteilt.

3) Biographisch-soziale Transformationen und Akkulturationsstress

Rapide kulturelle und soziale Veränderungen führen generell zu Stress, Destabilisierung und Überforderung. Die Auswirkungen dieser Veränderungen treffen Migranten aus dem orientalischen Raum besonders. Denn weitaus häufiger als Einheimische geraten sie in ihrem sozialen Alltag in Situationen der Uneindeutigkeit, in denen die innerhalb der Herkunftskultur eingelebten und routinisierten Handlungsformen versagen (vgl. Uslucan, 2000). Für die psychologische Erklärung dieser lebensweltlichen Verunsicherung eignen sich vorzugsweise stresstheoretische Ansätze. Wenn bspw. Migranten mit Anforderungen wie die Organisation des Alltags in einer modernen Gesellschaft, Integration in die Mehrheitsgesellschaft ohne Aufgabe eigener kultureller Überzeugungen und Bewältigung der eigenkulturellen Modernitätsdefizite konfrontiert werden und dabei die Grenzen ihrer Fähigkeiten spüren, wenn also Verunsicherungen auf mangelnde

Ressourcen stoßen, dann wird diese Problemkonstellation von den Betroffenen in der Regel als Streß wahrgenommen: Das Gefühl der Herausforderung, das Leben auch in der Fremde zu meistern, weicht dann dem Gefühl der Überforderung. Lazarus und Folkman (1987) zu Folge entsteht Streß generell dann, wenn Menschen im Umgang mit Anforderungen in persönlich wichtigen Bereichen wie Familie, Beruf oder auch Sozialbeziehungen nicht über ausreichende Bewältigungsressourcen verfügen. Streß läßt sich in dieser Konzeption als ein mehrstufiger Prozeß begreifen, wo am Beginn die wahrgenommenen Situationsanforderungen und die Einschätzung der Ressourcen stehen. Je nach Ausgang dieser Bewertung von Anforderungen und Ressourcen qualifizieren Subjekte eine Situation entweder als eine Herausforderung, eine Bedrohung oder als einen persönlichen Gewinn. Darauf folgen Bewältigungsversuche, die zum einen auf eine positive Veränderung der Problemlage, zum anderen auf eine Verbesserung der emotionalen Befindlichkeit gerichtet sind. Soziale und personale Ressourcen können dabei die Wirksamkeit stressinduzierender Belastungsfaktoren beeinflussen (vgl. Schwarzer & Jerusalem, 1994). Als personale Ressourcen sind hierbei Aspekte wie das individuelle Bewältigungsverhalten, formale Bildung, aber auch individuelle Verhaltensdispositionen wie Selbstwirksamkeit (vgl. Jerusalem, 1990) und Selbstwertgefühl zu verstehen. Als soziale Ressourcen werden soziale Netzwerke wie Familien- und Freundschaftsbeziehungen (landsmannschaftliche Gruppen bei Migranten bzw. Menschen, die aus derselben Region kommen) bezeichnet, die eine Person zur Verfügung hat bzw. in Notsituationen in Anspruch nehmen kann. Sie helfen der Person, unangenehme und negative Folgen bedrohlicher Anforderungen zu dämpfen. Stress entsteht also am Ende der vergleichenden Einschätzung im Falle des Missverhältnisses von Anforderungen und der zur Verfügung stehenden Ressourcen.

Ein Ortswechsel, ein Umzug, stellt stets eine Phase der Veränderung und des Überganges dar, der zunächst eine erhöhte Hilflosigkeit und Stress zur Folge hat. Und Stress steigert gleichzeitig die Anfälligkeit für Krankheiten und schwächt das Immunsystem. Der Wechsel der Heimat, wie ihn die Arbeitsmigranten aus der Türkei durchlaufen haben, ist jedoch wesentlich gravierender als bspw. gewöhnliche Wohnortswechsel von Deutschen innerhalb Deutschlands oder Türken innerhalb der Türkei. Türkische Migranten aus provinziellen Regionen müssen sich nicht nur die neue natürliche Umgebung aneignen, sondern zusätzlich das technologische wie soziale Entwicklungsgefälle, die Modernitätsdefizite des eigenen Herkunftsortes als auch die symbolisch-kulturelle (Sprache, Religion, Werte) Verschiedenheit verarbeiten; d.h. der ökologische Übergang gestaltet sich als schwieriger, weil sowohl ein radikaler Wechsel des Lebenskontextes als auch ein Wechsel der kulturellen Deutungssysteme stattfindet. Zwar ist der Akkulturationsstress dort stärker, wo die Diskrepanzen zwischen Herkunft- und Aufnahmekultur groß sind (vgl. Berry, 1997), wie im Falle der kulturellen Distanz zwischen Deutschland und der Türkei. Gleichwohl aber "puffern" pluralistische Gesellschaften wie die Bundesrepublik, die eine hohe Toleranzschwelle für andersartige Lebensweisen haben, also andere Norm- und Moralvorstellungen erlauben, einen Teil des Stresses auch ab, so dass trotz großer Differenzen Menschen unterschiedlicher Herkunftskontexte ihren Alltag relativ gut meistern können. Dabei bringt aus der Sicht der Migranten beispielsweise auch eine Rückzugstendenz in landsmannschaftliche Gruppen, in denen ein höherer sozialer Rückhalt erwartet wird und eine Gettoisierung – quasi als Imitat der Heimat - eine Entlastung und Bewältigung des Stresses mit sich. Denn das Leben in eigenethnischen Kontexten verleiht das Gefühl, die Situation eher kontrollieren und verstehen zu können, was sich zwar kurzfristig förderlich für die psychische Gesundheit und das Wohlbefinden auswirkt, langfristig jedoch sich als kontraproduktiv erweist, da es zu weiterer Separation von der Mehrheitsgesellschaft und zu sozialer Desintegration führt.

Es ist charakteristisch, dass die Anomie als ein Zustand sozialer Desintegration und Verunsicherung sich eher verstärkt, je länger der Aufenthalt dauert (vgl. Morone, 1997). So wird beispielsweise bei vielen türkischen Migranten mit der Zeit auch die Heimat zur Fremde, ohne dass gleichzeitig die Fremde zur Heimat wird. Denkbar ist, dass verunsicherte Menschen Situation und Interaktionen, die sie nicht beherrschen, eher vermeiden, dadurch aber gleichzeitig auch ihre Bewältigungskompetenzen geringer ausbilden. Sie können diese Gelegenheiten und Erfordernisse jedoch nicht ganz aus der Welt räumen und erfahren bei weiteren Begegnungen höhere Verunsicherungen.

Auf individueller Ebene wird Akkulturationsstress stärker von solchen Personen erlebt, die über geringe Sprachkenntnisse der Aufnahmekultur (vgl. Jerusalem, 1992) verfügen, eine nur wenig ausdifferenzierte Persönlichkeitsstruktur haben und in starkem Maße von den Veränderungen ihrer sozialen Umwelt abhängen. Die Belastungen steigen, wenn Menschen eher agrarischen lebensweltlichen Verhältnissen entstammen; denn vielfach ist der öffentliche Kontakt in der bäuerlichen Gesellschaft durch starke Rituale festgelegt und geregelt, wie etwa der Etikette der Anrede, Benimmregeln, soziale Hierarchien und Statusmerkmale etc. (vgl. Leyer, 1991). Durch starre Regeln werden aber auch - sofern man sich an diese hält - Interaktionskonflikte gemieden, weil alles klar geregelt und geordnet erscheint. Es wird für das Individuum wenig Ambiguität erzeugt; spontane Impulse, die die öffentliche Ordnung durcheinander bringen könnten, werden gemieden. Gleichwohl Begegnungen in einem neuen kulturellen Raum wie in der Bundesrepublik für Migranten auch fruchtbar sein und zu einer stärkeren Emanzipation aus alten Zwängen, Ritualen und Rollenbildern führen können, so ist doch festzuhalten, dass in der Fremde alte und neue Orientierungen vielfach nebeneinander existieren und dadurch starke Spannungen und neurotische Symptome auslösen. So ist bspw. die höhere Krankheitsanfälligkeit sozial benachteiligter Gruppen, verursacht u.a. durch höhere Stressbelastung, in der gesundheitspsychologischen Forschung gut dokumentiert (vgl. Schwarzer & Leppin, 1989). Migranten zeigen gegenüber der deutschen Bevölkerung deutlich mehr Risikozustände und Gesundheitsbelastungen auf (Firat, 1996). Collatz (1998) schätzt, gemessen an den "Life-events", den kritischen, stressverursachenden Lebensereignissen, eine 20-mal höhere Belastung von Migranten im Vergleich mit der einheimischen Bevölkerung. Ferner zeigen Befunde, dass türkische Migranten im Vergleich zu Deutschen deutlich stärkere Depressionssymptome zeigen (vgl. Diefenbacher & Heim, 1997). Generell spielen bei der Frage der psychischen Gesundheit von Migranten sowohl die ethnische Zugehörigkeit und der Status dieser Ethnie innerhalb der Mehrheitsgesellschaft, (ist sie von besonderer Ausgrenzung betroffen?), die eigene soziale Lage (Arbeitsmigrant in un- bzw. unterqualifizierten Berufssektoren oder gut dotierter Experte?) und die Umstände der Migration eine entscheidende Rolle (vgl. Faltermaier, 2001).

Für den erlebten Akkulturationsstress und Verunsicherung spielt auch der Grad der Freiwilligkeit für eine Migration eine entscheidende Variable; denn je unfreiwilliger und erzwungener eine Migration erfolgt, desto mehr wird Stress erlebt. So ist bekannt, dass sowohl Flüchtlinge als auch deren Kinder größeren Akkulturationsstress erleben als freiwillige (vgl. Garcia Coll & Magnusson, 1997). Des Weiteren hängt die Frage, wie gut eine Migration bewältigt wird, u. a. davon ab, mit welcher Motivation Personen sich zur Migration entschieden haben, welche Hoffnungen und Träume, aber auch Ängste an die Migration gekoppelt waren und welche Vorbereitungen es bereits im Herkunftsland gegeben hat (vgl. Berry, 1997). Ferner sind der Einfluss der familiären Situation und die soziale Unterstützung für die Bewältigung des Stresserlebens ein wichtiger Faktor. Personen, die sich in unterstützenden Netzwerken eingebettet fühlen, tendieren eher dazu, das Potential stressreicher Begegnungen als geringer einzuschätzen (vgl. Schwarzer & Leppin, 1989). Hinsichtlich der Migrationsbelastungen gibt es in der Literatur übereinstimmende Befunde, die zeigen, dass Personen, die mit Familien umziehen, die Situation besser bewältigen als alleinstehende oder geschiedene Menschen. Hier zeigen jedoch die Befunde in den siebziger Jahren für die erste Generation von Migranten (vgl. Schrader, Nikles & Griese, 1979), dass gerade etwa 6 % von ihnen mit ihren Familien zusammen ausgereist sind; d. h. die Migration nach Deutschland hat eine große Zahl von „zerrissenen Familien" als Folge gehabt. Nicht zuletzt sind für die Höhe des Stresserlebens auch frühere Erfahrungen mit Ortswechseln in der Heimat ausschlaggebend. Hier ist davon auszugehen, dass insbesondere Arbeitsmigranten der ersten Generation aus der Türkei vor einem Wechsel nach Deutschland bereits dort eine Binnenmigration vom Land in die Stadt durchgemacht haben. Anzunehmen ist auch, dass bei Menschen, die aus ländlich-agrarischen Kontexten in neue Metropolen ziehen, größere Verunsicherungen auftreten als bei Menschen, die urbanen Lebenskontexten entstammen. Menschen aus ursprünglich provinziellen Verhältnissen, die in einer überschaubaren Umgebung groß geworden sind, einen anderen Arbeitsrhythmus, ein anderes Verhältnis zur Zeit und eine andere Wahrnehmung menschlicher und gesellschaftlicher Räume haben, deren soziokultureller Habitus sie also wenig adaptiv macht für neue Lebensumstände, sind prädisponiert für soziale und kulturelle Anpassungsschwierigkeiten (vgl. Frigessi Castelnuova & Rossi, 1986). Dieser Aspekt ist insbesondere für türkische Migranten in Deutschland relevant: So nehmen Kürsat-Ahlers & Ahlers (1985) an, dass rund zwei Drittel aller türkischen Migranten in Deutschland der ersten Generation aus dörflichen Provinzen Anatoliens stammen.

Folgt man der familienpsychologischen Literatur, so lässt sich jede Familie sowohl durch Ressourcen als auch durch Vulnerabilitäten (Verwundbarkeiten) kennzeichnen (vgl. Schneewind, 1999), die auf ihre Akkulturation einwirken. Dabei werden bei Migranten drei Arten von Ressourcen voneinander unterschieden: Sozialstatus (z.B. finanzielle Mittel), politischer Status (z.B. Aufenthaltsstatus) und soziale Ressourcen wie soziales Netzwerk und Familienkohäsion (vgl. Rumbaut, 1997). Beispielsweise bildet familiäre Kohäsion eine wichtige protektive Ressource, wenn die Familie finanziell schlecht gestellt ist sowie intensive Diskriminierungen und extreme soziale Benachteiligungen erfährt. Außerdem lassen Forschungserfahrungen vermuten (vgl. Rumbaut, 1997), dass kohäsive Familien mit wenigen Eltern-Kind-Konflikten in Aspekten wie Wohlbefinden, Schulleistung der Kinder, soziale Unterstützung, Bildungsaspiration usw. konfliktreichen Familien überlegen sind.

4) Empirische Studie

Die vorliegende Studie behandelt in erster Linie lebensweltliche Verunsicherungen türkischer Migranten im Zusammenhang mit ihrer erfahrenen sozialen Unterstützung; d.h. sie eruiert die alltäglich wahrgenommenen Bedrohungs- und

Unterstützungspotentiale. Theoretisch wird dabei Bezug genommen auf das Konzept der Anomie bzw. der anomischen Verunsicherung, die hier als „soziale Verunsicherung" umschrieben wird. Anomie wird generell als eine Folge gesellschaftlicher Desintegration betrachtet, bei der Norm- und Orientierungslosigkeit vorherrscht. Insbesondere ist das in Krisenzeiten und Zeiten rascher Transformationen zu beobachten. Anomie zielt auf die Beschreibung der Prozesse beschleunigten Wandels unter der Perspektive normativer Bindungen des Individuums (vgl. Hochstim & Plake, 1997). Jedoch ist zu präzisieren, dass Anomie nicht lediglich auf Prozesse sozialen Wandelns zurückzuführen ist - denn jede Gesellschaft macht einen Veränderungsprozeß durch, - sondern mit Anomie geht eine spürbare und unkontrollierbare Beschleunigung des Wandels, mit der soziale Akteure nicht mehr Schritt halten können, einher (vgl. Atteslander, Gransow & Western, 1999). Das heißt: Anomische Verunsicherungen entstehen, wenn sich die Lebenswelt dramatisch verändert, ohne dass zugleich soziale Akteure die Regeln und Normen dieser veränderten Welt sich subjektiv aneignen können, also neuen konstituierten gesellschaftlichen Strukturen nicht gleichzeitig sozial verbindliche Regeln und Normen folgen. Genau diese Art von Veränderungen, einher gehend mit einem Verlust eigenkultureller Referenzpunkte und eigenkultureller Interpretationsmatrizen der gelebten Alltagswirklichkeit, lassen sich im Leben türkischer Migranten in Deutschland, als einer Art „anomic state of mind" (Li, Atteslander, Tanur & Wang; 1999), zeigen.

Vielen türkischen Migranten wird mit der Zeit auch die Heimat zur Fremde, ohne dass gleichzeitig die Fremde zur Heimat wird. Faktoren wie mangelndes Sprachverständnis und mangelnde Kenntnisse über Verhaltensregeln im Aufnahmeland fördern die Entstehung von Angst. Dann ist ein stärkerer Rückzug in eigenkulturelle bzw. eigenethnische Nischen zu vermuten, die die erfahrene Deklassierung und Entwertung reduziert, aber im gleichen Atemzug die Wahrnehmung der Mehrheitsgesellschaft als anomisch und undurchsichtig steigert. Hierbei ist jedoch daran zu erinnern, dass die subjektiv wahrgenommene Anomie nicht in einem direkten Verhältnis eine objektive Anomie bzw. objektive Regellosigkeit der Mehrheitsgesellschaft widerspiegelt.

In der empirischen Studie sollen Antworten auf folgende Fragen versucht werden: 1) Wie hoch ist das Ausmaß der erlebten sozialen Verunsicherung und der sozialen Unterstützung ausgeprägt? 2) Welche Unterschiede im Verunsicherungs- und Unterstützungserleben lassen sich hinsichtlich der verschiedenen Gruppen innerhalb der türkischen Migranten - wie etwa Alters-, Geschlechts- und Bildungseffekte- identifizieren? 3) Wie weit ist das Belastungs- und Unterstützungserleben von den unterschiedlichen Graden der Freiwilligkeit der Migration abhängig? und 4) Welche statistischen Zusammenhänge lassen sich zwischen sozialer Verunsicherung und Unterstützung aufzeigen?

Erwartbar ist zunächst, dass mit der Dauer des Aufenthaltes die sozialen Verunsicherungen abnehmen, weil eine Gewöhnung an das Leben in Deutschland eintritt bzw. mehr Gelegenheiten entstehen, sich einzuleben (vgl. Jerusalem, 1992). Ferner ist zu erwarten, dass bei steigendem Bildungsniveau mit geringeren Verunsicherungen zu rechnen ist, weil höhere kognitive Kompetenzen sowohl die Organisation des eigenen Lebens in der Fremde vereinfachen als auch das Verhalten anderer sozialer Akteure und die Veränderungen in der sozialen Lebenswelt eher antizipierbar und dadurch für das eigene Leben weniger bedrohlich und verunsichernd erscheinen lassen. Zuletzt ist zu erwarten, dass türkische Frauen stärkere Verunsicherungen erleben als türkische Männer, weil bei ihnen vermutlich die unfreiwillige Migration bzw. die Heiratsmigration überwiegt und sie in Deutschland noch stärker von Einheimischen abgeschottet leben.

Stichprobenkennzeichnung:
Um diese Zusammenhänge empirisch zu testen, haben wir im Rahmen einer standardisierten Fragebogenstudie in der Zeit von Oktober 2001 bis Mai 2002 Daten von 357 türkischstämmigen Probanden im Alter von 13 bis 66 Jahren (M = 34.3 J., SD = 12.3 J.) in Berlin erhoben, die in der Zeit von 1963 bis 2001 nach Deutschland gekommen sind. Die durchschnittliche Aufenthaltsdauer in Deutschland betrug 20.09 Jahre (SD = 7.95 J.). Die Befragung war anonym und freiwillig. Ein Teil der Probanden wurde aus türkischen internistischen Praxen (128 Probanden) rekrutiert; der größte Teil (229 Probanden) entstammte einer unausgelesenen Stichprobe (Schulen, Bekanntenkreis, Frauengruppen). Der Fragebogen wurde sowohl in türkischer als auch deutscher Sprache angeboten; eine deutliche Mehrheit (89.6 %) füllte ihn auf türkisch aus. Was die Staatsangehörigkeit betrifft, so gaben 257 (72 %) diese mit türkisch an, 80 (22.4 %) als deutsch, 12 (3.4 %) als bi-national und 8 (2.3 %) machten hierzu keine Angaben. Die geschlechtsspezifische Verteilung wies eine Überrepräsentanz von Frauen auf: 227 (63.6 %) der Probanden waren weiblich, 119 (33.3 %) waren männlich, 11 Personen (3.1 %) machten hierzu keine Angaben. Der Bildungshintergrund wies deutliche Unterschiede zur deutschen Bevölkerung auf: die meisten der Probanden hatten nur eine abgeschlossene Grundschulbildung als höchsten Schulabschluss (33.6 %), gefolgt von abgeschlossener Gymnasialbildung (26.3 %) und Realschul- bzw. Mittelschulbildung (25.6 %); der Anteil der Schüler betrug 6.4 %, und 3.6 % hatten eine Universitätsausbildung. Eine überwiegende Mehrheit

wohnte mit dem Ehepartner und den Kindern zusammen (65.2 %), gefolgt von jungen Menschen, die bei ihren Eltern wohnten (20.5 %) und Paaren (8.5 %). Lediglich 4.6 % der Befragten wohnte allein.

Messinstrumente:
Soziale Verunsicherung und soziale Unterstützung wurden mit bislang in der empirisch-sozialwissenschaftlichen Forschung bewährten Instrumenten gemessen; für die erlebte Verunsicherung kam die Anomieskala von Fischer & Kohr (1980) mit insgesamt zehn Items zum Einsatz; für die Messung der sozialen Unterstützung wurde die „Social Support Scale" von Bullinger, Kirchberger & von Steinbüchel (1993) mit insgesamt zwölf Items eingesetzt. Die Kennwerte (interne Konsistenzen) deuten auf eine hohe Zuverlässigkeit der Messinstrumente (Cronbach's alpha von 0.89 für soziale Verunsicherung und 0.92 für soziale Unterstützung) hin. Fragen nach der Zustimmungsintensität sind von „stimmt völlig" bis „stimmt überhaupt nicht", bzw. „trifft völlig zu" bis „trifft überhaupt nicht zu", Fragen nach der Häufigkeit von „nie" bis „immer" skaliert worden.
Um zu erfassen, welche Motive bei der Migration nach Deutschland ausschlaggebend waren und inwiefern die Migration freiwillig erfolgte, wurden die Probanden einleitend gebeten, anzugeben, warum sie nach Deutschland gekommen sind.

Tabelle 2: Einreisegründe nach Deutschland

Prozentuale Häufigkeiten

	Männlich	Weiblich	Gesamt
Arbeitsmigration	32.7	9.6	17.9
Ehezusammenführung	19.5	45.0	36.1
Studium	4.4	1.4	2.3
In Deutschland geboren	13.3	23.9	19.9
Familienzusammenführung	28.3	19.7	22.9
Flüchtling	1.8	0.5	0.9

Die Tabelle 2 verdeutlicht, dass mit rund 36 % der größte Teil der Probanden nach Deutschland kam, weil der Partner hier lebte; ca. 23 % sind als Kinder zu ihren in Deutschland lebenden Eltern zugezogen, knapp 20 % der Befragten sind in Deutschland geboren und 18 % sind zum Arbeiten nach Deutschland gekommen, 2.3 % sind ursprünglich zum Studieren, und etwa 1 % ist als Flüchtling nach Deutschland gekommen bzw. ist aus der Heimat vertrieben worden. In der geschlechtsspezifischen Auswertung wird deutlich, dass bei Männern die Arbeitsmigration überwiegt (32.7 %), bei Frauen dagegen Migration im Zuge der Ehe- bzw. Familienzusammenführung (45.0 %).

Gefragt, wo sie sich eher heimisch fühlten, antwortete die größte Mehrheit (39.1 %), daß sie sich sowohl in der Türkei als auch in Deutschland heimisch fühlt. Eher in der Herkunftskultur heimisch fühlten sich ca. 28.3 % der Befragten; eine annähernd gleich große Gruppe (26 %) fühlte sich eher in Deutschland heimisch. Bedeutend geringer waren die Ablehnungen beider kulturelle Bezüge (5.7 %) und die Präferenz eines ganz anderen Landes als Deutschland oder der Türkei (0.9 %).

Im Rückblick schätzte etwa jeder sechste der befragten türkischen Migranten (15.4 %) die Einreise nach Deutschland als einen biographischen Irrtum ein, eine etwa gleich große Anzahl (16.1 %) verhielt sich zu dieser Frage eher indifferent, wogegen die überwältigende Mehrheit (68.5 %) das Item, dass die Migration ein Fehler gewesen sei, ablehnte.

5) Ergebnisse

Die deskriptiven Befunde zeigen zunächst anhand sechs exemplarischer Items die allgemeine Ausprägung der erlebten sozialen Verunsicherung und der subjektiv wahrgenommenen Unterstützung.

Soziale Verunsicherung:

Abbildung 1

Deskriptive Angaben zu sozialer Verunsicherung

Beispielitems: **Soziale Verunsicherung**

1. In diesen Tagen ist alles so unsicher, dass man auf alles gefasst sein muss.
2. Moralische Grundsätze gelten heute nicht mehr.
3. Heute ist jeder mit sich beschäftigt, dass er nicht an morgen denken kann.
4. Den meisten Menschen fehlt ein richtiger Halt.
5. Früher waren die Leute besser dran, weil jeder wusste, was er zu tun hatte.
6. Wenn man die Ereignisse der letzten Jahre betrachtet, wird man richtig unsicher.

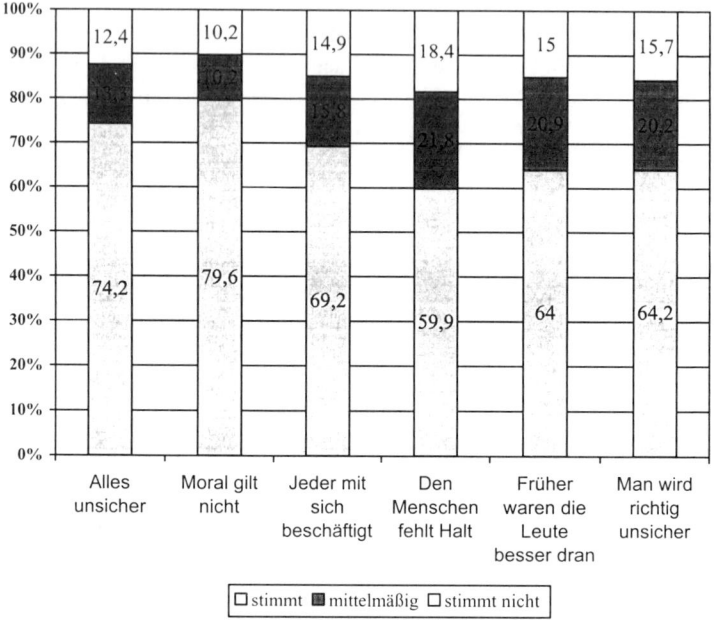

Die Abbildung 1 verdeutlicht, dass die Mehrheit der türkischen Migranten ihren sozialen Alltag als stark verunsichernd erlebt. Bei allen der hier vorgestellten exemplarischen Items antworteten zwischen 60 bis 80 Prozent aller Befragten, das soziale Leben in Deutschland sei für sie undurchschaubar, außerhalb ihrer persönlichen Kontrolle und eine Quelle von Verunsicherung. Insbesondere die Zustimmung zum Ausmaß des „moralischen Verfalls" ist mit fast 80 % extrem hoch.

Der wahrgenommenen hohen Verunsicherung steht jedoch auch ein beträchtliches Ausmaß an sozialer Unterstützung entgegen, wie aus Tabelle 3 deutlich wird. So antworteten knapp 70 % aller Befragten, dass ihnen „oft bis immer" jemand hilft, wenn sie bettlägerig sind; 76.1 % verfügten „oft bis immer" über eine Person, die sie zum Arzt bringt, wenn es nötig ist und über 80 % bekundeten, dass sie „oft bis immer" jemanden haben, der ihnen Liebe und Zuneigung zeigt. Etwas mehr als zwei Drittel aller Befragten verfügte „oft bis immer" über Personen, die ihnen helfen, undurchsichtige Situationen besser zu verstehen bzw. die ihnen mit Rat zur Seite stehen. Etwas geringer fiel allerdings mit knapp 64 %

das Antwortverhalten auf die Frage aus, ob die Befragten Personen haben, die ihre Probleme wirklich verstehen.

Tabelle 3:

Deskriptive Angaben zu sozialer Unterstützung

Prozentuale Häufigkeiten

Konstrukt	Antwortformat		
Soziale Unterstützung	*Nie-selten*	*gelegentlich*	*Oft-immer*
Gibt es in Ihrem Umfeld jemanden,			
der Ihnen hilft, wenn Sie bettlägerig sind?	19.0	11.9	69.1
der Sie zum Arzt bringt, wenn es nötig ist?	12.5	11.3	76.1
der Ihnen Liebe und Zuneigung zeigt?	9.9	8.7	81.4
der Ihnen Informationen gibt, um eine Situation zu verstehen?	15.1	16.0	68.9
dessen Rat Ihnen wirklich wichtig ist?	14.3	17.7	68.0
der Ihre Probleme versteht?	17.3	18.7	63.9

Betrachtet man die Ergebnisse nicht nur auf der Einzelitemebene, sondern auf der Skalenmittelwertsausprägung, so lassen sich folgende Zusammenhänge erkennen:
Türkische Frauen erlebten ihren Alltag deutlich stärker verunsichernd ($\underline{M}$ = 4.02, $\underline{SD}$ = 0.82) als türkische Männer ($\underline{M}$ = 3.79, $\underline{SD}$ = 0.81). Diese Differenzen sind statistisch hoch signifikant [$\underline{F}$ (1, 313) = 5.60, $\underline{p}$ = .018] und spiegeln Befunde anderer Studien wider, wonach Frauen im Allgemeinen stärkeren Akkulturationsbelastungen unterliegen, weil sie zusätzlich noch Rollenkonflikte bewältigen müssen (vgl. Berry, 1997). Auch bei einem Mediansplit der Gruppe in „hoch

verunsicherte" und „niedrig verunsicherte" (Median = 4.10) zeigte sich, dass mit 115 Personen eine deutlich größere Anzahl der Hochbelasteten unter den Frauen vorzufinden waren - etwas mehr als die Hälfte aller beteiligten Frauen -, während sie bei Männern mit 46 Personen etwa 40 % betrug ($\underline{Chi}^2$ = 4.44, $\underline{df}$ = 1, $\underline{p}$ = .035). Von diesen hochbelasteten Frauen waren wiederum mehr als die Hälfte (53 %) Heiratsmigrantinnen.

Ferner zeigte sich, dass Migranten, die alleine lebten, deutlich stärkere Verunsicherungen erlebten ($\underline{M}$ = 4.38, $\underline{SD}$ = 0.68) als Menschen, die mit ihrem Ehepartner ($\underline{M}$ = 4.03, $\underline{SD}$ = 0.85) oder mit ihrer Familie zusammenlebten ($\underline{M}$ = 3.94, $\underline{SD}$ = 0.83).

Hinsichtlich des Bildungshintergrundes ließ sich jedoch kein konsistentes Muster erkennen: Während Menschen mit einer Grundschulbildung, wie zu erwarten war, eine hohe Verunsicherung erlebten ($\underline{M}$ = 4.07, $\underline{SD}$ = 0.84), fühlten sich auch Gymnasiasten und Schüler stark verunsichert, sogar stärker als Personen mit nur einer Mittelschulbildung. Auf einem relativ hohen Niveau, aber geringer als die anderen Bildungsstufen war die soziale Verunsicherung bei Personen mit einer Universitätsbildung ausgeprägt. Dieser kontraintuitive Befund der hohen Belastung von Schülern und Gymnasiasten lässt sich vermutlich einerseits vor dem Hintergrund der unsicheren beruflichen Perspektive junger Menschen (insbesondere junger Migranten) in Zeiten knapper Ausbildungs- und Studienplätze erklären, zum anderen aber auch als ein Ausdruck des Generationen- und Kulturkonflikts türkischer Jugendlicher deuten. Denn von der Ambivalenz der Moderne, die einerseits eine generelle Öffnung der Chancen auf Selbstverwirklichung für Jugendliche, zugleich aber auch eine Verschärfung des ökonomischen Ungleichgewichts für bestimmte (Rand-)Gruppen der Gesellschaft bedeutet, sind türkische Jugendliche noch stärker betroffen. Sie müssen dabei nicht nur - wie ihre deutschen Altersgenossen - die nachteiligen Auswirkungen der Individualisierung, der Beschleunigung des Lebens und der erlebten Anomie etc. bewältigen, sondern auch die positiven Aspekte dieser Individualisierung (Chancen der Selbstverwirklichung) gegen ihre Eltern durchsetzen, die eine stärkere kollektivistische Orientierung favorisieren.

Dennoch ist aber auffällig, dass im Vergleich der Altersgruppen ältere Türken deutlich stärker verunsichert sind als jüngere ($\underline{M}$ = 4.24, $\underline{SD}$ = 0.73 vs. $\underline{M}$ = 3.84, $\underline{SD}$ = 0.74).

Die Annahme, soziale Verunsicherungserlebnisse würden mit der Dauer des Aufenthaltes allmählich nachlassen, erwies sich für die hier untersuchten türkischen Migranten nicht haltbar: so zeigten die Ergebnisse zweier nach unterschiedlicher Aufenthaltsdauer (weniger als zehn Jahre vs. mehr als dreißig Jahre) gebildeten Teilstichproben, dass diejenigen mit mehr als einer dreißigjährigen Migrationsgeschichte ($\underline{M}$ = 4.20; $\underline{SD}$ = 0.84; N = 35) gegenüber der Gruppe, die sich weniger als zehn Jahre in Deutschland befand ($\underline{M}$ = 3.93; $\underline{SD}$ = 0.76; N = 35), deutlich stärkere Verunsicherungen aufwiesen. Zusammenfassend ist festzuhalten, dass die Werte um einen Mittelwert von annähernd $\underline{M}$ = 4.0 deutlich den theoretisch erwartbaren Skalenmittelwert von $\underline{M}$ = 3.0 überschreiten. Somit lässt sich innerhalb der befragten türkischen Migrantengruppe eine stark ausgeprägte soziale Verunsicherung identifizieren. Eine hohe Verunsicherung, folgt man der Theorie der erlernten Hilflosigkeit (vgl. Seligman, 1979), lässt sich als ein Ausdruck von Ohnmacht und Kontrollverlust deuten, was besonders depressionsfördernd wirkt und zu weiterer Verunsicherung im Alltag führt.

Diese im Allgemeinen sehr hohen Belastungswerte der Migranten sind nicht allein auf fehlende persönliche Ressourcen zurückzuführen, sondern auch eventuell einer mangelnden Akzeptanz, geringerer Anerkennung (Jerusalem, 1992) oder offener Diskriminierung (vgl. Vahedi, 1996) seitens der Mehrheitsgesellschaft geschuldet und sind teilweise als ein realistischer Reflex gelebter unsicherer Verhältnisse zu verstehen, was bspw. die hohe soziale Verunsicherung betrifft. Denn nach wie vor ist das Leben vieler Migranten durch aufenthaltsrechtliche, familiäre (verschärfte Generationenkonflikte zwischen Eltern und Kindern) und finanzielle Unsicherheiten (mit über 20 % weisen Migranten eine deutlich höhere Arbeitslosigkeitsrate auf) gekennzeichnet.

Tabelle 4: Soziale Verunsicherung und soziale Unterstützung

Mittelwerte und Standardabweichungen

	Soziale Verunsicherung		Soziale Unterstützung	
	M	SD	M	SD
Männlich	3.79	0.81	3.86	0.92
Weiblich	4.02	0.82	3.80	1.00
Alleinlebend	4.38	0.68	2.97	1.20
Zusammenleben mit Ehepartner	4.03	0.85	3.87	1.10
Zusammenleben mit Ehepartner und Kinder	3.94	0.83	3.74	0.99
Grundschule	4.07	0.84	3.63	1.08
Mittelschule	3.77	0.86	3.81	0.98
Gymnasium	4.03	0.74	3.85	0.92
Universität	3.56	0.68	4.16	0.61
Schüler	3.80	0.88	4.0	0.62
Junior (<= 25 J.)	3.84	0.74	4.11	0.70
Senior (> 50 J.)	4.24	0.73	3.83	1.16
Gesamtstichprobe	**3.92**	**0.81**	**3.81**	**0.97**

Soziale Unterstützung:
Was die erlebte Unterstützung betrifft, so erfuhren - wie sie die Tabelle 4 verdeutlicht - Männer tendenziell etwas mehr Unterstützung als Frauen (M = 3.86, SD = 0.92 vs. M = 3.80, SD = 1.00); jedoch sind diese Differenzen statistisch nicht signifikant. Deutlich auffälliger dagegen waren die Unterschiede zwischen Alleinlebenden (M = 2.97, SD = 1.20) und Menschen, die ein einem ehelichen (M = 3.87, SD = 1.10) oder familiären Kontext lebten (M = 3.74, SD = 0.99): Alleinlebende erfuhren, wie zu erwarten war, eine geringere soziale Unterstützung. Hinsichtlich der Bildungsunterschiede ist der Befund auffällig (vgl. Tabelle

4), dass Personen mit abgeschlossener akademischer Bildung über deutlich höhere Unterstützungspotentiale berichteten als Menschen mit geringeren Schulabschlüssen. Die ebenfalls hohen Werte bei Schülern sind vermutlich der Verfügbarkeit von Eltern und Geschwistern als potentiellen Helfern in Notzeiten zurückzuführen. Im Vergleich der Altersgruppen wurde auch hier deutlich, dass ältere Migranten über deutlich weniger soziale Unterstützung verfügten als jüngere. Diese Differenzen waren statistisch signifikant ($p<.00$). Jedoch ist generell festzuhalten, dass bei einem theoretisch erwartbaren Skalenmittelwert von M = 3.0 die berichtete soziale Unterstützung weit darüber lag. Türkische Migranten erlebten also nicht nur hohe Verunsicherungen, sie verfügten auch über ein hohes Maß an sozialer Unterstützung.

Tab. 5: Verunsicherungs- und Unterstützungserfahrung in Abhängigkeit von der Freiwilligkeit der Migration

Mittelwerte und Standardabweichungen

	Soziale Verunsicherung		Soziale Unterstützung	
	M	SD	M	SD
Arbeitsmigration	4.13	0.82	3.85	0.96
Ehezusammenführung	4.10	0.75	3.58	1.08
In Deutschland geboren	3.85	0.73	4.14	0.64
Familienzusammenführung	3.60	0.91	3.86	0.96

Betrachtet man zuletzt das Ausmaß des Verunsicherungserlebens und der erlebten Unterstützung in Abhängigkeit von der Freiwilligkeit der Migration, so lassen sich für die vier großen Gruppen folgende Befunde festhalten[2]: Die stärkste Verunsicherung erlebten Arbeitsmigranten (M = 4.13; SD = 0.82), dicht gefolgt von Personen, die aufgrund einer Ehe mit einem in Deutschland lebenden Partner sich zur Migration gezwungen sahen (M = 4.10; SD = 0.75). Deutlich geringere Verunsicherungen erlebten dagegen in Deutschland geborene Personen, bei denen nur die Eltern einen Migrationshintergrund hatten (M = 3.85; SD = 0.73).

---

[2] Die Gruppe der Flüchtlinge und die Gruppe der Studenten wurden aufgrund extrem kleiner Fallzahlen (N=3 bei Flüchtlingen und N=8 bei Studenten) bei den Berechnungen nicht berücksichtigt, um die Statistiken nicht zu verzerren.

Am geringsten war jedoch die Verunsicherung bei jenen ausgeprägt, die aus der Türkei zu ihrer Familie in Deutschland nachzogen ($\underline{M}$ = 3.60; $\underline{SD}$ = 0.91), obwohl zu erwarten wäre, dass in Deutschland geborene Migrantenkinder aufgrund ihrer längeren und von Geburt an erfolgenden Interaktion mit der deutschen sozialen Umwelt die geringsten Verunsicherungen aufweisen müßten. Diese intuitiven Erwartungen ließen sich eher hinsichtlich der erlebten sozialen Unterstützung wiederfinden: Hier nahm die Gruppe der in Deutschland geborenen mit einem deutlichen Abstand die stärkste Unterstützung von ihrem sozialen Umfeld wahr ($\underline{M}$ = 4.14; $\underline{SD}$ = 0.64), gefolgt von Familiennachzüglern ($\underline{M}$ = 3.86; $\underline{SD}$ = 0.96). Arbeitsmigranten dagegen wiesen unerwarteter Weise deutlich höhere Unterstützungswerte ($\underline{M}$ = 3.85; $\underline{SD}$ = 0.96) auf als Personen, die im Rahmen der Ehezusammenführung nach Deutschland gekommen waren ($\underline{M}$ = 3.58; $\underline{SD}$ = 1.08). Es ist zu vermuten, dass insbesondere Heiratsmigrantinnen durch ihre Übersiedlung zu ihrem Partner in Deutschland wichtige soziale Netzwerke wie Freundschaft und Familie in der Heimat verloren haben und hier das unterstützende Netzwerk weitestgehend auf verwandtschaftliche Bezüge zur Familie des Mannes eingeschränkt ist.

Die Unterschiede innerhalb der Gruppen waren sowohl hinsichtlich der erlebten Verunsicherung ($F_{(3, 313)}$ = 7.29; p = 0.00) als auch hinsichtlich der erlebten Unterstützung ($F_{(3, 325)}$ = 5.17; p = 0.02) statistisch signifikant.

Diskussion der Zusammenhänge zwischen den Erhebungsvariablen:

Tabelle 6 verdeutlicht die korrelativen Zusammenhänge zwischen den Erhebungsvariablen.

Korrelationen zwischen den Erhebungsvariablen

(Pearson-Korrelationen; Korrelationskoeffizient $\underline{r}$)

	1	2	3	4	5	6
Soziale Verunsicherung (1)	1	-.20***	-.06	.01	.14*	.12*
Soziale Unterstützung (2)		1	.11*	.00	-.14*	-.03
Bildung (3)			1	-.06	-.33***	-.06
Aufenthaltsdauer (4)				1	.57***	-.24***
Alter (5)					1	-.21***
Geschlecht (6)						1

***: p < .001; **: p < .01; *:p < .05

Wie erwartet, zeigt soziale Verunsicherung einen negativen Zusammenhang (r = -.20) mit sozialer Unterstützung auf, d. h. hohe Verunsicherung geht einher mit einer geringen sozialen Unterstützung. Dieser Zusammenhang erwies sich für Frauen deutlich enger (r = -.25) als für Männer (r = -.11). Hierbei können keine Kausalitäten ausfindig gemacht werden. Denkbar ist, dass verunsicherte Menschen Schwierigkeiten haben, soziale Unterstützung zu mobilisieren, aber auch, dass fehlende Unterstützung zu einer stärkeren Verunsicherung führt. Ferner ließen sich zwischen sozialer Verunsicherung und den Variablen Alter und Geschlecht zwar kleine, aber statistisch signifikante Korrelationen aufzeigen; d.h. je älter Migranten waren, desto eher erfuhren sie Verunsicherungen, und Frauen waren eher dem Risiko ausgesetzt, Verunsicherungen zu erleben. Hinsichtlich der sozialen Unterstützung zeigen die Befunde, dass diese positiv mit Bildung korreliert (r = .11); d. h. ein höherer Bildungshintergrund geht mit einer höheren Unterstützung einher; ferner zeigen sich mit dem Alter negative Korrelationen (r = -.14); d.h. je älter Migranten werden, desto geringer wird die von ihnen erlebte Unterstützung. Überraschend ist der Befund, dass die zunehmende Aufenthaltsdauer entgegen den Erwartungen keinen mildernden Effekt auf das Verunsicherungserleben hatte. Damit wird ein in der Forschung zum Akkulturationsstress wichtiger Befund bestätigt: Aufenthaltsdauer allein, wie Jerusalem (1992) an türkischen Jugendlichen demonstrierte, erweist sich nicht generell als stress- bzw. verunsicherungsmindernd.

Dagegen scheint das Verunsicherungserleben deutlich stark von der Freiwilligkeit der Migration abzuhängen: Betrachtet man bspw. Arbeitsmigration als eine Form erzwungener Migration aufgrund ökonomischer Notlage im eigenen Land, so wird deutlich, dass diese eher unfreiwillig migrierten Personen das Leben in der Fremde deutlich bedrohlicher erleben als jene, die in Deutschland geboren oder zu ihren Familien gekommen sind. Ähnliche Zusammenhänge lassen sich auch bei der Heiratsmigration feststellen: Es ist davon auszugehen, dass die meisten der Heiratsmigranten Frauen sind, die nicht nur aus Liebe, sondern vielfach von dem Motiv geleitet, der ökonomischen Not und der provinziellen Enge des eigenen Lebenskontextes zu entfliehen, einen türkischen Partner in Deutschland heiraten. Sie erfahren jedoch eindeutig die höchsten Verunsicherungen und scheinen eine Risikogruppe für psychosoziale Belastungen darzustellen.

Die bisherigen Ergebnisse synoptisch zusammenfassend betrachtet, zeigt sich eine ausgesprochen starke soziale Verunsicherung innerhalb der türkischen Bevölkerung. Inwieweit diese auch von der Haltung der Mehrheitsgesellschaft „provoziert" worden ist, konnten wir nicht ermitteln. Dies ist eine Aufgabe künftiger Forschung. Gleichfalls lässt sich ebenfalls eine hohe soziale Unterstützung ausfindig machen. Diese kann als eine protektive Ressource gegenüber migrationsbedingten Stressoren fungieren. Insofern ist davon auszugehen, dass bspw. ein hoher Familialismus der Migranten (Loyalität, Solidarität und Reziprozität der Familienmitglieder untereinander) nicht nur ein Integrationshemmnis darstellt, sondern auch als ein Protektivfaktor gegenüber Stresssituationen wirkt. Die starke Familienorientierung in der Migrationssituation kompensiert die vielfach erfahrene soziale Isolation im Alltag (vgl. Leyendecker, 2003).

Was das Ausmaß der sozialen Verunsicherungen betrifft, so lassen sich die Befunde mit anderen Daten nicht direkt vergleichen, da es in der Bundesrepublik kaum Studien gibt, die explizit das Verunsicherungserleben mit quantitativen Verfahren messen. Insofern stellen die Ergebnisse auch eine Referenzquelle für künftige Forschungen dar, um Aussagen über Veränderungen und Stabilität der sozialen Verunsicherung türkischer Migranten machen zu können.

Auch wenn die hier vorgestellten Daten möglicherweise etwas verzerrt sind, weil sie aus dem Berliner Raum, einer Gegend mit einer hohen ethnischen Dichte entstammen und nicht als repräsentativ für die Bundesrepublik gelten können, so lassen sich doch diese Zusammenhänge für andere ähnliche Regionen mit einem hohen Anteil an türkischen Migranten unproblematisch übertragen.

Als ein relevantes Ergebnis dieser Studie wie auch als eine methodische Herausforderung kann die Erfassung eines soziologisch wie sozialpsychologisch äußerst bedeutsamen, aber nur schwer greifbaren Konzepts wie Anomie mit empirisch psychologischen Messmethoden betrachtet werden; und dies an einer Population, die - als eine Minderheit - von ihrer Ausgangslage eher geneigt ist, stärkeren Verunsicherungserfahrungen ausgesetzt zu sein. Damit wird ein wichtiger Lebensaspekt von Migranten in Deutschland einer breiteren Öffentlichkeit vertraut gemacht und hilft, die nicht immer im gewünschten Tempo erfolgende Integration etwas besser zu verstehen. Künftige sozialwissenschaftliche und gesundheitspsychologische Forschung mit Migranten sollte stärker längsschnittliche Analysen vornehmen, um spezifische Risiken im Verlauf des Eingliederungsprozesses ausfindig zu machen und darauf aufbauende politische bzw. gesundheitspolitische Empfehlungen abgeben zu können. Diese Arbeit stellt einen ersten Schritt in diese Richtung dar.

Kritisch ist zuletzt daran zu erinnern, dass gerade in Studien zu Migranten das methodische Problem der Konfundierung von ethnischer Zugehörigkeit und sozialer Schicht stärker zu beachten ist: häufig überschneiden sich hier Schichtzugehörigkeit (z. B. Unterschicht) und ethnische Zugehörigkeit; Phänomene, die eventuell nur vor dem Hintergrund unterschiedlicher sozialer Zugehörigkeiten zu verstehen wären, werden unreflektiert ethnisiert. Gerade mit einem Anteil von weit über 30 % an bloßer Grundschulausbildung von (insbesondere) älteren Migranten ist dieser Aspekt höchst relevant.

Literatur

Atteslander, P., Gransow, B. & Western, J. (1999) (Eds.): Comparative Anomie Research. Aldershot - Brookfield: Ashgate.

Atteslander, P. (1999): Social Change, Development and Anomie. In P. Atteslander, B. Gransow & J. Western. (Eds.), Comparative Anomie Research (pp. 3-16). Aldershot - Brookfield: Ashgate.

Berry, J. W. & Kim, U. (1988): Acculturation and mental health. In P. R. Dasen, J. W. Berry & N. Sartorius (Eds.), Health and cross-cultural psychology (pp. 207-236). London: Sage.

Berry, J. (1997): Immigration, acculturation and adaptation. Applied Psychology: An International Review, 46, 5-34.

Bourhis, R.Y., Moise, L.C., Perreault, S & Senécal, S. (1997): Towards an Interactive Acculturation Model: A social Psychological Approach. International Journal of Psychology, 32, 369-386.

Bullinger, M., Kirchberger, I. & von Steinbüchel, N. (1993): Der Fragebogen Alltagsleben - ein Verfahren zur Erfassung der gesundheitsbezogenen Lebensqualität. Zeitschrift für Medizinische Psychologie, 3, 121-131.

Collatz, J. (1998): Kernprobleme des Krankseins in der Migration - Versorgungsstruktur und ethnozentrische Fixiertheit im Gesundheitswesen. In M. David, Th. Borde & H. Kentenich (1998) (Hrsg.), Migration und Gesundheit. Zustandsbeschreibung und Zukunftsmodelle (S. 33-59). Frankfurt am Main: Mabuse.

Diefenbacher, A. & Heim, G. (1997): Kulturspezifische Einstellung zum Körper. Somatisierung bei türkischen und deutschen Depressiven. T & E Neurologie und Psychiatrie, 11, 870-873.

Faltermaier, T. (2001): Migration und Gesundheit: Fragen und Konzepte aus einer salutogenetischen und gesundheitspsychologischen Perspektive. In P. Marschalck & K.H. Wiedl (Hrsg.), Migration und Krankheit (S.93-112): IMIS-Beiträge. Osnabrück: Universitätsverlag Rasch.

Firat, D. (1996): Migration als Belastungsfaktor türkischer Familien. Hamburg: Dr. Kovac.

Fischer, A. & Kohr, H. (1980): Politisches Verhalten und empirische Sozialforschung. München: Juventa.

Frigessi Castelnuova, D. & Risso, M. (1986): Emigration und Nostalgie. Frankfurt: Cooperative-Verlag.

224

Garcia Coll, C. & Magnusson, K. (1997): The psychological experience of immigration: A developmental perspective. In A. Booth, A. C. Crouter & N. Landale (Eds.), Immigration and the family (pp. 91-132). Mahwah, NJ: Erlbaum.

Hochstim, P. & Plake, K. (1997) (Hrsg.): Anomie und Wertsystem. Nachträge zur Devianztheorie Robert K. Mertons. Beiträge aus dem Fachbereich Pädagogik der Universität der Bundeswehr Hamburg.

Hoffmann-Nowotny, H.-J. (1989): Weltmigration – eine soziologische Analyse. In W. Kälin & R. Moser (Hrsg.), Migrationen aus der Dritten Welt (S. 29-40). Bern: Haupt.

Jerusalem, M. (1990): Persönliche Ressourcen, Vulnerabilität und Stresserleben. Göttingen: Hogrefe.

Jerusalem, M. (1992): Akkulturationsstress und psychosoziale Befindlichkeit jugendlicher Ausländer. Report Psychologie, 2, 16-25.

Kürsat-Ahlers, E. & Ahlers, I. (1985): Kulturelle, soziale und familiäre Lebensbedingungen in der Türkei und Ursachen der Emigration türkischer Familien. In J. Collatz, E. Kürsat-Ahlers & J. Korporal (Hrsg.), Gesundheit für alle. Die medizinische Versorgung türkischer Familien in der Bundesrepublik (S. 11-40). Hamburg: EB-Verlag Rissen.

Lazarus, R. S. & Folkman, S. (1987): Transactional theory and research on emotions and coping. European Journal of Personality, 1, 141-169.

Leyendecker, B. (2003): Frühe Entwicklung im soziokulturellen Kontext. In H. Keller (Hg.), Handbuch der Kleinkindforschung (S. 381-431). Bern: Huber.

Leyer, E. M. (1991): Migration, Kulturkonflikt und Krankheit. Opladen: Westdeutscher Verlag.

Li, H., Atteslander, P., Tanur, J. & Wang, Q. (1999): Anomic Scales: Measuring Social Instability. In P. Atteslander, B. Gransow, & J Western (1999) (Eds.), Comparative Anomie Research (pp. 23-45). Aldershot - Brookfield: Ashgate.

Morgenroth, O. & Merkens, H. (1997): Wirksamkeit familialer Umwelten türkischer Migranten in Deutschland. In B. Nauck & U. Schönpflug (Hrsg.), Familien in verschiedenen Kulturen (S. 303-323). Stuttgart: Enke.

Morone, T. (1997): Die Bewältigung des Kulturwechsels; zur Psychologie der Lebenskrisen. Ethnopsychologische Mitteilungen, 6, 32-40.

Rumbaut, R. G. (1997): Ties that bind: Immigration and immigrant families in the United States. In A. Booth, A. C. Crouter & N. Landale (Eds.), Immigration and the family (pp. 3-46). Mahwah, NJ: Erlbaum.

Schneewind, K. (1999): Familienpsychologie. Stuttgart: Kohlhammer.

Schrader, A., Nikles, B. & Griese, H. M. (1979): Die zweite Generation. Sozialisation und Akkulturation ausländischer Kinder in der Bundesrepublik. Kronberg: Athenäum.

Schwarzer, R. & Leppin, A. (1989): Sozialer Rückhalt und Gesundheit. Göttingen: Hogrefe.

Schwarzer, R. & Jerusalem, M. (1994) (Hrsg.): Gesellschaftlicher Umbruch als kritisches Lebensereignis. Weinheim: Juventa.

Seligman, M. E. P. (1979): Erlernte Hilflosigkeit. München: Urban & Schwarzenberg.

Uslucan, H. H. (2000): Gewalt in türkischen Familien. Frühe Kindheit, 4, 20-24.

Vahedi, N. (1996): Diskriminierung und gesundheitliches Wohlbefinden bei türkischen Industriearbeitern. Psychosozial, 63, 71-92.

Gesellschaftliche Transformationen/ Societal Transformations

hrsg. von /edited by Eckhard Dittrich, Nikolai Genov, Raj Kollmorgen, Ingrid Oswald, Heiko Schrader, Melanie Tatur

Heiko Schrader (Ed.)
Trust and Social Transformation
Theoretical approaches and empirical findings from Russia
Literature on trust has experienced a continuous growth from the 1970s onward. The focus of sociological and political science theories is not so much on what trust *is* rather than what trust *does* (its function), where it comes from (its origin) and how it changes in course of time. Books on transformation in Eastern Europe, however, are mainly related to questions of system transfer and institutional change, rather than interpersonal relations within society that can constitute both an opportunity for, and an obstacle to social transformation. With this book German and Russian scholars intend to fill this gap. This collection includes theoretical papers, articles that link topics of trust and empirical/historical observations, and empirical research on trust and transformation.
Bd. 1, 2004, 208 S., 19,90 €, br.,
ISBN 3-8258-7866-x

Nikolai Genov (Ed.)
Ethnic Relations in South Eastern Europe
Problems of Social Inclusion and Exclusion
Peaceful interethnic relations together with the implementation of minority rights individually and through collective schemes are of utmost importance for peace and stability of the countries in South Eastern Europe and therefore on the European continent. This is the reason why ethnic minority rights need particular attention on the part of governments, of national and international NGOs

as well as of the academia in and outside the sub-region.
Bd. 4, 2004, 152 S., 19,90 €, br.,
ISBN 3-8258-7869-4

Rainer Neef; Philippe Adair (Eds.)
Informal Economies and Social Transformation in Romania
Informal economies, growing throughout the 1990s, make a central determinant of social transformation in Eastern Europe. In this book, the various patterns of informal economies and the causes of its growth in Romania are explored from quantitative and qualitative research: the difficult social transformation; informal consumption and labour of households, their incomes, developments and strategies; the impact of informalisation in different branches, related to the Romanian economy as a whole; in the end, comparisons with Eastern European countries are included, and methodological procedure is explained.
Bd. 5, 2005, 248 S., 19,90 €, br.,
ISBN 3-8258-8296-9

Nikolai Genov (Hg.)
Ethnicity and Educational Policies in South Eastern Europe
The crosscutting area of interethnic relations and educational policies is the locus of most intriguing scientific and practical issues in South Eastern Europe. They concern economic, political and cultural dimensions of social action and social order, touch upon sensitive relationships between individual and collective human rights and imply integration or disintegration of societal systems.
Bd. 7, 2005, 216 S., 24,90 €, br.,
ISBN 3-8258-8594-1

Wissenschaftliche Paperbacks
Politikwissenschaft

Hartmut Elsenhans
Das Internationale System zwischen Zivilgesellschaft und Rente
Gegen derzeitige Theorieangebote für die Erklärung der Ursachen und die Auswirkungen wachsender transnationaler und internationaler Verflechtung setzt das hier vorliegende

LIT Verlag Münster – Berlin – Hamburg – London – Wien
Grevener Str./Fresnostr. 2 48159 Münster
Tel.: 0251 – 62 032 22 – Fax: 0251 – 23 19 72
e-Mail: vertrieb@lit-verlag.de – http://www.lit-verlag.de

Konzept eine stark durch politökonomische Überlegungen integrierte Perspektive, die auf politologischen, soziologischen, ökonomischen und philosophischen Ansatzpunkten aufbaut. Mit diesem Konzept soll gezeigt werden, daß der durch Produktionsauslagerungen/ Direktinvestitionen/ neue Muster der internationalen Arbeitsteilung gekennzeichnete (im weiteren als Transnationalisierung von Wirtschaftsbeziehungen bezeichnete) kapitalistische Impuls zur Integration der bisher nicht in die Weltwirtschaft voll integrierten Peripherie weiterhin zu schwach ist, als daß dort nichtmarktwirtschaftliche Formen der Aneignung von Überschuß entscheidend zurückgedrängt werden können. Das sich herausbildende internationale System ist deshalb durch miteinander verschränkte Strukturen von Markt- und Nichtmarktökonomie gekennzeichnet, die nur unter bestimmten Voraussetzungen synergetische Effekte in Richtung einer autonomen und zivilisierten Weltzivilgesellschaft entfalten werden. Dabei treten neue Strukturen von Nichtmarktökonomie auf transnationaler Ebene auf, während der Wiederaufstieg von Renten die zivilgesellschaftlichen Grundlagen funktionierender oder potentiell zu Funktionsfähigkeit zu bringender, dann kapitalistischer Systeme auf internationaler und lokaler Ebene eher behindert.
Bd. 6, 2001, 140 S., 12,90 €, br., ISBN 3-8258-4837-x

Klaus Schubert
Innovation und Ordnung
In einer evolutionär voranschreitenden Welt sind statische Politikmodelle und -theorien problematisch. Deshalb lohnt es sich, die wichtigste Quelle für die Entstehung der policy-analysis, den Pragmatismus, als dynamische, demokratieendogene politisch-philosophische Strömung zu rekonstruieren. Dies geschieht im ersten Teil der Studie. Der zweite Teil trägt zum Verständnis des daraus folgenden politikwissenschaftlichen Ansatzes bei. Darüber hinaus wird durch eine konstruktiv-spekulative Argumentation versucht, die z. Z. wenig innovative Theorie- und Methodendiskussion in der Politikwissenschaft anzuregen.
Bd. 7, 2003, 224 S., 25,90 €, br., ISBN 3-8258-6091-4

Politik: Forschung und Wissenschaft

Klaus Segbers; Kerstin Imbusch (eds.)
The Globalization of Eastern Europe
Teaching International Relations Without Borders
Bd. 1, 2000, 600 S., 35,90 €, br., ISBN 3-8258-4729-2

Hartwig Hummel; Ulrich Menzel (Hg.)
Die Ethnisierung internationaler Wirtschaftsbeziehungen und daraus resultierende Konflikte
Mit Beiträgen von Annabelle Gambe, Hartwig Hummel, Ulrich Menzel und Birgit Wehrhöfer
"Die Ethnisierung der internationalen Wirtschaftsbeziehungen und daraus resultierende Konflikte" lautete der Titel eines Forschungsprojekts, das diesem Band zugrunde liegt. Es geht um die Themen Handel, Migration und Investitionen. In drei Fallstudien werden die Handelsbeziehungen zwischen den USA und Japan, die Einwanderung nach Deutschland bzw. Frankreich und das auslandschinesische Unternehmertum untersucht. Die Ergebnisse des Projekts sehen Hummel und Menzel in den späteren Ereignissen bestätigt: Ethnisierende Tendenzen können sich in der Handelspolitik und der Investitionstätigkeit von Unternehmen nicht durchsetzen, während die Ethnisierung im Bereich der Migration andauert.
Bd. 2, 2001, 272 S., 30,90 €, br., ISBN 3-8258-4836-1

Theodor Ebert
Opponieren und Regieren mit gewaltfreien Mitteln
Pazifismus – Grundsätze und Erfahrungen für das 21. Jahrhundert. Band 1
Das grundlegende und aktuelle Werk eines Konfliktforschers, der über Jahrzehnte in

LIT Verlag Münster – Berlin – Hamburg – London – Wien
Grevener Str./Fresnostr. 2 48159 Münster
Tel.: 0251 – 62 032 22 – Fax: 0251 – 23 19 72
e-Mail: vertrieb@lit-verlag.de – http://www.lit-verlag.de

pazifistischen Organisationen, in sozialen Bewegungen und in Gremien der Evangelischen Kirche gearbeitet hat. Ebert breitet in anschaulichen Berichten und doch in systematischer Ordnung die Summe seiner Erfahrungen aus und entwickelt Perspektiven für eine Welt, die mit der Gewalt leben muss, doch Gefahr läuft, an ihr zugrunde zu gehen, wenn sie auf die Bedrohungen keine neuen, gewaltfreien Antworten findet. Aus dem Vorwort: "Es gibt eine pragmatische Befürwortung des gewaltfreien Handelns in innenpolitischen Auseinandersetzungen durch eine Mehrheit der Deutschen, und dies sollten wir als tragenden Bestandteil der Zivilkultur nicht gering schätzen. Doch die Frage, wie man mit gewaltfreien Mitteln regieren und sich gegenüber gewalttätigen Extremisten durchsetzen kann und wie man sich international behaupten und Bedrohten helfen kann, ist bislang kaum erörtert worden ... Dieses Buch soll klären, was unter politisch verantwortlichem und doch radikal gewaltfreiem Pazifismus zu verstehen ist, und wie mit gewaltfreien Mitteln nicht nur opponiert, sondern auch regiert werden kann."
Bd. 3, 2001, 328 S., 20,90 €, br.,
ISBN 3-8258-5706-9

Theodor Ebert
Der Kosovo-Krieg aus pazifistischer Sicht
Pazifismus – Grundsätze und Erfahrungen für das 21. Jahrhundert. Band 2
Mit dem Luftkrieg der NATO gegen Jugoslawien begann für den deutschen Nachkriegspazifismus ein neues Zeitalter. Ebert hat sich über Jahrzehnte als Konfliktforscher und Schriftleiter der Zeitschrift "Gewaltfreie Aktion" mit den Möglichkeiten gewaltfreier Konfliktbearbeitung befasst. Von ihm stammt der erste Entwurf für einen Zivilen Friedensdienst als Alternative zum Militär. Aus dem Vorwort: "Wer sich einbildet, auch in Zukunft ließe sich aus großer Höhe mit Bomben politischer Gehorsam erzwingen, unterschätzt die Möglichkeiten, die fanatische Terroristen haben, in fahrlässiger Weise. Jedes Atomkraftwerk ist eine stationäre Atombombe, die von Terroristen mit geringem Aufwand in ein Tschernobyl verwandelt werden kann. Wir haben allen Grund, schleunigst über zivile Alternativen zu militärischen Einsätzen nachzudenken und die vorhandene Ansätze solch ziviler Alternativen zu entwickeln."
Bd. 4, 2001, 176 S., 12,90 €, br.,
ISBN 3-8258-5707-7

Wolfgang Gieler
Handbuch der Ausländer- und Zuwanderungspolitik
Von Afghanistan bis Zypern
In der Literatur zur Ausländer- und Zuwanderungspolitik fehlt ein Handbuch, dass einen schnellen und kompakten Überblick dieses Politikbereichs ermöglicht. Das vorliegende Handbuch bemüht sich diese wissenschaftliche Lücke zu schließen. Thematisiert werden die Ausländer- und Zuwanderungspolitik weltweiter Staaten von Afghanistan bis Zypern. Zentrale Fragestellung ist dabei der Umgang mit Fremden, das heißt mit Nicht-Inländern im jeweiligen Staat. Hierbei werden insbesondere politische, soziale, rechtliche, wirtschaftliche und kulturelle Aspekte mitberücksichtigt. Um eine Kompatibilität der Beiträge herzustellen beinhaltet jeder Beitrag darüber hinaus eine Zusammenstellung der historischen Grunddaten und eine Tabelle zur jeweiligen Anzahl der im Staat lebenden Ausländer. Die vorgelegte Publikation versteht sich als ein grundlegendes Nachschlagewerk. Neben dem universitären Bereich richtet es sich besonders an die gesellschaftspolitisch interessierte Öffentlichkeit und den auf sozialwissenschaftlichen Kenntnissen angewiesenen Personen in Politik, Verwaltung, Medien, Bildungseinrichtungen und Migranten-Organisationen.
Bd. 6, 2003, 768 S., 98,90 €, gb.,
ISBN 3-8258-6444-8

LIT Verlag Münster – Berlin – Hamburg – London – Wien
Grevener Str./Fresnostr. 2 48159 Münster
Tel.: 0251 – 62 032 22 – Fax: 0251 – 23 19 72
e-Mail: vertrieb@lit-verlag.de – http://www.lit-verlag.de

Harald Barrios; Martin Beck;
Andreas Boeckh; Klaus Segbers (Eds)
Resistance to Globalization
Political Struggle and Cultural Resilience
in the Middle East, Russia, and Latin
America
This volume is an important contribution
to the empirical research on what globalization means in different world regions.
"Resistance" here has a double meaning: It
can signify active, intentional resistance to
tendencies which are rejected on political
or moral grounds by presenting alternative
discourses and concepts founded in specific
cultural and national traditions. It can also
mean resilience with regard to globalization
pressures in the sense that traditional patterns
of development and politics are resistant to
change. The book shows the that the local,
sub-national, national, and regional patterns
of politics and development coexist with glo-
balized structures without yielding very much
ground and in ways which may turn out to be
a serious barrier to further globalization. Case
studies presented focus on Venezuela, Brazil,
the Middle East, Iran, and Russia.
Bd. 7, 2003, 184 S., 20,90 €, br.,
ISBN 3-8258-6749-8

Michael Neu; Wolfgang Gieler;
Jürgen Bellers (Hg.)
**Handbuch der Außenwirtschaftspoliti-
ken: Staaten und Organisationen**
Afrika, Amerika, Asien, Europa,
Ozeanien
Das vorliegende Handbuch ist die erste um-
fassende Darstellung der Außenwirtschafts-
politiken der Staaten dieser Welt. Die klar
strukturierten Beiträge sind in verständlicher
Sprache verfasst. Sie geben Wissenschaftlern,
Studierenden und sonstigen interessierten
Personen des öffentlichen und privaten Le-
bens einen fundierten und soliden Überblick
über die nationalen Wirtschaftsstrukturen und
Außenwirtschaftsbeziehungen der einzelnen
Länder. Darüber hinaus werden in diesem

Zusammenhang relevante internationale Orga-
nisationen behandelt.
Bd. 8 (2 Bde.), 2004, 1136 S., 149,90 €, br.,
ISBN 3-8258-6920-2

Ellen Bos; Antje Helmerich
Neue Bedrohung Terrorismus
Der 11. September 2001 und die Folgen.
Unter Mitarbeit von Barry Adams und
Harald Wilkoszewski
Die terroristischen Anschläge des 11. September 2001 haben die Weltöffentlichkeit
erschüttert. Ihre weitreichenden Auswirkungen auf die Lebenswirklichkeit des Einzelnen,
den Handlungsspielraum der Nationalstaaten und das internationale System stehen im
Mittelpunkt des Sammelbandes. Er basiert
auf einer Ringvorlesung, in der sich Wissenschaftler der Ludwig-Maximilians-Universität
München aus den Fächern Amerikani-
stik, Jura, Geschichte, Politik-, Religions-,
Kommunikations- und Wirtschaftswissen-
schaft mit den geistigen Hintergründen und
den Konsequenzen des Terrorismus auseinan-
dersetzten.
Bd. 9, 2003, 232 S., 19,90 €, br.,
ISBN 3-8258-7099-5

Heinz-Gerhard Justenhoven; James
Turner (Eds.)
**Rethinking the State in the Age of Glo-
balisation**
Catholic Thought and Contemporary
Political Theory
Since Jean Bodin and Thomas Hobbes, political theorists have depicted the state as
"sovereign" because it holds preeminent authority over all the denizens belonging to its
geographically defined territory. From the Peace of Westphalia in 1648 until the beginning
of World War I in 1914, the essential respon-
siblities ascribed to the sovereign state were
maintaining internal and external security and
promoting domestic prosperity. This idea of
"the state" in political theory is clearly inadequate to the realities of national governments
and international relations at the beginning
of the twenty-first century. During the twen-
tieth century, the sovereign state, as a reality

LIT Verlag Münster – Berlin – Hamburg – London – Wien
Grevener Str./Fresnostr. 2 48159 Münster
Tel.: 0251 – 62 032 22 – Fax: 0251 – 23 19 72
e-Mail: vertrieb@lit-verlag.de – http://www.lit-verlag.de

and an idea, has been variously challenged from without and within its borders. Where will the state head in the age of globalisation? Can Catholic political thinking contribute to an adequate concept of statehood and government? A group of German and American scholars were asked to explore specific ways in which the intellectual traditions of Catholicism might help our effort lo rethink the state. The debate is guided by the conviction that these intellectual resources will prove valuable to political theorists as they work to revise our understanding of the state.

Bd. 10, 2003, 240 S., 19,90 €, br.,
ISBN 3-8258-7249-1

Gesine Foljanty-Jost (ed.)
Japan in the 1990s
Crisis as an impetus for change
The 1990s in Japan have been a period of far-reaching changes in Japanese society, which have not come to an end yet. These developments demand a reexamination of our accumulated knowledge of Japan. This volume looks at them from different perspectives; the contributions deal with issues from the fields of economy, education, political and social science. The volume is a collection of papers from the 2002 meeting of the German Association of Social Scientific Research of Japan (VSJF) at Halle-Wittenberg University.

Bd. 11, 2004, 224 S., 24,90 €, br.,
ISBN 3-8258-7346-3

Wolfgang Gieler; Dietmar Fricke (Hg.)
Handbuch Europäischer Migrationspolitiken
Die EU-Länder und die Beitrittskandidaten
Migrationspolitik ist ein zentrales Thema in der politischen Diskussion. Es ist zu erwarten, dass sowohl die Diskussion um eine restriktivere Migrationspolitik als auch die sich dort abbildenden Befürchtungen und Stereotype in der Bevölkerung mit der EU-Osterweiterung neue Nahrung erhalten. Andererseits ist das allgemeine Wissen über die jeweilige Migrationspolitik der EU insgesamt und noch mehr die der einzelnen EU-Länder als auch

die der Beitrittskandidaten sehr gering. Das vorliegende Handbuch möchte hier ein Lücke schließen und zur Versachlichung der Diskussion beitragen. Die Publikation versteht sich als ein grundlegendes Nachschlagewerk, das eine schnelle und differenzierte Orientierungshilfe in dem komplexen Feld der europäischen Migrationspolitiken ermöglichen soll.

Bd. 12, 2004, 320 S., 29,90 €, gb.,
ISBN 3-8258-7509-1

Stephan Bierling; Karlfriedrich Herb; Jerzy Maćków; Martin Sebaldt
Politischen Wandel denken
Herausforderungen der Demokratie in europäischer und globaler Perspektive.
Antrittsvorlesung Institut für Politikwissenschaft der Universität Regensburg 26./27. Januar 2004
Dass Wandel mit Fortschritt einhergeht, ist ein moderner Gedanke. Er hat heute seine Selbstverständlichkeit verloren. Den vielfältigen Fragen des politischen Wandels geht die gemeinsame Antrittsvorlesung nach, mit der sich die Professoren des Regensburger Instituts für Politikwissenschaft am 26. und 27. Januar 2004 präsentierten. Politischen Wandel denken. Herausforderungen der Demokratie in europäischer und globaler Perspektive – so lautete die gemeinsame Fragestellung. In ihrer Vielfalt und Eigenheit spannen die Vorträge den Bogen von der Reflexion auf das Verhältnis von Wandel und Fortschritt bis hin zu den Herausforderungen, denen die Demokratie heute begegnet.

Bd. 14, 2004, 72 S., 9,90 €, br.,
ISBN 3-8258-7920-8

Lutz Roemheld (Hg.)
Erinnerung an P.-J. Proudhon
Zur Aktualität seines Denkens für die Zukunft der Sozialdemokratie
P.-J. Proudhon – „nur der Kleinbürger, der beständig zwischen dem Kapital und der Arbeit, zwischen der politischen Ökonomie und dem Kommunismus hin- und hergeworfen wird"? (K. Marx: Elend der Philosophie, 1847). Diese Diskriminierung hat wohl am meisten zur

LIT Verlag Münster – Berlin – Hamburg – London – Wien
Grevener Str./Fresnostr. 2 48159 Münster
Tel.: 0251 – 62 032 22 – Fax: 0251 – 23 19 72
e-Mail: vertrieb@lit-verlag.de – http://www.lit-verlag.de

Verdrängung Proudhons aus dem kollektiven Gedächtnis von Sozialisten und Sozialdemokraten beigetragen. Nach dem Scheitern des Sozialismus Marx-Engels'scher Provenienz kann ein Erinnern an Proudhons libertären Sozialismus Hinweise auf die Möglichkeit der Entwicklung einer „sozialpflichtigen Moderne" (Gerhard Senft) im 21. Jahrhundert geben.

Bd. 15, 2005, 296 S., 24,90 €, br.,
ISBN 3-8258-8292-6

Jürgen H. Wolff
Entwicklungshilfe: Ein hilfreiches Gewerbe?
Versuch einer Bilanz
Die Lebensbedingungen auf der Welt, insbesondere in den Entwick-lungsländern, sollen sich, so hört man es oft, laufend verschlechtern. Insbesondere Institutionen, die von und für die Entwicklungs-hilfe leben, vertreten diese These. Mit reichem Datenmaterial belegt der Verfasser, daß fast überall auf der Welt die Lebenserwartung steigt, sich Bildungsstand und Ernährungslage verbessern, kurz, der Wohlstand zunimmt. Mit einer Ausnahme: Schwarzafrika. Wolff geht weiter, er warnt vor dem Trugschluß, dies sei auf Entwicklungshilfe zurückzuführen und erfolgreiche Entwicklungsprojekte seien mit erfolgreicher Entwicklung gleichzusetzen. Reformvorschläge für die Entwicklungshilfe schließen den Band ab.
Bd. 18, 2005, 320 S., 19,90 €, br.,
ISBN 3-8258-8162-8

Wolfgang Gieler (Hg.)
Internationale Wirtschaftsorganisationen
Entstehung – Struktur – Perspektiven.
Ein Handbuch
Das „Handbuch Internationale Wirtschaftsorganisationen" informiert über die Außenwirtschaftspolitiken internationaler Organisationen. Zur besseren Handhabbarkeit verfügen die einzelnen Beiträge über einen vergleichbaren Aufbau – Gründungsgeschichte und Gründungsmotivation, vertragliche Grundlage und Struktur, integrationstheoretische

Einordnung und Perspektiven sowie eine Auswahlbibliographie. Der Band wendet sich an einen breiten Benutzerkreis in Forschung und Lehre, in Politik, Verwaltung und Medien sowie an alle politisch Interessierten.
Bd. 19, 2005, 416 S., 24,90 €, br.,
ISBN 3-8258-8532-1

Studies on South East Europe
edited by Prof. Dr. Karl Kaser (Graz)

Miroslav Jovanović ; Karl Kaser;
Slobodan Naumović (Eds.)
Between the archives and the field
A dialogue on historical anthropology of the Balkans
The present volume binds together papers presented at the International Colloquium on Historical Anthropology held at the Faculty of Philosophy in Belgrade 1 – 2. 10. 1996. The Colloquium offered to researchers coming from different scientific communities (Austrian and Serbian) and disciplines (historical anthropology, social history and social anthropology) an opportunity to exchange ideas and opinions in direct dialogue.
Bd. 1, 2004, 280 S., 29,90 €, br.,
ISBN 3-8258-6438-3

Slobodan Naumović; Miroslav Jovanović (Eds.)
Childhood in South East Europe
Historical Perspectives on Growing Up in the 19th and 20th Century
Rapid growth of interest in the research of childhood during the last several decades can be regarded not only as an indicator but also as an important factor in the long-term processes of changes, which have radically transformed history as a scientific discipline. With the growth of the history of childhood as a discipline a series of problems neglected until then has been opened, and along the questions about the new sources and equivalent methods of research. This is especially true for historiography in the South East European countries, where social history and

LIT Verlag Münster – Berlin – Hamburg – London – Wien
Grevener Str./Fresnostr. 2 48159 Münster
Tel.: 0251 – 62 032 22 – Fax: 0251 – 23 19 72
e-Mail: vertrieb@lit-verlag.de – http://www.lit-verlag.de

historical anthropology is still marginal. The volume comprises 18 contributions to the topic with authors from all countries of the region, focussing on the 19th and 20th century. Topics like "upbringing of female children in Serbia" or "rural childhoods in mountain regions of Austria and Greece" are as well touched as "children and war" and "children and migration". This is the first volume that provides an international readership with an overall picture on childhood in South Eastern Europe.

Bd. 2, 2004, 304 S., 29,90 €, br., ISBN 3-8258-6439-1

Miroslav Jovanović;
Slobodan Naumović (Eds.)
Gender Relations in South Eastern Europe
Historical Perspectives on Womanhood and Manhood in 19th and 20th Century
Gender studies are undoubtedly one of the fastest growing domains of contemporary cultural and social research. Ignited by early feminist thought, contextualized and given argument by anthropological insights into the logic of the cultural construction of gender roles and relations, theorized and radicalized by consecutive waves of feminism, the study of gender relations now inspires reflection and debate in the majority of social sciences and humanities. This book bears witness to the multi-disciplinary character of contemporary reflection on the topic of gender. The approaches of social history, historical anthropology, oral history, anthropology and ethnology, sociology, history of literature, political science and pedagogy, all work together to provide an overview of various aspects of gender relations in South Eastern Europe in the 19th and 20th century. The volume comprises 20 contributions on various facets of gender relations in the region, written by the most profiled authors in this field like Andrea Pető, Kristina Popova, Radina Vučetić, Ana Stolić or Krassimira Daskalova.

Bd. 3, 2004, 416 S., 29,90 €, br., ISBN 3-8258-6440-5

Ulf Brunnbauer (ed.)
(Re)Writing History. Historiography in Southeast Europe after Socialism
The authors of this volume analyse the development of historiography in Southeast Europe after the collapse of socialism. On the one hand, they discuss efforts at reevaluating the past. On the other hand, their contributions reveal that recent historiography has often been characterised by a high degree of continuity despite social and political transformation. Neither the methodology nor the topics of mainstream historiography have changed. Nevertheless, new approaches have developed that do not view the past from a narrow political and national perspective. They connect to international discourse and break out of the parochialism of much of traditional historical writing in Southeast Europe.

Bd. 4, 2004, 384 S., 29,90 €, br., ISBN 3-8258-7365-x

Region
Internationales Forum für lokale und globale Entwicklung
hrsg. von Prof. Dr. Winfried Böttcher

Winfried Böttcher (Hg.)
Internationales Forum für lokale, regionale und globale Entwicklung
Jahrbuch 03/04. Subsidiarität – Regionalismus – Föderalismus. Schwerpunkt: Kaliningrad
Das deutsch-russische Jahrbuch REGION will ein internationales Forum für lokale, regionale und globale Entwicklungen sein. Neben drei grundsätzlichen Artikeln zur Regionsräson, zum russischen Föderalismus und den Rezentralisierungstendenzen in Russland hat dieser Band Kaliningrad zum Schwerpunkt. Russische und deutsche Experten setzen sich , mit der Situation der Oblast nach der Ost-Erweiterung, dem Regionalbewußtsein, dem kulturellen Erbe und der ökonomischen Entwicklung auseinander.

Bd. 1, 2003, 432 S., 35,90 €, br., ISBN 3-8258-6752-8

LIT Verlag Münster – Berlin – Hamburg – London – Wien
Grevener Str./Fresnostr. 2 48159 Münster
Tel.: 0251 – 62 032 22 – Fax: 0251 – 23 19 72
e-Mail: vertrieb@lit-verlag.de – http://www.lit-verlag.de